The Police and Criminal Evidence Bill

Policing by Coercion

Louise Christian

GLC Police Committee Support Unit

Contents

Preface

Section A   **Introduction**

Section B   **The Background to the Bill**
     1   The Police Lobby and the Criminal Justice System/8

Section C   **New Powers on the Streets and in the Home**
     2   Stop and Search of Persons/19
     3   The Present Law on Stop and Search and its History/26
     4   Stop and Search of Vehicles and Roadblocks/31
     5   Does Stop and Search Prevent Crime?/35
     6   Search of Premises/41
     7   The Law and Procedure on Search Warrants/50
     8   Complaints about Searches of Premises/56
     9   Arrests/63
     10   Complaints About Arrests/68

Section D   **New Powers in the Police Station**
     11   The Detention of Suspects/71
     12   The Admissibility of Confession Evidence/82
     13   The Treatment of Suspects in the Police Station/88
     14   The Judges' Rules, the Codes of Practice and Exclusion of Evidence/99
     15   Complaints about the Detention and Treatment of Suspects/109

Section E   **Police Powers and Police Methods**
     16   Stereotyping – How do Police Identify "Criminal Types"?/115
     17   Community Policing, Crime Prevention and Social Control/124
     18   The Policing Strategies of Sir Kenneth Newman/136
     19   Policing and Surveillance/147
     20   Policing and Coercion/154

CONTENTS

Section F **The Safeguards**
21 Records of Reasons for Police Exercise of their Powers/160
22 The Independent Assessor of Police Complaints and Statutory Police Liaison Committees/167
23 The Police Complaints System, the Double Jeopardy Rule and Proposals for Change/175
24 The Royal Commission on Criminal Procedure Report and the Concept of "Balance"/187
25 Omissions – An Independent Prosecution Service, Tape Recording and Lay Visitors/193
26 Police Accountability and the Police Bill/205

Appendix – Summary of the Provisions of the Police and Criminal Evidence Bill (As Amended by Standing Committee J)/211

Index/220

Preface

This book looks at the issues raised by the Conservative Government's Police and Criminal Evidence Bill. Although the Bill fell when a General Election was called in June 1983, the Government has said it will be introduced in substantially the same form in the 1983-4 parliamentary session. The book analyses the new powers proposed by the Bill and places them in the context of new policing strategies being promoted by the Metropolitan Police Commissioner, Sir Kenneth Newman. It argues that the Bill discarded the basic legal principle governing police power in England and Wales – that the police are merely "citizens in uniform" – and that the Bill would legitimise policing by coercion.

The GLC Police Committee was established in May 1981 in response to a crisis of policing in Greater London which has intensified since that time. The first discussion paper produced by the Committee's Support Unit, *A New Police Authority for London,* presented the options for achieving proper police accountability and identified a preferred option for London. This is the second in the series. Details of the work of the Unit are at the back of the book.

Louise Christian is a solicitor working in the GLC's Police Committee Support Unit.

A. Introduction

The purpose of this book is to examine the issues raised by the Police and Criminal Evidence Bill which fell when a General Election was announced in June 1983 by the Conservative government. Subsequently the government was re-elected and has made known its intention to introduce a new Police and Criminal Evidence Bill as soon as possible. It is likely that most of the provisions in it (particularly those giving new powers to the police) will either be very similar or identical to those in the old Police Bill.*

Public awareness of the provisions of the Bill was slow to develop after its publication in October 1982. It was only in the closing stages of its progress through Standing Committee in the House of Commons that serious public opposition was expressed through the media. This opposition focused on clauses in the Bill allowing the police access to or rights of search of confidential files kept by social workers, councillors, advisers, doctors or journalists.

Professional bodies forced the government to promise withdrawal of the offending clauses affecting their members. But the surrounding publicity also began to draw people's attention to other even more drastic new powers in the Bill which would affect ordinary people, not endowed with the same political clout as the professionals.

In the closing stages of the Bill a broad-based opposition to the other new police powers in the Bill was emerging. Even the *Daily Express* devoted an editorial to it headlined:

''Kill this Tawdry Bill''.

---

*References to that Bill reflect so far as is possible all amendments made or promised by the government before it was dropped. The Bill applied only in England and Wales and not to Scotland or Northern Ireland. A summary of the Bill is contained in the Appendix. References to debates in Parliament (including those of Standing Committee J) are to debates on the old Bill, taking place before the General Election.

warning its readers against the Police Bill, calling it a:

"tawdry, illiberal and ill-conceived piece of legislation".

The editorial concluded:

"Mrs Thatcher should ditch the Bill and present a new one".[1]

The *Daily Mail* said the Bill would give too much power to the police[2] and the *Sun* called on the then Home Secretary, William Whitelaw, to withdraw it.[3] Alone among the national daily newspapers, the *Daily Telegraph* defended the Bill.[4] Public meetings all over London were called and a national conference in Hackney attracted large numbers. Meanwhile a national demonstration against the Bill went ahead, despite the fact that by then the country was already in the midst of a General Election campaign.

It is hoped that the public debate about the new police powers will continue. Events are likely to force policing to the top of the political agenda sooner or later. There have been disturbing reports in the press of new conflicts between police and public in depressed areas of London and elsewhere.

Policing stategies are intimately connected to social and economic conditions. High unemployment, bad housing and lack of job prospects create tension and anxiety on the streets in working class areas, particularly among youth. The police increasingly see themselves as an agent of social control, as part of a repressive rather than redistributive welfare state which stigmatises its recipients as both "scroungers" and "criminals". As discussed in Chapter 17 there are significant pointers to these developments in the Police Bill. At the same time the product of the "heavy" policing tactics of recent years is the systematic criminalisation of a section of society. The psychology of police identification of "criminal types" is one of the issues discussed in connection with the new powers in Chapter 16. Black people suffer disproportionately from the indiscriminate exercise of police power because of police attitudes although the number of black people unemployed is obviously a factor too. Meanwhile racist attitudes are becoming institutionalised in the police not just as a matter of "police sub-culture" but also as an intrinsic part of the new strategies being introduced by Sir Kenneth Newman, the Commissioner of the Metropolitan Police.

Those strategies aim to reorganise policing around the perceived priority of social control rather than crime detection. This redefining of the police role by senior officers demands a re-orientation of police powers. Requirements that powers should be directed at specific crimes have fast become inconvenient impediments and were discarded by the Bill. Instead it developed two criteria: the maintaining of order on the streets (eg new powers of arrest); and the gathering of intelligence (eg new powers to search people's homes). These criteria frequently overlap, such as in the new power to set up roadblocks which will serve the dual purpose of the control of traffic into the area and the collection of information. The relationship between the new powers and the Newman strategy, together with the impact of increased use of technology by the police is considered in Chapters 18-19.

The provisions of the Bill would not only affect black people disproportionately. The young, the unemployed and the homeless who are out on the streets will all become "targets" for the police. Trade unionists and political activists could find powers of stop and search and road blocks used to control and/or prevent political protests or pickets.[5] Gay men and lesbians could be singled out for extraordinary powers of arrest on the grounds of "affronting public decency".[6] Women could be subjected to "intimate body searches" in police stations, especially if classified as prostitutes.[7]

The starting point of any examination of the *new* powers must be the present widespread abuse by the police of their *existing* powers. This is documented here by quotation from complaints received by the GLC Police Committee. These complaints are growing in number and becoming increasingly serious. The step from institutionalised abuse of power to the legitimation proposed by the Bill is not a negligible one. Failure to obtain satisfaction is as little compared to an inability to complain at all. Random stops and searches, speculative raids on houses, arbitrary arrests and detention without charge for long periods all happen now. But they are not supposed to happen; the public know it and can complain and the police know it and will abuse their powers only selectively if they are wise.

This selectivity is what former Metropolitan Police Commissioner, Sir David McNee, may have meant in the often quoted passage from his evidence to the Royal Commission on Criminal Procedure:

"Many police officers have, early in their careers learned to use methods bordering on trickery or stealth in their investigations because they were deprived of proper powers by the legislature".[8]

It is also what Les Curtis, the Chairman of the Police Federation, may have meant when he said recently that police were currently operating with

"one hand tied behind their back".

If the Bill becomes law in its old form, much of the onus on the police to exercise at least some restraint will be removed. Standards of power laid down in legislation quickly become norms of behaviour. If a general power to search houses for evidence is allowed, it is extremely unlikely that this will be used only in exceptional circumstances, as the government claim. Such claims do not correspond with the judgement of Les Curtis that the Bill

"provides for the first time a framework which will make it possible for the police to make a real impact on the fight against crime".[10]

The only way that the police can live up to this extravagant supposition is by using the new powers in the Bill to the hilt so that, for example, every serious offence will justify searches of the homes of all those who are in any way connected with the victim or circumstances of the crime.

The Bill discarded once and for all the basic legal principle governing police power in England and Wales that police are merely "citizens in uniform". In the Bill the police were given specific powers to use force wholly unrelated to the prevention of specific crimes, in a situation where it would be illegal for an ordinary citizen to attack anyone or anything. What these provisions add up to is the legitimisation of brutal friskings on the street and destructive rampages through people's homes. In the police station, the Bill effectively legalised police assault on suspects in giving power to take compulsorily body samples, fingerprints and, even more abhorrently, to carry out intimate body searches. These measures ignore the extent to which police rely on public co-operation for the prevention and detection of crime. The new powers in the Bill are not simply an attack on civil liberties; they are also an attack on society's ability to counter crime and violence. The legitimisation of violence by the police, even though for specific purposes, may well legitimise violence generally in society.

The attack on civil liberties in the Bill does not stop with policing. Its effects are likely to permeate the whole of the criminal justice system. For example, a further slackening of the requirements to be satisfied in order for police to obtain search warrants will surely have an effect on the magistrates who grant them. Moreover magistrates are to grant warrants for further detentions authorising suspects to be held without charge in sittings of the court not open to the public, a dangerous precedent. As Lord McCluskey said in respect of other similar (but less drastic) provisions during the Second Reading debate in the Lords of the Criminal Justice (Scotland) Bill:

> "I detect shades of South Africa here, and indeed of the police state, in allowing successive periods of detention on a mere magistrate's warrant"[11]

The provisions allowing detention of suspects without charge for questioning would be a substantial erosion of the right to silence, a long-established principle of criminal law. This erosion will affect the whole system of administration of criminal justice as new rules on confession evidence in the Bill demonstrate. The result is likely to be an increasingly heavy reliance on the questioning of suspects and confession evidence even in relation to relatively minor crimes. The background to this part of the Bill is a powerful police lobby which has argued for drastic changes in the criminal justice system for some ten years or more. Its recent victories include the new Criminal Justice Act and government commitments to restrict eligibility for jury service.

Parallels have been made between the Police Bill and "emergency" legislation on policing and criminal justice in force in Northern Ireland. Current policing practices there (including the systematic gathering of intelligence) are said to be a rehearsal for the exercise of the new powers here. In his review of the Prevention of Terrorism Act, Lord Jellicoe recommended its extension to other non-Irish terrorists and this was incorporated in the Prevention of Terrorism Bill published in July 1983.[12] Suspects held under the Prevention of Terrorism Act were exempted from the small protections in the new Police Bill. Ironically terrorism was frequently cited by Tory MPs during debates in Parliament as the justification for new powers such as the intimate body search.[13] What is certain is that the new Bill will become the norm against which further "emergency" legislation is measured.

The Bill supposedly balanced new and increased powers with safeguards, following the approach of the widely criticised Report of the Royal Commission on Criminal Procedure. Yet the safeguards were even weaker than they recommended and most of the increased powers they sanctioned were extended still further. The Royal Commission naively thought that requiring police to write down reasons for exercise of powers would somehow act as a check despite the difficulty of getting legal aid for subsequent challenge. However they did say that increased powers should only be available to combat specific "grave offences".[14] But the powers in the Bill, such as detaining without charge, were instead applicable to "serious arrestable offences" which were very loosely defined.[15]

There was no provision in the Bill whatsoever for exclusion of evidence obtained in breach of restriction on police power. The Home Office may have been duped into believing that police behaviour can be controlled without an exclusion provision, by granting them the new powers they want and thus gaining the support of senior police officers for control of abuse. But even senior police officers are powerless against institutionalised abuse of power, which is why they have condoned it in the past. Moreover the new powers were often so wide that any safeguards would be meaningless. The so-called "right" of access to a lawyer, for example, was in fact not a right at all for the first 36 hours of detention. This is where the Royal Commission's concept of "balance" was also seriously defective.

The Bill relied on the police complaints and internal discipline systems for enforcement of the quite inadequate safeguards in it, fundamentally leaving the police to investigate themselves. The provisions relating to police complaints could only be described as "tinkering" with the system. The introduction of an "independent assessor" (who will be Chair or Vice-Chair of the Police Complaints Board) would be hardly likely to inspire public confidence. This has been realised by both the Police Federation and the Law Society who are demanding a team of investigators who would be seconded police officers.[16]

Criticism of this part of the Bill should not however be confined to saying that safeguards and redress mechanisms were inadequate. Careful examination is needed of the concept of "balance" itself. There is a serious danger that if the government strengthens some of the safeguards, opposition to the Bill will collapse on the basis that such measures will somehow cancel out new powers. With this in mind, this book examines not only the provisions which were in the Bill, but also the proposals for an independent prosecution service and tape recording of interviews which were not included, to see what impact they would have.

The book concludes with a brief examination of the constitutional position of the police and the concept of police accountability. It shows that the theory of policing exemplified by the Bill ("policing by coercion") not only cannot be balanced by democratic control but runs contrary to it, prejudicing and preventing such control by the abrogation of power into the hands of dangerously autonomous self governing bodies - the police forces of England and Wales.

Notes

1. *Daily Express* 27.4.83.
2. *Daily Mail* 15.3.83.
3. *Sun* 4.4.83.
4. *Daily Telegraph* 5.5.83.
5. See Chapter 4.
6. See Chapter 9.
7. See Chapter 13.
8. Part I of the *Written Evidence of the Commissioner of Police of the Metropolis to the Royal Commission on Criminal Procedure*, Scotland Yard, 1978, P2.
9. *Today* programme BBC Radio 4 25.3.83.
10. *Guardian* 25.3.83.
11. Quoted in *Policing the Police* ed Peter Hain (John Calder 1981) vol 2 P183.
12. *Review of the operation of the Prevention of Terrorism (Temporary Provisions) Act 1976* (Cmnd 8803) 9.2.83.
13. See for example *Hansard* Standing Committee J 17.2.83 col 707 Eldon Griffiths MP.
14. *Royal Commission on Criminal Procedure Report* (Cmnd 8092) Jan 1981 paras 3.5 - 3.9.
15. See Chapter 11 P78.
16. *Guardian* 15.6.83.

B. The Background to the Bill

1. The Police Lobby and the Criminal Justice System

David Leigh wrote in *The Observer* that:

> "The real inside story of the Police Bill is a murky one, stretching back almost 20 years, that does not show the British political process in a very comforting light. It is a history of secret lobbying, intellectual confusion and vicious infighting largely conducted behind the public's back".[1]

The proposals in the Police Bill have not been the only result of this process. The jury system has been under constant attack since 1967 when majority verdicts were introduced. In the 1970s it was discovered that prosecutors were secretly "vetting" jury lists.[2] Last year the inclusion of black people on juries was publicly attacked by a senior judge.[3] The government was preparing proposals to exclude all persons convicted of any offence from juries, because of disquiet at the extent to which juries increasingly disbelieve police evidence.[4] Meanwhile the Northern Ireland (Emergency Provisions) Act 1973 completely abolished juries in Northern Ireland for those charged with terrorist offences because of concern about the difficulty of getting juries to convict.[5]

These changes have come about, at least partly, due to a strident "law and order" lobby who constantly assert that criminals are acquitted too easily and that sentences are too short. Since at least 1972 this lobby has been actively encouraged by some senior police officers and police organisations such as the Association of Chief Police Officers (ACPO) and the Police Federation. Its more recent successes have also included the Criminal Justice Act 1982 which introduced "more flexible" custodial sentencing for young people (including "short sharp shocks" which have led to an increase in the use of detention centre orders), curfew orders as part of supervision orders and (by an amendment introduced into the House of Lords) the abolition of the right of the accused to make a statement in the dock. One of the main demands of the lobby is the restoration of capital punishment. The decisive defeat of the pro-hangers in July 1983 has led them to make renewed demands for increased sentences and other changes to the criminal justice system.

The demands for increased police powers are therefore only part of a larger set of pressures. These demands were strengthened by the increase in power of the individual Chief Constables following the amalgamation of the police forces in 1966 when the number of police forces was reduced from 117 to 49 (subsequently to 43). Police historian, T A Critchley, wrote of the importance of Chief Constables:

> "This was a forseeable - and forseen - result of the change to fewer and larger forces. At the same time the change has provided the opportunity for greater cohesion between Chief Constables, under the machinery of the central conference and elsewhere, in policy making. Theoretically, at least, it would seem that they are able to speak with greater authority than ever before - both locally and nationally. And this trend can only have been reinforced by the abolition or dismemberment of many police authorities with the consequent loss of experience."[6]

The first to realise the potential political role which could be played by Chief Constables was Sir Robert Mark, who was Commissioner of the Metropolitan Police from 1972 to 1977. Mark is best known for his attempts to rid the force of corruption. But he also built up an efficient communications and public relations role for the police, negotiating arrangements with newspapers and television. In the foreword to Critchley's book, Mark himself wrote:

> "The post war years have seen a gradual change in our role from mere law enforcement to participants in the role of social welfare and even more importantly to that of contributors in the moulding of public opinion and legislation."[7]

While still Chief Constable of Leicester, Mark was already calling for changes in the criminal justice system to restrict the right of silence of an accused person, introduce majority verdicts by juries (later implemented) and compel prior disclosure of the defence case.[8]

When Mark became Commissioner, the Eleventh Report of the Criminal Law Revision Committee had just appeared after eight years of deliberation by the Committee. This Report was to provide the "law and order" lobby with one of its most powerful intellectual supports. The group of judges and lawyers who sat on the Committee had set out with the intention of seeing how far changes in the rules of evidence "justify making the law less favourable to the defence" and "to go as far in getting rid of restrictions on admissability of evidence as is possible in the modern conditions".[9] The attitudes of the Committee were clearly demonstrated when they referred to the suspect in their Report as "the criminal".[10]

The result was a set of recommendations changing the form of caution to be given by police prior to questioning, allowing courts to draw unfavourable inferences from suspects remaining silent in the police station and changing the rules of evidence to restrict the extent to which it could be excluded. This wholesale attack on the right to silence provoked strong protests from civil libertarians on the one hand and adulation from the police on the other. Lord Devlin said of the Report:

> "The Report pictures the police as men with open minds under a duty to question persons for the purpose of discovering whether and by whom an offence has been committed. The picture is true enough up to the point of arrest. But after that it changes, as the Judges' Rules which it is proposed to supersede so clearly recognised. Once the police have got their man the prime object of further questioning is to secure a conviction. The methods employed are not always scrupulous.
>
> One cannot ignore, though I do not stress, the notorious scandals to which the Report refers. I am thinking of humbler practitioners who browbeat, who use bail as an inducement and a night in the cell as an intimidation and who, often overworked, look upon a confession as a short cut to justice.
>
> There is a school of thought which regards as purely sentimental the British reluctance to allow a man to convict himself out of his own mouth. They think it legitimate to get anything that can be got out of the suspect without ill-treatment. This is the inquisitorial system. To some extent we have it already. Into what is fundamentally an adversarial system we have introduced an inquisitorial power, placing it in the hands of the police. This hybrid device has worked tolerably well because we have demanded and largely obtained from the police a higher degree of impartiality than we have any right to expect and because it is subject to stringent control through the Judges' Rules. If

the compromise has broken down, the answer is not to abolish the rules and leave it all to the police."[11]

The Report was not implemented at the time primarily because of the strength of police resistance to its proposals for tape recording of all interviews in police stations. But the Report has never really been shelved; the proposals in the Police Bill on detention and admissability of evidence, the abolition of dock statements in the Criminal Justice Act 1982 and the proposals on juries are all piecemeal implementations of it.

In January 1973 Sir Robert Mark was invited to give the Dimbleby lecture on BBC Television and used the opportunity to express forceful and provocative views on the criminal justice system. Mark asserted that the rate of acquittals was far too high and that the rules of evidence placed an intolerable burden on the prosecution:

"It is of course right that in a serious criminal case the burden of proof should be upon the prosecution. But in trying to discharge that burden the prosecution has to act within a complicated framework of rules which were designed to give every advantage to the defence. The prosecution has to give the defence advance notice of the whole of its case, but the accused, unless he wants to raise an alibi, can keep his a secret until the actual trial. When the police interrogate a suspect or charge him they have to keep reminding him that he need not say anything. If he has a criminal record the jury are not ordinarily allowed to know about it. Most of these rules are very old. They date from a time when, incredible as it may seem, an accused person was not allowed to give evidence in his own defence, when most accused were ignorant or illiterate. There was no legal aid and, perhaps most important, if someone was convicted he would most likely be hanged or transported. Under these conditions it is not surprising that the judges who made the rules were concerned to give the accused every possible protection. But it is, to say the least, arguable that the same rules were not suited to the trial of an experienced criminal, using skilled legal assistance, in the late twentieth century."[12]

In the lecture Mark also attacked the "bent" lawyers whom he said took advantage of the technical rules to invent false defences. Subsequently he claimed:

"Experienced and respected metropolitan detectives can identify lawyers in criminal practice who are more harmful to society than the clients they represent".[13]

Martin Kettle has written:

> "Mark's campaigns and statements were intended to achieve specific results. These intended results were occasionally long-term as in the case of his Dimbleby lecture. He could hardly have expected to win the changes he wanted in criminal procedure overnight. But he could try to stir things up so that the Criminal Law Revision Committee's proposals did not sink into oblivion."[14]

Mark justified his outspoken views on the basis that the criminal law system was a whole and policing could not be separated from the criminal law and the courts. He claimed that senior police officers were uniquely placed to comment on the whole system. His views were taken up by his successor as Commissioner, Sir David McNee. In his first annual report as Commissioner, McNee signified his approval of the line which had been taken by his predecessor:

> "Whilst I acknowledge and defend the need to maintain a proper balance between the rights and liberties of the suspect on the one hand and the powers conferred on the police for the effective discharge of their responsibilities on the other, I am firmly of the opinion that the task of the police is being made unwarrantably difficult by certain restraints of criminal procedure."[15]

He also adopted many of the arguments put forward by Mark. Thus Mark had attacked the Judges' Rules on the grounds that they deflected from spontaneity and that the establishment of "truth" rather than the determination of technical "guilt" should be the objective of the criminal justice system.[16] This theme was subsequently taken up by McNee, who, in his evidence to the Royal Commission on Criminal Procedure, contrasted the position of the defence lawyer, who is bound to act for his client, with that of the police officer:

> "The police officer is duty bound to attempt to discover the truth whether that truth discloses the innocence or the guilt of the suspect."[17]

He therefore argued that increased powers to compel the truth could only be for the benefit of all. McNee also began to reflect on an implied threat which had been contained in Sir Robert Mark's Dimbleby lecture:

> "Unwillingness to make the law more effective will inevitably provoke demands for harsher punishments and will increase the pressures on the police to use more arbitrary methods."[18]

McNee was forced at an early stage to give attention not only to the question of criminal procedure, but also to that of police powers. At the end of Sir Robert Mark's time as Commissioner a political scandal had been caused by the revelations of the judicial inquiry into the Maxwell Confait murder case. Three juveniles had been wrongly convicted on the basis of confession statements and the Inquiry Report by Sir Henry Fisher revealed that the police systematically ignored or broke the Judges' Rules for interrogating suspects (see also p 99).[19] The Labour government then in power decided to set up a Royal Commission on Criminal Procedure to enquire into what changes were needed. The composition of the Royal Commission was intended as a compromise - a mixture of police, eminent lawyers and "radicals".

Under McNee the police lobby concentrated on influencing the Royal Commission. According to one commentator:

> "Desperate for unanimity, according to its members, the liberal and radical members of the Commission started horsetrading with the police, trying to sense what compromises would satisfy them."[20]

McNee prepared his own detailed evidence to the Royal Commission by setting up a working party at Scotland Yard. The result was a detailed set of proposals which applied the sort of arguments used by Sir Robert Mark to the area of police powers.[21] McNee's argument was that the police were already abusing their powers, it was essential for them to continue and they intended doing so, and therefore Parliament should legitimise their actions. The difficulty, as McNee saw it, was not that the police were breaking the rules, but that they could no longer get away with it. McNee therefore combined the demands of Sir Robert Mark for the curtailment of the right to silence with proposals for sweeping new powers to arrest, search and fingerprint. These included search for evidence, random roadblocks, compulsory fingerprinting of whole areas and detention for 72 hours with unlimited extensions. Many of these new powers, along with part of the recommendations of the Eleventh Criminal Law Revision Committee, were adopted by the Royal Commission (others not adopted by the Royal Commission appeared subsequently in the Police Bill).

Undoubtedly the police exercised an enormous influence on the Royal Commission's deliberations. As Martin Kettle wrote:

"McNee's proposals have dominated public perception of the work of the Royal Commission. They have strongly influenced the proposals emerging from the rest of the police. They are undoubtedly the most influential set of recommendations received by the Commission, and the most detailed modern manifesto of police intentions in the exercise of their principal task, the enforcement of the criminal law."[22]

Kettle considered the Royal Commission had done well to resist some of McNee's proposals. Nevertheless when the Commission's Report was published many civil liberties and radical lawyers groups decisively rejected its findings. One left wing lawyer was quoted as saying of the Commission's "radicals":

"We know what happened. They were puffed up and flattered by the police into making managerial and political compromises that were really the job of the Cabinet."[23]

The Royal Commission had propounded the notion of "balance" (see p 187). In real terms this consisted in trading off an acceptance of police demands for increased powers against "safeguards", including an independent police complaints and public prosecutor system and tape recording of inteviews in police stations. David Leigh has described the police reaction:

"As soon as the report was published, a series of secret memoranda flowed into the Home Office fortress in St Anne's Gate from the Association of Chief Police Officers' Crime Committee. It is chaired by Peter Imbert, Chief Constable of Thames Valley, but the names of the remaining Chief Constables on the Committee are, rather ludicrously, kept secret. The ACPO memoranda, according to sources close to the Home Office, said that the Chief Constables would not accept a system of independent prosecutors."[24]

Since that time it would appear that the Home Office has been striving to overcome police resistance to public prosecutors, tape recording and more independence in the complaints system. At the same time, presumably as a result of further negotiations with senior police officers, more provisions, similar to McNee's proposals, crept into the Police Bill, even though not included in the Royal Commission Report.

After publication of the Report in January 1981 and following the intensive lobbying by ACPO, the Home Office produced, in the summer of 1982, a "consultative" memorandum – allowing precisely two months for consultation.[25] The memorandum was the first indication that the Home Office was inclined to go further in the area of police powers than had the Royal Commission. For example, the definition of "grave offences" (a list of very serious offences said by the Royal Commission to justify greater police powers) was said to be "impracticable" and was subsequently replaced in the Bill by the much wider "serious arrestable offences". Other proposals emanating from the police parallelling those of McNee were for greater powers of fingerprinting and taking names and addresses, to set up roadblocks at will and to hold suspects in detention for longer periods without independent check.

Some proposals which appeared in the Bill had not even been considered in the Royal Commission Report, for example the notorious new power for police to search confidential files of doctors etc (subsequently withdrawn by the government). Provisions on admissability of confession evidence and requiring disclosure of "expert" defence evidence were in the first instance an implementation of some of the proposals of the Eleventh Report of the Criminal Law Revision Committee and in the second of proposals made by Sir Robert Mark.[26]

Policing London speculated on the influence of the police on the new powers in the Bill:

> "If the new powers did not come from the Royal Commission or the Home Office's response to it where did they come from? Some of the proposals are so exceptional that it is important to speculate how much influence Sir Kenneth Newman, drawing on his Northern Ireland experience, had on the drafting of the Bill. It is likely that he was consulted in view of his background and pending appointment to head London's police. Similarly, how much influence did the experience of Northern Ireland have on the officials in the Home Office, particularly when faced with the prospect of mass long-term unemployment in the inner city areas? Another influential group is likely to have been the Association of Chief Police Officers (ACPO). On 16 December, the Home Secretary announced that the Government had undertaken 'extensive consultations with, among others, the Association of Chief Police Officers' . . . It is likely, however, that ACPO's voice would have received a more sympathetic hearing at the Home Office than the others to whom the Home Secretary referred. The Association has, in recent years, been vociferous in its demands."[27]

Meanwhile some of those who had supported the Royal Commission's "compromise package" began to realise that a sort of confidence trick had been played on them. The quid pro quo for the drastic new proposals was scarcely in evidence. Tape recording experiments carried out in police stations in Scotland proved disastrous (see p 200) and discussions about an independent prosecutor system were still going on in the background – the police being particularly unhappy about the Royal Commission's idea of locally based prosecutors. One of the Commission's supposedly "radical" members took to the pages of the *Times* to express his own sense of betrayal.[28]

Police lobbying on the criminal justice system has not been confined to senior police officers. The Police Federation (the organisation of police constables – they are not allowed to form a trade union) has been mounting "law and order" campaigns demanding changes in the criminal justice system and the restoration of capital punishment since the mid 1970s. These campaigns have often coincided with election periods. As Martin Kettle pointed out, such lobbying by the Federation has by no means always been in harmony with that done by senior police officers. Recently Sir Robert Mark (now retired) wrote about why he is opposed to capital punishment. His reasoning is that if the death penalty is restored this will mean that safeguards in the judicial process protecting the suspect, which he believes to be unnecessarily cumbersome, will have to be retained or restored to prevent the state from hanging the wrong person. Sir Robert wrote that:

"I believe that the best deterrent to deliberate crime is not the severity of punishment, unlikely to be applied because of excessive safeguards to prevent injustice, but the likelihood of being caught followed by a high probability of conviction. Acquittal for the experienced criminal is encouraging and an incentive to commit further crime. A greater likelihood of conviction of wrongdoers would lessen rather than increase the need for severity of punishment".[29]

Despite Sir Robert's remarks the Police Federation have reacted to Parliament's recent decisive rejection of capital punishment by demanding increased sentences and that "life should mean life".

In practice the two demands for withdrawal of safeguards in the judicial process and for increased custodial sentences are often made together by the police. The recent abolition of the dock statement was clearly connected to its successful use in the course of the trial in 1982 of the Bradford 12, whose acquittal infuriated police.[30] The demands for disqualification of convicted offenders from juries, ostensibly made on the grounds of alleged cases of interference with juries, have been deliberately encouraged by police who are worried about the increasing tendency for jurors to disbelieve police evidence.[31] Doubtless demands for further such measures, together with increased sentencing, will continue. And in policing terms, the passing of a new Police Bill will be likely to be succeeded by further demands. It is possible that the police suggested the new powers to search confidential files which the government have now substantially dropped. They may well return to this demand as well as to the remaining proposal of the Criminal Law Revision Committee not implemented; that the form of caution be amended to remove altogether the right to silence.

Notes

1. *Observer* 27.3.83.
2. *Justice Deserted* by Harriet Harman and John Griffith (NCCL, 1979).
3. Lord Denning *What next in the Law* (Butterworths 1982).
4. *New Statesman* 5.7.82.
5. Northern Ireland (Emergency Provisions) Act 1973 S 2.
6. *A History of Police in England and Wales* by T A Critchley (Constable 1978) p 300.
7. *Op cit* p xiii.
8. *The Politics of Policing and the Policing of Politics* by Martin Kettle in *Policing the Police,* ed P Hain (John Calder 1981) vol 2 p 17.
9. Eleventh Report of the Criminal Law Revision Committee (Cmnd 4991) June 1972, p 13 paras 22 and 24.
10. *Ibid passim* eg, p 29 para 50.
11. *The Listener* Vol 101, 1979, p 441-2.
12. Quoted by Martin Kettle *Op cit*
13. *In the Office of Constable* by Sir Robert Mark (Fontana 1979) p 163.
14. Martin Kettle *Op cit* p 32.
15. *Ibid* p 23.
16. *Ibid*.
17. *Written Evidence of the Commissioner of Police of the Metropolis to the Royal Commission on Criminal Procedure,* Scotland Yard, 1978.
18. Martin Kettle, *Op cit* p 26.
19. *Report of an Inquiry by the Hon. Sir Henry Fisher into the circumstances leading to the trial of three persons on charges arising out of the death of Maxwell Confait and the fire at 27 Doggett Road, London, SE6.* HC 90 13.12.77 para 2.17.
20. David Leigh *Op cit*
21. *Written Evidence of the Commissioner of Police of the Metropolis to the Royal Commission on Criminal Procedure, op cit.*
22. Martin Kettle *Op cit* p 27.
23. David Leigh, *Op cit*.
24. *Ibid*.

25.   Home Office Consultative Memorandum on the Report of the Royal
        Commission on Criminal Procedure July 1981.
26.   Police and Criminal Evidence Bill (as Amended by Standing Committee J)
        clauses 59, 62.
27.   *Policing London* No. 5, GLC, January 1983.
28.   *Times* 19.11.82.
29.   *Observer* 10.7.83.
30.   The Bradford 12 were a group of Asian youths charged with conspiracy to
        cause explosions. The trial became a test case for community self-defence.
31.   *New Statesman* 5.7.82.

C. New Powers on the Streets and in the Home

2. Stop and Search of Persons

The new police powers in the Police Bill were all in the first part of it; Clause I established new powers of stop and search. At present there are powers to stop and search persons in public places for stolen goods in London and other metropolitan areas.[1] The Royal Commission on Criminal Procedure had recommended extension of the power of stop and search to anything the possession of which in a public place is in itself a criminal offence, subject to requirements that grounds for the search should be recorded by police.[2] The Bill adopted the substance of this recommendation by extending the power to offensive weapons and items made or adapted for use in the course of or in connection with burglary, theft, taking a motor vehicle without authority and obtaining property by deception.[3] The Bill did not attempt to define the "reasonable suspicion" on which the power of stop and search is dependent. The Royal Commission on Criminal Procedure stated that:

> "Clarification of powers will help but the principal safeguard must be found in the requirements for and stricter application of the criterion of reasonable suspicion".[4]

Perhaps it was not surprising that they went on to find that it was "impracticable" to define "reasonable suspicion" and to rely on the supposed safeguarding which would result from the recording of reasons by the police officer. The Greater London Council's response to the Royal Commission Report asked:

> "If the Commission with all its expertise was unable to arrive at some agreed standards to define 'reasonable suspicion' . . . how can the recording of reasons – undoubtedly in standard form – be challenged?".[5]

The Bill did not relate the criterion of "reasonable suspicion" to the commission of a particular offence. This part of the Bill therefore represented a return to the idea of "suspicious persons" embodied in the old "sus" law. It was made clear in Committee debates that a police constable would not have to suspect that a particular offence had been or was about to be committed. It would be sufficient to search for an offensive weapon if:

> "A young man known to have a record for that type of offence . . . is seen in circumstances in which he has committed the offence before in company with people with whom he has committed the offence before",[6]

or for drugs if, a person is known to be:

> "a regular drug carrier".[7]

The proposed use of the stop and search powers in new police tactics of "targeting and surveillance" is examined in Chapter 18.

The emptiness of the criterion of "reasonable suspicion" was further demonstrated by the necessity to prove intent in relation to the carrying of offensive weapons. Many perfectly innocent items can be offensive weapons but only if the prosecution proves an intention to use them as such.[8] In addition the power to confiscate items would also be extended by the Bill to those which the police believed would be used offensively by someone other than the person stopped, even though carrying such items is not an offence.[9] It is difficult to know how "reasonable suspicion" could be formed in relation to an article concealed in a person's pocket, when the police officer could not know how it is to be used. Would the mere fact of carrying such an item (eg a bunch of keys, a comb, a penknife or a pair of scissors) always be sufficient to justify a stop and search?

The power of stop and search could therefore amount to a requirement that people out on the streets (particularly youth) justify to the police the possession of any item in their pockets. If they failed to do so the police could then confiscate the item and/or charge them with an offence.

Meanwhile the safeguards in the Bill were considerably weakened by failures in definition. They consisted of a requirement that police officers record the reasons for the search so that it could supposedly be challenged in a court. Arguably however the test of "reasonable suspicion" would only be capable of becoming anything like objective if it was properly defined. The likely effect of the requirement that police officers record their reasons for search is examined in Chapter 21.

The prime illustration of the total devaluation of the criterion of "reasonable suspicion" required by stop and search has been the incidence of random searches. The Royal Commission on Criminal Procedure recognised concern about this but failed to meet their own finding that:

> "There must be safeguards to protect members of the public from random, arbitrary and discriminatory searches";[10]

Operation Swamp '81 which precipitated the Brixton riots must have contained a large number of such searches, as 943 were carried out in one week in Brixton.[11] But Commander Fairbairn's evidence to the Scarman Enquiry may cast some doubt as to whether he accepted that searches should not be random:

> **Lord Scarman:** "Mr Fairbairn, you are being asked about the exercise of the statutory power to stop – not just accosting somebody in the street – and that person impliedly agreeing to stop and converse and answer questions. You are being asked about the statutory power of stopping. It is quite clear and we do not need to waste time about it, that that can be done legally or can be done illegally."
> **Mr Fairbairn:** "Yes. However I would have thought that if a policeman saw fit to stop a person in the exercise of his powers under the Metropolitan Police Act, he would be doing so legally.[12]

"Reasonable Force"

The Bill would have allowed a constable to use "reasonable force if necessary" both in carrying out a stop and search and in detaining a person in order to carry it out.[13] A similar provision also related to search of premises.[14] At present police officers are not by law permitted to use any more force against the person than anyone else, although the practice has been said to diverge enormously from theory.[15] The law governing the present situation is as follows:

> "A person may use such force as is reasonable in the circumstances in the prevention of crime, or in effecting or assisting in the lawful arrest of offenders or suspected offenders or of persons unlawfully at large".[16]

The Bill's provisions were a significant departure from the notion of policing by consent, which has underpinned the legal theory of police power up to now. The danger of such specific provisions would be that the courts may feel bound to interpret them less restrictively than the existing law quoted above. Because of the rules of judicial interpretation, the provisions in the Bill allowing the use of force in specific instances by police officers would be interpreted to extend and add to the existing law. Thus the use of force *without* reference to the "prevention of crime or in effecting or assisting in the lawful arrest of offenders" would be specifically legitimised.

Clearly the government envisaged that "frisking" might be necessary even where there was no resistance. The then Minister of State, Patrick Mayhew, MP, said that the police could not be expected:

> "To invite someone to empty his or her pockets or bag when that person is, for example, suspected of carrying an offensive weapon or a packet of drugs, which he could simply take out of his pocket and drop down a grating".[17]

The provisions were highly dangerous because it allowed a police officer to use force at the outset regardless of whether or not the person was committing an offence or resisting. The provisions clearly allowed the exercise of force in circumstances in which ordinary citizens would be acting illegally in carrying out stops and searches by force.

There are at present no guidelines laid down by the courts as to what is a "reasonable" exercise of a special power to use force given to the police, since in the past the "reasonableness" criterion has always been related to the stated purpose of preventing crime or apprehending offenders (see Chapter 20).

Apart from the difficulty of proving "reasonable suspicion" the loose definitions of the "offensive weapon"[18] and "equipment for stealing"[19] charges were problems in themselves. The case of *R v. Dayle* establishes a distinction between "offensive weapons per se", eg a flick knife, and those where the prosecution must prove intent to use a particular item offensively.[20] Unfortunately such intention is all too often established in the case of common everyday items, such as a small penknife, by "verballing", eg the following series of questions and answers cited by the Haldane Society in their evidence to the Royal Commission on Criminal Procedure:

"Question: Do you carry your penknife to fight with?

Answer:	No
Question:	If you were attacked would you use it?
Answer:	I suppose so
Question:	Do you think you might get attacked?
Answer:	Probably
Question:	So you might use it then in a fight?
Answer:	Yes
Officer:	I'm arresting you for being in possession of an offensive weapon".[21]

Given that a majority of young teenage men and boys carry penknives, the implications of this are alarming. In the country the carrying of a penknife by boys is encouraged (the "boy scout" mentality) but in working class urban areas, it can lead to criminalisation. Examples of innocent items carried in the pockets alleged to be "offensive" weapons include a pair of scissors, gloves, pipecleaners, tools for work and a nail file. The *Daily Mail* reported a case of a 16 year old boy being locked in a cell for two hours after police accused him of carrying an offensive weapon, ie a silver-headed cane. The report stated that the police released the boy after they realised he was only a "snappy dresser".[22]

The offence of "going equipped for stealing" is equally problematical. An article "made or adapted for use . . ." may be a screwdriver, a spanner, keys, a credit card, any thin piece of plastic, car tools, or work tools. Once possession of this kind of item has been proved, the burden of proof actually shifts to the defendant to show that the article was in his or her possession for purposes other than burglary or theft.[23]

For these reasons such offences have in some areas of London acquired a reputation similar to the old "sus" law. To this can be added the factor of the emotive nature of the "offensive weapon" charge in view of increasing racial attacks on black people, in respect of which there are constant complaints of lack of police protection. There have also been widely publicised instances of prosecutions on offensive weapons charges of women carrying items which they stated they would use for self protection if attacked late at night. Under the Bill stops and searches could be used even more widely to look for small everyday items such as penknives and spanners.

A pamphlet on the "sus" law by Clare Demuth of The Runnymede Trust referred to a police practice of "double charging", ie, associating sus charges with other offences:

"In the first category the offences most commonly associated with 'sus' are attempted theft and 'going equipped to steal'. Both provide possible alternative methods of prosecution. In the second category searching the suspect may lead to the discovery of an offensive weapon, such as a penknife, contrary to the Prevention of Crimes Act 1953".[24]

It concluded that:

"The range of charges associated with 'sus' indicates that although deleting 'sus' from the statute book might lead to a decrease in the number of convictions for intent to steal, it would not necessarily limit the power of the police either to arrest those whom they think are about to make a theft or more generally to assert their control over the streets".[25]

Finally a problem with the provisions in the Bill much debated in Standing Committee J was that they allowed stops and searches to be carried out by plain clothes officers. In Parliament MPs questioned how a member of the public would be able to tell police officers from thieves and Ian Mikardo MP described vividly what his reaction would be if he or his car were searched late at night by a plain clothes man.[26] It is however unlikely that these provisions will be changed because Newman's plans for District Support Units (which will be carrying out many stops and searches) involve them in far more plain clothes operations (see Chapter 18).

Notes

1. S66 Metropolitan Police Act 1839.
2. Royal Commission on Criminal Procedure *op cit* para 3.20.
3. Police and Criminal Evidence Bill (as amended by Standing Committee J) Clause 1(5).
4. *Op cit* para 3.25
5. Greater London Council: Report by the Head of the Police Committee Support Unit PC23 2.3.82.
6. *Hansard* Standing Committee J, 16.12.82, Col 81 Patrick Mayhew MP.
7. *Hansard* Standing Committee J. 9.12.82. Col 19 Sir Nicholas Bonsor MP.
8. Prevention of Crimes Act 1953 S 1.
9. *Hansard* Standing Committee J, 9.12.82, Col 22 Patrick Mayhew MP.
10. *Op cit* para 3.24.
11. *The Brixton Disorders 10-12 April 1981* Report by Lord Scarman OBE (Cmnd 8427) November 1981, para 4.40.
12 Before Lord Scarman: In the matter of S32 Police Act 1964 and in the matter of a Local Inquiry into the Brixton Disturbances on 10 to 12 April 1981. Transcript of the shorthand notes of Marten Meredith and Company Limited and Walsh Cherer and Company Limited Volume 11 Page 17.
13. *Op cit* Clause 2(5); the phrase "such reasonable force as is necessary" was to

be replaced by "reasonable force *if* necessary" under a government amendment tabled at Report Stage. The same amendment allowed "reasonable force if necessary" to conduct a search *or* to detain a person or vehicle for the purpose of carrying out a search.

14. *Op cit* Clause 9(1). Again a government amendment tabled at Report Stage would have substituted "reasonable force *if* necessary" for "such reasonable force as is necessary".

15. See for example *Constitutional and Administrative Law* by de Smith: 4th edition edited by Harry Street and Rodney Brazier (Penguin 1981) P 382-3.

16. S3 Criminal Law Act 1967.

17. *Hansard* Standing Committee J, 21.12.82, Col 140 Patrick Mayhew MP.

18. Prevention of Crimes Act 1953.

19. Theft Act 1968 S25.

20. R v. Dayle (1973) ALL ER 1151.

21. *The Police, the Law and the People* by Nick Blake (Haldane Society of Socialist Lawyers 1981) P 20.

22. *Daily Mail* 5.11.82.

23. Theft Act 1968 s25 and *Stones Justice Manual* (Butterworth and Company 1982) Vol 2 page 4891.

24. *Sus a report on the Vagrancy Act 1824* by Clare Demuth (Runnymede Trust April 1978) P 49.

25. *Ibid* P 50.

26. *Hansard* Standing Committee J, 9.12.82, Col 7 Ian Mikardo MP.

3. The Present Law on Stop and Search and its History

In the Standing Committee on the Bill the question of whether stop and search powers were really necessary, or did anything to prevent crime, was never really debated at all. Throughout the debates on it in Parliament, only one MP said he did not believe stop and search powers were necessary.[1] The Opposition's objections to the Bill were because it extended stop and search powers, not because it did not abolish them. Subsequently the Labour Party's manifesto in the General Election promised only to restrict but not abolish these powers.[2]

S66 Metropolitan Police Act 1839 covering the Metropolitan Police District provides that:

> "Every such constable may also stop, search and detain any vessel, boat, cart or carriage in or upon which there shall be reason to suspect that anything stolen or unlawfully obtained may be found and also any person who may be reasonably suspected of having or conveying in any manner anything stolen or unlawfully obtained."

The provision was re-enacted to cover other Metropolitan areas, such as Liverpool.[3] In addition there are more modern statutory powers to stop and search for specific items; firearms,[4] birds' eggs,[5] fish[6] and drugs.[7]

Yet before leaping to the conclusion that stop and search powers are necessary because they already exist, there should be examination as to whether the legal and historical justification for those powers still applies and whether police officers really require such powers. If a police officer has "reasonable suspicion" that an offence has been committed, s/he can arrest a person for the offence. Subsequent to the arrest, the person can be searched at the police station, under rules governing searches after arrest. The grounds justifying stop and search of a person by a police constable on the street are identical to those justifying arrest, namely "reasonable suspicion".

In the Standing Committee debates on the Police Bill, Roy Hattersley MP asked whether stop and search powers were intended to be an "alternative" to arrest but this question was never satisfactorily answered or explored.[8] In fact there seem to be two separate arguments for the retention of stop and search: one is the historical reason for the original incorporation into English criminal law of stop and search powers for stolen goods; and the other is an argument developed since and propounded by the Royal Commission on Criminal Procedure.

The historical justification for stop and search powers for stolen goods was that these powers were needed to operate a form of legal proceeding introduced at the same time (1839[9]). Under this anyone carrying goods reasonably suspected to be stolen could be hauled up in front of a magistrate and required to give a satisfactory explanation. If no explanation was forthcoming they would be convicted of an offence or "misdemeanour". The logic behind this was that carrying stolen goods need not necessarily be an offence in itself if the person carrying them had acquired them innocently. It applied not only in London but also in other large cities, where local stop and search powers for stolen goods were also given to the police.

The rationale for this form of legal proceeding is now, however, officially discredited. The relevant legislation was repealed by the Criminal Law Act 1977. The reason was that it ran contrary to a basic principle of English law, that what is called "the burden of proof" should be on the prosecution. This means that it is up to the prosecution to show that an accused person is guilty, not up to the accused to show that they are innocent. Moreover the "reasonable suspicion" justifying an arrest must be referable to a specific offence not just suspicious circumstances. L H Leigh in his textbook on police powers explains the modern attitude to the old form of proceeding:

> "Such provisions are an intolerable and, it is submitted, unnecessary departure from the normal rules of criminal evidence and proof and should be abolished".[10]

Victorian values

If the reversal of the "burden of proof" has been officially discredited, its shadow lingers on. Together with the Vagrancy Act of 1824 the provision was a part of that body of Victorian law which was considered necessary for the purposes of social control and which discriminated between persons according to their social status. Since many of the provisions in the Police Bill appear to be a return to that mentality and since in some respects Sir Kenneth Newman's new policing strategies might be said to be simply an updated version of it, this theme will be discussed later.[11] But the way in which the original justification for the "sus" law[12] was transformed into an argument on the inadequacy of the law governing attempted crimes may be compared with modern justifications advanced for stop and search powers.[13]

The Royal Commission on Criminal Procedure did not base their acceptance of the necessity for stop and search powers on any argument about crime prevention or social control. They stated fairly and squarely that the purpose of the powers was "the detection of crime and the arrest of offenders".[14] However they rejected the idea that the police powers of arrest should be sufficient to allow them to carry out their functions if stop and search were abolished because, they said:

"Although the grounds for exercising the power to stop and search and the power of arrest may in some circumstances be the same, that is not necessarily always so, and the powers are exercised at distinct stages in the process of investigation. If this proposal were put into effect, it might lead to an increased use of arrest, and this is something which we wish to preclude, both because it can involve a more significant deprivation of liberty than that involved in stop and search and because of the consequences that flow from it. To guard against this it would be necessary to make the power to search dependent upon the power to arrest and this would do no more than create by another means the power to stop and search. It would be a cumbersome expedient. We conclude that, provided better safeguards can be developed, it would be simpler and clearer to rely upon an explicit statutory power to stop and search prior to arrest".[15]

The Royal Commission begged several questions in their reasoning. First, they did not have the benefit of the Home Office Research Report discussed subsequently and assumed that stop and search was valuable in detecting crime.[16] Second, they missed the issue of the identical criterion of "reasonable suspicion" for arrest and stop and search. Logically either stop and search should require lesser criterion or arrest a greater. In practice, as will be argued later, the police constantly adopt a lesser criterion for stop and search. It must therefore be considered whether a lesser criterion is acceptable or can justify the exercise of coercive powers. The lesser criterion will inevitably be the sort which would be unarguable in a court of law, ie, the police constable's "hunch" based on their subjective notions of "suspicious" appearance or behaviour.

One of the most eminent English constitutional lawyers, Professor Glanville Williams, has therefore argued for the abolition of all stop and search powers because they add nothing to the ordinary powers of arrest and search after the person has been arrested. He argued that the advantages of the extra power are illusory, based on the erroneous assumption that the police:

> "are empowered to search anyone whose behaviour is at all out of the usual, even though they have no solid grounds of suspicion".[17]

Third the Commission assumed that dealing with all situations where a police constable has "reasonable suspicion" of an offence, by way of arrest, would be detrimental to the public. They ignored the advantages of requiring a person to be arrested before they are searched – it is only by this means that the criterion of "reasonable suspicion" can be defined and made a real requirement. An arrest is a formal legal process which carries some safeguards (eg, the right to sue the police for false imprisonment) and which the Royal Commission recommended should carry more, on a necessity principle.[18]

Finally, and perhaps most importantly, the Royal Commission ignored the ability of the police to search a person on the street with the *consent* of that person as an alternative to the exercise of their powers. If the police are going to arrest a person but that person is able to avoid arrest by submitting voluntarily to a search and proving their innocence, the chances are that they will consent voluntarily to a search. The advantage of this is that it puts the onus on the police to ask people if they will consent to be searched in the first instance, where they are uncertain of the grounds for "reasonable suspicion". Blanket powers of stop and search, on the other hand, may have the opposite effect: they allow police to frisk people by force, without bothering to ask permission.

If stop and search powers were abolished, it would appear that existing powers of arrest are quite adequate to deal with all the circumstances. Theft, burglary and deception are all "arrestable" offences, so is the offence of "going equipped to steal".[19] Arrest without warrant is also possible for the offence of carrying an offensive weapon, if either the suspect's name and address cannot be ascertained or to prevent an offence in which an offensive weapon might be used.[20] It could be argued that the offence of possession of an offensive weapon should be made fully arrestable, but it would certainly be preferable to do this than to extend stop and search powers.

It is suggested that if stop and search powers were abolished, many of those searches on the street which do not produce result would be carried out voluntarily. Of the remainder some – those where there are no real grounds for "reasonable suspicion" – would not occur at all. The net result would be only a small increase in the number of arrests overall, vastly increased protection for the individual, and the removal of one of the biggest impediments to better police-community relations.

Notes

1. *Hansard* Parliamentary Debates 30.11.82 Col 181-2, Robert Kilroy-Silk MP.
2. *Labour's Plan – The New Hope for Britain* (The Labour Party, March 1983) para 136.
3. Liverpool Corporation Act 1921 S 507(1).
4. Firearms Act 1968 S 47.
5. Protection of Bird Act 1967 S 11.
6. Salmon and Freshwater Fisheries Act 1923 S 54(3) and 68, Salmon and Freshwater Fisheries Act 1972 S 11.
7. Misuse of Drugs Act 1971 S 23.
8. *Hansard* Standing Committee J, 9.12.82, Col 15 Roy Hattersley MP.
9. Metropolitan Police Courts Act 1839 S 24.
10. *Police Powers in England and Wales* by L H Leigh (Butterworths 1975) p 137.
11. See Chapter 18..
12. Section 4 of the Vagrancy Act 1824.
13. See *Sus – a report on the Vagrancy Act 1824* by Clare Demuth (Runnymede Trust, April 1978) p 46-7. See also the Criminal Attempts Act 1981 passed on the abolition of the "sus" law.
14. Royal Commission on Criminal Procedure, *Op cit,* para 3.17.
15. *Ibid* para 3.19.
16. *The use, effectiveness and impact of police stop and search powers* by Carole F Willis (Home Office Research and Planning Unit Paper 15 1983). Discussed in Chapter 5.
17. *Statutory powers of search and arrest on the grounds of unlawful possession* Glanville Williams (1960) Criminal Law Review 598.
18. *Op cit* para 3.75 *et seq*. See also Chapter 9.
19. Theft Act 1968 S 25(4).
20. Prevention of Crime Act 1953 S 1.

4. Stop and Search of Vehicles and Roadblocks

The provisions in the Police Bill relating to stop and search of persons would apply equally to stop and search of vehicles, except that vehicles would only be stopped by a police officer in uniform. This is true of the existing power to stop and search vehicles for stolen goods in London.[1] In addition there is an existing power under the Road Traffic Act 1972 to stop vehicles at random.[2] However there is no power to set up roadblocks at random under existing law. Undoubtedly roadblocks do take place but because police usually have to rely on public co-operation rather than on legal powers they may have been considerably more circumspect in doing so in the past than they will be in the future. The significance of roadblocks is that they would be the first ever legal power given to police to prevent or control systematically the flow of all traffic into an area.

The Bill called roadblocks "road checks" and defined them as:

> "the obstruction of a road in order to stop –
> (a) all vehicles passing along it, or
> (b) vehicles selected by any criterion."[3]

It allowed them to be set up on the authority of a superintendent unless a police officer of any rank considered that one was needed as a matter of urgency.[4] In that case it had to be reported to a superintendent as soon as possible who would decide if it should continue.[5]

They were to be set up for a period of not exceeding seven days but could be renewed indefinitely. A police officer could set one up on two grounds. The first was if he or she reasonably suspected that someone committing a "serious arrestable offence", or an escaped prisoner was in the area. The second was if:

> "having regard to a pattern of crime in that area, a serious arrestable offence is likely to be committed in that area within the period for which the road check would be set up."[6]

The Royal Commission stated in relation to roadblocks:

"If such checks are to be allowed, they should be confined to a particular type of serious crime and should be regularised by the introduction of a measure of supervisory control".[7]

They went on to propose that:

"a police officer of rank not less than Assistant Chief Constable should be empowered to authorise in writing the setting up of road checks for a limited and specified period in the following circumstances: when a person whose arrest is sought in connection with a grave offence is believed on reasonable grounds to be moving in a particular area; and when there is reason to suppose that a grave offence . . . may be committed in a defined area over a specified period".[8]

The limitations on this power proposed by the Royal Commission were omitted from the Bill. First the power was to be exercised by reference to "a pattern of crime" and not to the commission of a particular serious offence. This was directly contrary to the Royal Commission's proposals. Second, the period for which roadblocks were to be set up was not "limited and specified" but for a seven day period *renewable indefinitely*. Third, the area within which roadblocks may be set up was not "defined" but left wide open. Fourth the Bill allowed a superintendent, or in an emergency *any* police officer, to give authority for a roadblock, rather than an Assistant Chief Constable, as proposed by the Royal Commission. Finally the Bill did not give a person being stopped at a roadblock any right to know of the reasons for the stop even though the Royal Commission recommended that, "the reason for the check would be incorporated in the written authorisation and should be explained to persons whose freedom of movement has been temporarily restricted at a check point."[9]

The Royal Commission gave some recognition to the dangers of giving police very wide powers to stop and search vehicles and to impede the flow of traffic along a road. They also criticised the existing power under the Road Traffic Act 1972 to stop vehicles at random and its use as "a subterfuge for exercising the power of stop upon suspicion".[10] However their proposals for roadblocks paved the way for the very wide powers in the Bill. During the Standing Committee debates it was pointed out that the provisions in the Bill would effectively give the police power to set up roadblocks at random whenever they liked. As Christopher Price, MP said:

"I should have thought that the pattern of crime in the Metropolitan
Police areas would justify any policeman to say at any time that a
serious arrestable offence may be committed . . . If the police want to
set up road checks anywhere or any time within the Metropolitan
Police area, I believe that they are absolutely legally free to do so and to
renew the powers every seven days throughout the year. I should not be
surprised if the Metropolitan Police simply put in a standing order
requesting road checks anywhere in the Metropolitan Police area to be
renewed every seven days".[11]

It should also be noted that because the police were not required to
give reasons for setting up a roadblock, it would not be possible for an
aggrieved member of the public to ascertain whether they had been
properly stopped.

The proposed new powers to set up roadblocks are particularly
alarming if considered in conjunction both with other powers in the
Bill and the new priority to be given to intelligence gathering under Sir
Kenneth Newman's strategies. Roadblocks could be set up around
areas where demonstrations are taking place, (eg, Greenham
Common, factory closure picket lines) and used to gather intelligence
on demonstrators as well as to prevent them reaching their
destination. Police would be able to search both the vehicles of
demonstrators stopped in roadblocks and the demonstrators
themselves. In this way the police would be able to control and
prevent social and industrial protest as well as to deter those who are
wanting to take part.

But the power to seal off areas by roadblocks is not confined to
those areas where specific political demonstrations are taking place.
It is possible that the police would use the new power in an attempt to
control certain areas, specifically those inhabited by black people,
which as noted before are invariably those defined as "high crime
areas" even though they are not necessarily those with the highest
recorded crime rates.[12] The process of arriving at these definitions is
by necessity a mystical one, looking at the "pattern of crime" – a
phrase invented by the police. It was described by Eldon Griffiths MP
(who represents the Police Federation as well as his constituency,
Bury St Edmunds) thus:

"On the subject of the pattern of crime, as a matter of experience one
has to take into account a wide range of matters. The volume of crime is
the most critical, but the nature of the crime is also important. There is
a great difference between the theft of cars and the use of knives. There
is a great difference too, in the intensity of crime. For example, in an

area with a number of old people's homes crimes against the elderly, which is common practice these days, must be taken into account. It depends on the neighbourhood and a lot of other circumstances. The English language is well used when it takes the word 'pattern' to try to comprehend the wide range of circumstances involving volume, the nature of the crime, the background, the intensity of it and so on. For example, 'pattern of crime' would be a good description of the reason why roadblocks are necessary in Northern Ireland."[13]

Finally the new power could be used to increase the quality and extent of information stored on the Police National Computer. As in Northern Ireland it could be used to build up a systematic picture of a particular community and its movements, as well as to isolate and "ghettoise" it. If they use roadblocks to control the population in this way, the police would simply be imitating the activities of the British army and the Royal Ulster Constabulary in Northern Ireland for many years. This subject will be further explored in Chapter 19 on "Policing and Surveillance".

Notes

1. Metropolitan Police Act 1839 S 66.
2. Road Traffic Act 1972 S 159.
3. Police and Criminal Evidence Bill (as amended by Standing Committee J) Clause 4(2).
4. *Ibid* Clause 4(5).
5. *Ibid* Clause 4(6).
6. *Ibid* Clause 4(3).
7. Royal Commission on Criminal Procedure *Op cit* para 3.31.
8. *Ibid* para 3.32.
9. *Ibid*.
10. Royal Commission on Criminal Procedure *Op cit* para 3.31.
11. *Hansard* Standing Committee J, 20.1.83 Col 211.
12. See Chapter 18 page 142.
13. *Hansard* Standing Committee J, 20.1.83 Col 209 Eldon Griffiths MP.

5. Does Stop and Search Prevent Crime?

All the evidence shows that stop and search does little to prevent crime. Figures published by the Royal Commission on Criminal Procedure showed that in 1978 searches for drugs resulted in a 27% arrest rate outside London and a 38% arrest rate in London.[1] However police records divide stops into those for drugs and those "re movements". The latter category has been described as "stops made on grounds which police officers find it hard to specify"[2] and includes stops on suspicion of carrying stolen goods. The percentages in this latter category are, as will be seen, much lower and should be reduced still further by the large number of unrecorded stops. Further figures for the Metropolitan Police District recording all stops showed arrest rates of only 12% and 13% in two one-month periods in 1978/79.[3]

More evidence comes from the Scarman Enquiry and the Metropolitan Commissioner's Reports. In Operation Swamp '81 in Brixton in April 1981 which led to the riots, 943 stops were made and 118 people arrested, out of which 75 charges resulted, many for offences such as "threatening behaviour", assault and obstruction. Only 22 persons were charged for offences such as robbery, theft and burglary.[4] The Metropolitan Police Commissioner's Report shows that in 1981 the Special Patrol Group detained 19,908 pedestrians and 16,982 vehicles. In the same period SPG arrests (related and unrelated) were 3,341 for crime, 1,775 "other" arrests and 1,250 persons reported for traffic offences.[5] In 1982 the SPG stopped 20,804 pedestrians and 13,678 vehicles. They made 3,846 arrests for crime and 2,499 "other" arrests[6] ("other" arrests are simply those which are for offences not classified as serious). These figures were only for SPG arrests. The following table shows stop and searches recorded in E District (Camden) alone, in which arrest rates were less than 10%.

Persons and vehicles stopped and resultant arrests*
E District (Camden) Metropolitan Police

Year	Persons or vehicles stopped	Resultant arrests*	Arrests as % of stops made
1979	24,374	2,344	9.6
1980	24,635	1,862	7.6
1981	25,759	2,200	8.5
1982	32,065	2.632	8.2

*Persons proceeded against by means of a charge, referral to juvenile bureau, a caution or in some other way; arrests not followed by any action are not included.
Source: Hansard 27.7.83 col 470.

By far the strongest evidence that stop and search does little to prevent crime came to light after Parliament considered the Police Bill. At the time Standing Committee was considering Clause 1, it was known that a Home Office research project on stop and search was under way and MPs asked unsuccessfully for it to be made available. The project is reputed to have been completed at the time but not released because it was under careful consideration by the Home Office. As Melanie Phillips stated:

"Suspicions were inevitably aroused that its conclusions were too embarrassing for the government to make known ... The Home Office researchers are undoubtedly caught in a web of political and professional pressures imposed by politicians, officials and their academic peers".[7]

However the Report, published in April 1983, contained the most convincing reasons why the continued use of stop and search should be questioned. Not only did it show that the so-called "safeguards" in the Bill requiring police officers to write down reasons would be useless and that stop and search powers were used discriminatorily against black people, it is also demonstrated that exercise of the powers does very little to prevent crime by catching criminals.

The Home Office researchers collected detailed information about stops from Kensington and Peckham police stations in London and Watford and Luton outside London. The findings were that the percentage of recorded stops resulting in prosecutions was 8% for the

Metropolitan stations but only 2% for the provincial stations. The researchers commented that:

> "Since it has been estimated that up to one half of all stops made are not recorded, this suggests that the percentage of prosecutions resulting from all stops could be as low as 4% in London and 1% elsewhere"[8].

A major defect in the Report appears to be its failure (and of course the police's failure) to distinguish between stops and stop and searches. Thus the Report states that:

> "Recorded stops need not necessarily end in a search, but very few stop records at any of the stations visited mentioned whether the person or vehicle stopped was searched"[9].

It goes on to say that officers at the four stations researched estimated that "at most a quarter of all stops they made resulted in a search"[10]. It is not clear what effect this has, but it is suggested that many of the arrests may arise from stops rather than stop and searches. The difference between a stop and a stop and search is vital, because if stop and search powers were abolished stops would still be made and result in arrests.

Another factor not dealt with by the Report is the extent to which stop and search *creates* crime. This could be measured in part by counting the number of offences, such as obstruction or assault on police, which can be said to arise out of the stop and search itself. However, the Report barely hints that these kind of offences may figure large in the Metropolitan Police District when it says:

> "In the MPD, arrests from stops made up a substantial proportion (perhaps as much as half) of all relevant arrests that are made. The result is more likely to be due to the greater importance of stops in the clear-up of offences in London than to the particular effectiveness of stop and search there. It follows that the removal of existing powers of stop and search would greatly reduce the number of arrests for certain offences (particularly the less serious) in the MPD".[11]

However a useful passage in the Report puts paid once and for all to the claim that the police need new powers in order to prevent football hooligans carrying offensive weapons. Both Luton and Watford have football grounds where searches are carried out inside the grounds under the regulations of the football clubs (ie, *not* under the police's statutory powers) or as in Luton, by co-operation outside the ground, failing which admittance is refused. In relation to this the Report says, "co-operation was usually forthcoming therefore".[12]

Despite its defects, the Report effectively demolishes all claims that stop and search prevents crime by catching criminals. But it manages to skirt the true implications of its findings only by avoiding asking the crucial question: are stop and search powers really necessary?

Deterrence and Pressure

In evidence to the Scarman Enquiry police officers responsible for Swamp '81, unable to defend the figures for that operation from the arrest rates, contended instead that it had somehow "deterred" criminals. That is not what instructions to officers prior to the exercise had said. They were told that:

> "The purpose of this operation is to flood identified areas in 'L' District to detect and arrest burglars and robbers. The essence of the exercise is therefore to ensure that all officers remain on the streets and success will depend on a concentrated effort of 'stops' based on powers of surveillance and suspicion preceded by persistent and astute questioning"[13].

On the first day of the Scarman Enquiry Deputy Assistant Commissioner Walker, questioned by Mr Simmonds, admitted that the operation had not been successful in catching burglars or robbers but claimed a deterrent effect.[14]

Lord Scarman concluded that although operations like Swamp '81 might result in a fall off of crime figures, the effect would only be temporary and would probably only relocate burglaries and thefts outside the affected areas.[15]

The notion that putting "pressure" on an area of high crime deters criminals is however widely held among police. Deputy Assistant Commissioner David Powis wrote in his training manual:

> "Never be disappointed because your stops are not always recorded as arrests. Who is to say that an apparently unsuccessful stop is not a crime prevented? Real effort will give your police area a reputation that it is a hot place for criminal loiterers and persons foolishly risking the conveyance of stolen property or contraband across it. Arrests and captures are important of course, but activity by uniformed officers in speaking to loiterers and suspicious persons is what is required to reduce the incidence of serious crime".[16]

The Home Office Research Study cited above found that:

> "Across police districts in 1981, the annual recorded stop rate was found to be significantly related to the recorded crime rate for notifiable offences, ie, stop and search powers are used particularly in high crime areas. It was also related to the percentage of the population which was black; police districts with large black populations are the districts where greatest use is made of stop".[17]

As will be discussed the correlation between what the police decide are "high crime areas" and those with a large black population is not borne out by the recorded crime statistics, as was found by another Home Office Research Study.[18] Yet the notion of putting pressure on such areas has led to their virtual sealing off and to "operations" such as Swamp '81. For example on 3 November 1981 the police in Notting Hill sealed off All Saints Road for 30 to 45 minutes. About 50 police searched everyone and all cars on the street. Some people were searched twice and one or two people were told to get out of the area. The given reason – the execution of a search warrant – was used in effect to issue a police warning to a whole community.

Meanwhile in Brixton the same police attitudes persist in relation to stop and search. The *Guardian* revealed that 728 stops in Brixton (up to 11 January 1983) had resulted in 280 arrests; 161 of which were for drug offences. The next most common categories were for drunkenness and offensive weapons. The article commented:

> "It sounds like a doubtful crusade against petty crime, with cannabis smokers elevated to public enemy number one. What about the most worrying local crimes – robbery and burglary?"[19]

The response of the Chief Superintendent in charge was reported to be:

> ". . . This kind of operation can't expect to catch the big robbers and burglars but it helps to keep *that kind of people* away".[20] (our emphasis).

One conclusion that can be drawn from this is that stop and search is not about preventing or detecting crime as such but about the police maintaining control on the streets. Chapter 16 examines the alleged police stereotyping of suspects and the possibility that control means clearing the streets not of offenders, but people identified as "criminal types" because of their appearance or behaviour.

Notes

1. *The Investigation and Prosecution of Criminal Offences in England and Wales: The Law and Procedure* HMSO Cmnd 8092, 1.1.81. (The Royal Commission on Criminal Procedure).
2. *The use, effectiveness and impact of police stop and search powers* by Carole F Willis *Op cit* p 15.
3. *Ibid*.
4. *Op cit* para 4.40.
5. *Report of the Commissioner of Police of the Metropolis for the year 1981* (HMSO Cmnd 8569) p 32.
6. *Report of the Commissioner of Police of the Metropolis for the year 1982* (HMSO Cmnd 8928) p 37.
7. *Guardian* 19.4.83.
8. Willis, *op cit,* p 17.
9. *Ibid* p 13.
10. *Ibid*.
11. *Ibid* p 23.
12. *Ibid* p 20.
13. Report of Lord Scarman *Op cit* para 4.39.
14. Transcript by shorthand writers *Op cit* Vol 1.
15. Report of Lord Scarman *Op cit* para 4.78.
16. *The Signs of Crime: Field Manual for Police* by David Powis (McGraw Hill 1977) p 104.
17. *Op cit* p 12-13.
18. *Race, crime and arrests* by Philip Stevens and Carole F Willis (Home Office Research Study No. 58, HMSO, August 1979).
19. *Guardian* 2.2.83.
20. *Ibid*.

6. Search of Premises

The Bill set out the conditions which had to be satisfied for the police to obtain search warrants of premises.

For the first time ever the Bill allowed search under warrant of premises for *evidence* of a serious arrestable offence regardless of whether the occupiers are suspected of the offence (or any other offence). The Bill specifically provided that this consideration should be immaterial.[1] The Royal Commission on Criminal Procedure stated that:

> "A compulsory power of search for evidence should be available only as a last resort. It should be granted only in exceptional circumstances and in respect of grave offences."[2]

The Royal Commission's proposals did pave the way for the provisions in the Bill, but the Bill also went far beyond what the Commission envisaged. Under the provisions in the Bill, searches for evidence would be made routinely. In relation to search of ordinary people's homes, there was also no provision for applying for an order for production of specific evidence in the first instance as envisaged by the Commission. And searches for "evidence" without a warrant would also be possible after arrest of the occupier.

The debates in the Committee and the public reaction to the provisions regarding search of premises have been remarkable, not only for the understandable opposition to the new powers regarding confidential information, but also for the relative lack of comment about those powers affecting ordinary people. It was left to a Tory MP, Sir Nicholas Bonsor, to point out that:

> "What we are doing, however, enables the police to go into the houses of innocent people, wholly unrelated to the crime, to search them, in some instances without giving prior warning to the owner of those premises, and with no opportunity given to him to put forward any reason why his home should not be searched."[3]

and to state *his* belief that the Committee and the House:

"should view with some suspicion and much careful thought, any proposals to extend the powers of officials of the state to go into private houses."[4]

There were very few safeguards attached to this new power and no reason to suppose that magistrates would do anything other than "rubberstamp" applications for search warrants, as is the practice now. Because of the nature of the procedure, it is indeed difficult to see how they could do anything else (see Chapter 7). The provision was a validation of raids on innocent people's homes in "fishing expeditions" for evidence. The police may be tempted to carry out speculative raids on the homes of friends and associates of suspects, even though they have no basis for doing so. The Bill would legitimise such arbitrary methods of "investigation". Application was not to be to a circuit judge but to an ordinary magistrate, who need only be satisfied that evidence of a "serious arrestable offence" was on the premises (see p 78 for definition of such offences). Alleged abuse of police power to search people's homes in unjustified or intimidatory raids is becoming increasingly well documented. Some examples are given in Chapter 8.

In the Standing Committee debates on the Police Bill, the Minister of State, Patrick Mayhew MP, attempted to assert that a general power to search for evidence, regardless of whether the occupier was suspected of a crime, was "not a new principle".[5] He went on:

"There has not been a general power to enter and search for evidence, but there are specific powers, which are dealt with in Appendix 5 of the first volume of the Royal Commission report."[6]

In fact a perusal of Appendix 5 reveals that *general* powers to search for evidence are granted only in exceptional cases, eg, in relation to an offence under the Official Secrets Act 1911, where the case is one of great emergency and immediate action is necessary in the interests of the state. There is no power to search for evidence of murders or rapes. The provisions in the Bill were therefore, as a government backbench MP, Sir Nicholas Bonsor, described them:

"an entirely new departure from any previous law which the House of Commons has seen fit to pass over the centuries."[7]

Precisely how and why is examined in more detail in the next chapter.

The Bill also provided that the magistrate issuing the search warrant should be satisfied that there was reasonable ground for believing that a serious arrestable offence had been committed and "that anything that might be produced in evidence at a trial for that offence" is on the premises.[8]

It was remarked in the Standing Committee in the House of Commons that "anything that might be produced in evidence" was not the same as anything which might lawfully be admitted into evidence. Some things might be produced but would be excluded under the rules of evidence. Nevertheless the police would still seek such items and use them in their investigations. Arthur Davidson MP for the Opposition Front Bench pointed out that:

> "it is difficult to sustain the argument, as I expect the Minister will try to do, that the clauses as they stand distinguish between evidence and information."[9]

Before the Bill fell the government said they would change the definition. But even so, all sorts of things might be admitted lawfully in evidence which would be of little relevance to the offence.

A further government amendment was that the evidence would have to be of "substantial" value (whether by itself or together with other evidence) to the investigation in connection with which the application is made[10]. But, as we shall see, there was no requirement in the Bill specifying the information to be given to magistrates to enable them to decide whether this was so before granting a search warrant.

The provisions would give an express power to police constables to use reasonable force if necessary in carrying out a search. This illustrated the disturbing nature of the new powers to search premises (the power would also apply where search warrants for confidential information were granted). Since the person whose premises are to be searched would not have to be suspected of any offence, existing powers for police to use force would not be sufficient. But as with stop and search the word "necessary" is not reassuring because it could be interpreted in varying ways. Polite requests to produce the required evidence or indeed even care to prevent unnecessary damage would be likely to be ruled out, not just on grounds of resistance from the occupier, but also because of the nature of the circumstances. The brutality to the occupiers which can accompany these raids at present may be validated and even encouraged.

Confidential Files

Much press attention has focused on the provisions in the Bill dealing with police access to confidential information obtained in the course of employment or paid or unpaid office. The Bill generally allowed police to apply to a circuit judge for an order for access to specified confidential evidence *or* for a search warrant. The judge could only issue the search warrant if they were satisfied that serving an order for production would be likely to result in the concealment, loss, alteration or destruction of the evidence. In any event, whether they issued an order or a warrant, they should be satisfied that the evidence required related to a "serious arrestable offence" and that other methods have either been met with no success or have not been tried, "because it appeared that they were bound to fail."[11]

Professional organisations, such as the British Medical Association and the British Association of Social Workers, and church organisations, vociferously condemned this section of the Bill before it was changed. Some bishops even said they would be prepared to go to prison rather than disclose confidential information. Just before the Bill fell the government promised to exempt all "personal records" ie, files from which an individual can be identified.[12] In addition it promised astonishingly wide concessions to journalists to exempt all material "acquired or created for the purposes of journalism".[13] The Guild of British Newspaper Editors has actually declared that it did not want these exemptions. It said:

"Journalism in Britain has gained much of its strength from enjoying the rights, but no more than the rights offered to every citizen."[14]

A *Guardian* editorial of 30.8.83 pointed out the dangers:

"People who look at the global problems of press freedom know that the hoariest, most dangerous gambit in the book of repression is a legal definition of journalism and journalists. Once you have a definition of a profession (as Franco, like many before him, found) and if you hold the levers of the legal system, then you can make sure that journalists you would rather shut up can't work as journalists at all."

The extent of the opposition to the provisions on confidential information was not surprising, as these represented a serious attack on the confidentiality of information and the whole *raison d'être* of the professional adviser. A welfare state which turned all of its agencies into potential sources of information would become a sinister system of social control. There are other developments in this direction even without these provisions (see Chapter 17). But what was surprising was the lack of public information about the even more dangerous provisions affecting ordinary people.

Limitations on Searches

Searches for "evidence" were limited only in that the evidence would have to be of "a serious arrestable offence". However as noted in Chapter 11 on detention, the definition of "serious arrestable offence" was a very wide one (see p 78). If the person whose premises were being searched was not required to be suspected of the offence in question, it would be a useless safeguard. It would be no justification that the police were investigating a serious crime if they were allowed to use the opportunity to search innocent people's homes.

Although the Bill provided that a search under a warrant "may only be a search to the extent required for the purpose to which the warrant was issued"[15] this provision was not made enforceable by any requirement that evidence obtained in breach be excluded. This was remarkable because it was the one instance where the Royal Commission on Criminal Procedure did support enforcement by exclusion of evidence:

"We appreciate that the obligatory exclusion of evidence at trial may appear an inflexible restriction, but the right of members of the public to be free from general searches must be respected."[16]

The omission of any exclusionary rule was compounded by a power to seize any article which was reasonably believed by police to be evidence of *any* offence.[17] Thus the police could obtain a warrant to search for stolen television sets. However, if, contrary to a provision in the Bill requiring them to search only in a manner necessary for the purpose of the search, they searched the bathroom cabinet and discovered prohibited drugs, they could seize and use them in evidence against the occupier.[18]

Evidence of wholly trivial offences such as allegedly stolen library books or unpaid parking fines could also be seized. The "reasonable suspicion or belief" test would be totally devalued as the police would be permitted to use a search to inquire into trivial activity wholly unconnected with the purpose of the warrant.

These provisions again went far beyond what the Royal Commission proposed, which was that only items specified in the warrant, items which it is an offence to possess and evidence of a *grave offence,* should be able to be seized.[19] In a letter to Opposition MP, Christopher Price, the then Minister of State, Patrick Mayhew MP set out the reasons for such a wide power. First he said that it would be impracticable to restrict it to evidence of "serious arrestable offences" because of the very wide definition of those offences in the Bill. This could of course be remedied by adopting the Royal Commission's definition instead. He then argued that restrictions on the power of seizure would have little practical effect because "if a police officer found an article which he was not empowered to seize under Clause 14, he would seize it as a consequence of arresting the person concerned". Mayhew said that:

". . . Paradoxically I fear that a consequence of a limitation on seizure powers might be simply to increase the number of arrests that take place."[20]

His comments were reminiscent of the justification for stop and search. The answer is of course that it would be better to have a small increase in arrests (which will only be those not resulting in charges) and to deter the police from seizing articles, which they have no real basis for believing to be evidence of a crime.

The police training manual *The Signs of Crime* by Deputy Assistant Commissioner David Powis gives a good indication of police attitudes to search of premises. It contains absolutely no injunctions to be careful of people's property or to prevent unnecessary damage or distress but advises:

"Search every pocket of every article of clothing in wardrobes. Look in shoes and especially in ladies' shoes. Property is often hung by a string from a clothes hanger and is concealed by the folds of dresses. Contraband, stolen money and incriminating documents are sometimes placed at, or taped to, the back of wooden drawers. All drawers should be taken out, then the sides, top and bottom of the aperture left should be carefully examined. All lofts should be entered and illuminated. Look along horizontal beams. Breakfast food packets and food have often contained unexpected articles. Is there anything taped under the table? Electric table lamps frequently are used to conceal small articles – examine these lamps closely."[21]

It goes on to advise the use of dogs in all searches:

> "Do not be prejudiced against the use of dogs. Of course they have failures and make mistakes and can embarrass you in good quality premises, but on a profit and loss accounting they are infinitely worth-while."[22]

Railton Road Raids

The impression created by the manual has recently been confirmed by the release of the Police Complaints Board Report on the raids carried out by police on 11 premises in Railton Road, Brixton immediately after the July 1981 riots. The Board's Report found that there was "institutional disregard for the niceties of the law" and "serious lapses from professional standards".[23] The Inquiry into the raids was carried out by Deputy Assistant Commissioner Dear on behalf of the Metropolitan Police Commissioner, who then presented his findings to the Board.[24]

The Board's report of September 1982 was however initially suppressed. It was not disclosed to Parliament until April 1983 after questions had been raised about it.[25]

The operation in Railton Road on 15 July 1981 involved 176 CID and uniformed officers employed actually to enter the premises and a further 391 officers either held in reserve or employed in cordoning off the area. Five warrants for five properties had been obtained under the Criminal Damage Act 1971 and six for six more properties under the Licensing Act 1964. Assistant Commissioner Dear's Report revealed that the instructions given to officers did not differentiate between the different kinds of warrant and that all officers were advised also to look for stolen property. During the briefing session given by senior officers, sledge hammers and crow bars were also issued to all those taking part. The results of the operation were that the properties were forcibly entered at 2.00am and external doors and windows and internal doors were forced open, wall panelling was broken, and property was smashed. However no evidence was found of the manufacture of petrol bombs or of the premises being used for illegal drinking. Seven people were arrested, all for minor offences.[26]

In a letter to Deputy Commissioner Kavanagh, the Secretary to the Police Complaints Board voiced their concern about the manner in which the searches had been carried out:

> "The Board's view, which appears to be shared by Mr Dear, is that only the search authorised by the warrant is lawful though evidence of

other offences discovered in such a search can be used in criminal proceedings. The Board note that _____ was responsible for a briefing which caused the wider searches to be conducted."[27]

The officer responsible for the briefing was not named by the Board. Their letter continued:

"They considered that there was evidence to justify a disciplinary charge against him, but were of the opinion that in view of the wider implications of this operation, he should not be singled out. The Board note that the evidence was available to have sought a warrant for 60 Railton Road under the Criminal Damage Act but that the searches of 35, 37 and 47 Railton Road were under Licensing Act warrants and that only the search authorised by these warrants should have been conducted. In none of the premises was there authority to search for drugs or stolen property. The Board's view is that the unauthorised searches cannot be attributed to _____'s error alone. Other senior officers were concerned in the planning and supervision of these raids. The Board understand that for a search to be lawful, the warrant should be in the hands of the officer conducting the search and it is difficult not to come to the conclusion that *every senior officer in possession of a warrant regarded it as a licence to enter* the premises and, once having gained entry, to search for evidence of any crime. The Board find it difficult to believe that this can be attributed entirely to ignorance of the law."[28]

Despite the Board's very strong words there do not appear to have been any proposals made for reviewing the way in which searches are carried out or search warrants issued (see Chapter 7).

The proposals in the Police Bill, far from placing limitations on this kind of police abuse, would specifically legitimise and encourage it.

Notes

1. The Police and Criminal Evidence Bill (as amended by Standing Committee J) Clause 14(3).
2. Royal Commission on Criminal Procedure Report *Op cit* para 3.42.
3. *Hansard* Standing Committee J, 27.1.83, Col 370, Sir Nicholas Bonsor MP.
4. *Ibid.*
5. *Hansard* Standing Committee J, 27.1.83, Col 349, Patrick Mayhew MP.
6. *Ibid.*
7. *Hansard* Standing Committee J, 27.1.83, Col 370, Sir Nicholas Bonsor MP.
8. Police and Criminal Evidence Bill (as amended by Standing Committee J) Clause 9.
9. *Hansard* Standing Committee J, 27.1.83, Col 343, Arthur Davidson MP.
10. New Clause 2: Mr Secretary Whitelaw Order paper Committee of the Whole House 3.5.83.

11. Police and Criminal Evidence Bill (as amended by Standing Committee J) Clause 10.
12. New Clauses 3 and 5 Mr Secretary Whitelaw Order paper Committee of the Whole House 3.5.83.
13. *Ibid* New Clause 3.
14. *The Times* 4.4.83.
15. Police and Criminal Evidence Bill (as amended by Standing Committee J) Clause 13(8).
16. Royal Commission on Criminal Procedure Report *Op cit* para 3.49.
17. Police and Criminal Evidence Bill (as amended by Standing Committee J) Clause 14(1).
18. *Ibid* Clause 13(8).
19. Royal Commission on Criminal Procedure Report *Op cit* para 3.49.
20. Letter from Patrick Mayhew MP to Christopher Price MP 8.4.83.
21. *The Signs of Crime, Op cit,* p 136.
22. *Ibid* p 144.
23. Letter dated 11.8.82 from the Secretary to the Police Complaints Board, P E Bolton, to P B Kavanagh Esq, CBE, QPM, Deputy Commissioner of the Met.
24. *Report of Inquiry by Deputy Assistant Commissioner Dear into police operations in Railton Road, Brixton on Wednesday 15 July 1981. Summary of Events and Main Conclusions.*
25. *Hansard* 28.4.83.
26. Report by Dear *Op cit*.
27. *Op cit*.
28. *Ibid*.

7. The Law and Procedure on Search Warrants

The present law on search is contained in the common law and is generally accepted to be vague and unsatisfactory. Thus there are no statutory requirements as to what information should be given in an application for a search warrant and a magistrate has an absolute discretion as to whether to issue one. A magistrate merely has a duty "to satisfy himself that in all the circumstances it is right to issue a warrant".[1] In addition to common law powers, a number of statutes, such as the Misuse of Drugs Act, confer extra powers.

The broad grounds that govern the issue of search warrants are that the occupier should be suspected of an offence and that officers should be looking for the "fruit" or "instrument" of that offence. The principle at stake here was put by Lord Denning in *Chic Fashions (West Wales) Ltd v Jones (1968)*:

"We have to consider, on the one hand, the freedom of the individual. The security of his home is not to be broken except for the most compelling reason. On the other hand we have to consider the interest of society at large in finding out wrongdoers and repressing crime".[2]

In 1969 a judgement of Lord Denning in the case of *Ghani v Jones* extended the power of seizure on search.[3] The case concerned the seizure of the passport of an Asian suspect (the officer in question was strangely enough the same officer who investigated the Confait case – see p 110). He laid down the following grounds which would justify the *taking* of an article:

"Firstly. The police officers must have reasonable grounds for believing that a serious offence has been committed – so serious that it is of the first importance that the offenders should be caught and brought to justice.
Secondly. The police officers must have reasonable grounds for believing that the article in question is either the fruit of the crime (as in

the case of the stolen goods) or was the instrument by which the crime was committed (as in the case of the axe used by the murderer) or is material evidence to prove the commission of the crime (as in the case of the car used by a bank robber or the saucer used by a train robber).

Thirdly. The police officers must have reasonable grounds to believe that the person in possession of it had himself committed the crime, or is implicated in it, or is accessory to it, or at any rate his refusal must be quite unreasonable.

Fourthly. The police must not keep the article, nor prevent its removal, for any longer than is reasonably necessary to complete their investigation or preserve it for evidence. If a copy will suffice, it should be made and the original returned. As soon as the case is over, or it is decided not to go on with it, the article should be returned.

Finally. The lawfulness of the conduct of the police must be judged at the time, and not by what happens afterwards".[4]

In the Standing Committee debates the government relied on *Ghani v Jones* as paving the way for the new power of search in the Bill. But it should be noted that it related not to searching premises so much as seizing a particular item in the course of a search.

Nicholas Lyell MP proposed, from the government front bench, an amendment that he said was intended to cover the third ground in *Ghani v Jones* quoted above. The amendment made the granting of a search warrant conditional on satisfying the magistrate:

(a) that it is not reasonably practicable to communicate with any person entitled to grant entry to the premises or access to the evidence believed to be in the premises *or,*

(b) that any such person has unreasonably refused such entry or access to a constable *or,*

(c) that the evidence is likely to be concealed, disposed of, altered or destroyed if such entry or access is sought without a warrant".[5]

Nicholas Lyell recognised that the amendment did not refer to any requirement that the person be suspected of an offence. He justified this omission as follows:

"I think that it is wise not to mention that in the drafting because, before one goes to the justice, if the justice has to be satisfied that there has been an unreasonable refusal to allow the police to enter and search for the evidence, it must follow, *a fortiori,* that the police have already gone and asked for admission or that it is one of these cases that we all recognise where, if they went and asked for admission to search, any evidence inside would promptly be destroyed, disposed of or otherwise concealed or done away with".[6]

However it is quite clear that the "refusal" mentioned by Lord Denning in the third ground of *Ghani v Jones* set out above was a refusal to hand over the item in question, not a refusal to allow a general search of property. Confusion arose by interpreting *Ghani v Jones* as extending the powers of search rather than seizure, which is what it was really dealing with. On the information which the justices (magistrates) would have before them and on an application by the police alone, there would simply not be the opportunity to be satisfied that a refusal was quite unreasonable. In any event it is difficult to see how a refusal to allow a search could be unreasonable if the person concerned was wholly innocent of any offence.

Clearly however *Ghani v Jones* laid the basis for subsequent Royal Commission recommendations that, in exceptional circumstances, it would be acceptable for the police to have a power to search for evidence rather than just the fruit or the instrument of crime. The Royal Commission said applications to search for evidence should be to a circuit judge and not a magistrate.[7] However once again the Bill did not follow the Commission's "safeguarding" recommendations and, under the Bill, a magistrate would continue to hear *all* applications for warrants.[8] It is interesting that the provisions in the Bill about reviews of the detention of suspects were changed because magistrates were unhappy about sitting alone without a (legally qualified) clerk and hearing representations from one party only. Yet applications for search warrants are made in private in identical circumstances.

There are certainly magistrates who will not question the police case and will tend simply to "rubber stamp" applications. The scrutiny of circuit judges who are legally trained would provide more protection. In their 1983 Triennial Review Report the Police Complaints Board said they were concerned at "the ease with which on occasion courts or individual magistrates grant search warrants on the basis of minimal and often uncorroborated facts presented by the police" and that they had seen a number of cases "in which we were frankly surprised that justices granted warrants on the information supplied".[9] The Report of the Police Complaints Board on the raids on Railton Road in 1981 (see Chapter 6) provided the basis for their concern. One hundred and seventy six officers entered 11 properties armed with sledge hammers and crow bars to carry out search warrants granted under the Criminal Damage Act 1971 and the Licensing Act 1964. The Police Complaints Board criticised the issuing of the warrants on scant information:

"The Board's concern arises primarily from the manner in which the warrants were obtained and executed. The Board have no criticism of the decision to seek warrants under the Criminal Damage Act 1971 in the light of the information which had been given by the informer, but they are concerned that the information on which search warrants under the Licensing Act was sought was scant. The Board are surprised that the warrants were granted on _____'s unspecific information and are glad to note that he is to be warned about his methods. The Board accept that criticism should perhaps be directed primarily at the court and they will be taking separate action in this respect".[10]

Subsequently the Board also criticised strongly the manner in which the searches were carried out (see also Chapter 6).

The Royal Commission proposed that the police would normally have to apply for an order for production of specific evidence in the first instance rather than a search warrant. They recommended that the magistrate should satisfy themself as to the following conditions before making such an order for production of specific evidence:

"(a) other methods of investigation have been tried and failed, or must in the nature of things be bound to fail;
(b) the nature of the items sought is specified with some precision;
(c) reasonable grounds are shown for believing that the items will be found on the premises; and
(d) reasonable grounds are shown for believing that the evidence will be of substantial value, and not merely incidental; that it will enable those responsible for a particular crime to be identified or the particulars of offences thought to have been committed by particular individuals to be determined."[11]

There was no provision in the Bill for application for an order of production in the first instance. Moreover even in relation to search warrants only conditions (a) and possibly (d) above were to be included in the Bill. (The government introduced at Report stage an amendment to the effect that the evidence should be of "substantial" value).[12]

For the issue of a *warrant* (as opposed to an order) the Royal Commission recommended that the following additional criteria should apply – either:

"(a) A final order, after appeal, has been made and disobeyed.
or
(b) There is reason to believe that the evidence sought will be disposed

of or disappear if there is delay or if the interest of the police in it becomes known."[13]

This was included in the Bill in respect of confidential information but there was nothing to spare ordinary people the experience of having their homes searched under search warrant. Thus the police would be encouraged by the law to treat alike suspected criminals and innocent people who were suspected to be in possession of "evidence".

Finally, as we have seen, the Royal Commission recommended that the restrictions on search should be enforced by a rule that evidence obtained illegally should be excluded.[14] The Bill went dramatically in the other direction by giving a power to seize evidence of *any* offence however trivial.[15]

The reason for all the safeguards proposed by the Royal Commission was that the powers of search proposed by them and included in the Bill would be very wide indeed. When the Royal Commission Report came out even the Chief Constable of Thames Valley, Peter Imbert, acknowledged the need for safeguards in respect of search powers. He said in a lecture to the Canadian Institute for the Administration of Justice that the "stringent safeguards" proposed by the Royal Commission "seem reasonable". He commented:

> "We, as a police service, cannot expect a *carte blanche* power especially in this area of such a delicate nature. The need should arise infrequently and would be used responsibly, the decision to adopt the procedure being taken at a high level, but it could be an invaluable tool when needed and should greatly assist in our efforts to detect serious crime when other methods failed or cannot be used."[16]

Thus he admitted that the need for the power would rarely arise; apparently only when all other methods failed.

American law applies principles of "particularity" and "adequacy" to the issue of search warrants. Before one can be issued, the articles to be seized must be described with particularity *and* adequate facts must be established to generate a reasonable belief that the articles relate to an offence. In this context it is insufficient for police to say they are merely acting on "information received".[17]

Unfortunately "particularity" and "adequacy" do not feature in present English law or in the Bill's provisions. The provisions were still far too vague. The articles only had to be specified "so far as is possible" and the police officer making the application merely had to state the ground on which they made the application.[18] They would not have to satisfy the magistrate in detail that there was *adequate* information to suppose that evidence of a serious arrestable offence was on the premises. Nor would they have to reveal the source and nature of their information. There is no reason why this could not be done, as in the USA, in a private hearing before a magistrate (or better, a judge). Only then could magistrates have any real possibility of questioning the application. Even if such wide powers of search for evidence were not being granted, provisions for adequacy and particularity would still be necessary to prevent the magistrate's role being simply illusory.

Notes

1. *Stones Justices Manual, Op cit,* Vol 1, p 34.
2. Chic Fashions (West Wales) Ltd. v Jones (1968) 2 QB 299.
3. Ghani v Jones 1969 3 ALL ER 1700.
4. Ghani v Jones *Op cit.*
5. Police and Criminal Evidence Bill (as amended by Standing Committee J) Clause 9(2).
6. *Hansard* Standing Committee J, 27.1.83, Col. 357.
7. Royal Commission on Criminal Procedure Report *Op cit* para 342.
8. Police and Criminal Evidence Bill (as amended by Standing Committee J) Clause 9.
9. Police Complaints Board *Triennial Review* Report 1983 (HMSO Cmnd 8853) para 4.9.
10. Letter from Secretary of the Police Complaints Board to Deputy Assistant Commissioner Kavanagh *Op cit.*
11. Royal Commission on Criminal Procedure Report *Op cit* para 3.43.
12. See Chapter 6 p 43.
13. Royal Commission on Criminal Procedure Report *Op cit* para 3.43.
14. *Ibid* para 3.49.
15. Police and Criminal Evidence Bill (as amended by Standing Committee J) Clause 14.
16. *The Police Journal* vol. LV Number 2, April-July 1982, p 138.
17. *The Law of Arrest, Search and Seizure* by J Shane Creamer.
18. Police and Criminal Evidence Bill (as amended by Standing Committee J) Clause 12.

8. Complaints about Searches of Premises*

Mr X

"My wife was making a bottle for my 16 month old son when she heard a crash at the front door. The door splintered and broke open and three men in ordinary dress came in, one holding an axe, one a gun and the other was unarmed. My wife was halfway up the stairs at the time. They ran towards her, all three passed her on the stairs. At this time my daughter hearing the noise, came out of her bedroom and saw the three men running towards her mother with an axe. She ran into the bedroom where I was. The officers burst into the bedroom where I was comforting my little girl in my arms. The man with the gun cocked it and told me to 'put the f------ child away'. My little daughter, who is five, hid under the bed because of her fright. I was handcuffed at this time. I was only wearing my underpants and vest. I was pushed against the wall. After complaints from my wife I was allowed to get dressed. All this time the man with the gun kept it trained on me. No identification or warrant was shown despite our requests. I was cautioned, and told I was being arrested for a conspiracy to commit robbery going back to 1970. The house was searched and my wife accompanied them while they searched. Nothing was taken. After the house was searched one of the three men (the one who had entered the house with the axe) went outside and flagged down a transit van driven by a woman police officer. There was another male police officer in the van. I asked where I was being taken so that my wife could contact my solicitor. But this request was refused. I was taken to a police station where I was detained until about 6.00pm on Sunday 20 November."

---

*Accounts given to the GLC or reports in the press of alleged police abuse.

Mrs Y (white woman with black children)

"In January 1982, around 3.00pm, myself, my daughter, my son-in-law, my daughter and two grandchildren were taking down Christmas decorations in the sitting room when there was a knock on the front door. I went to the door, opened it and saw two coloured boys. . . . They asked me if a boy called Tony lived here. I said no Tony lives here, try next door. After that I went to the kitchen to check on some meat that was on the stove. When I came back I saw that someone was looking through the front door letter box. I was a bit annoyed about that and opened the front door to find out who it was. I found five or six policemen standing outside the door. 'Have two boys come here', they asked. 'No', I said, 'Yes', the police said, 'we have seen two boys come in here with a television'. I said that two boys knocked and asked for someone called Tony and that I had suggested that they tried next door. One policeman then said to his companions, 'let's see if they have gone next door'. But then my daughter and her boyfriend came into the passage, from the sitting room, to see what was going on and the police, apparently seeing that they were coloured just pushed their way into the house.

They started searching the house; first everywhere downstairs and then upstairs. They were asking me where the televisions were. They said that they had seen two boys come in with one. But the boys who knocked on my door never had any television and I told the police this.

When we all came downstairs again my front door was wide open and another lot of policemen were coming into the house. They started searching the house all over again. This lot of policemen just ignored me as if I was not there. Most of my Xmas decorations were broken because of the way they handled the plastic bags in which I had carefully put them in and two of my ornaments were broken as well. When I told them about this they just laughed.

My son-in-law then told me that he had seen the police taking a boy out of the house from the passage. How did he get there, I asked; there was no boy there when I was down in the kitchen when the first lot of policemen searched the house (all I could think was that he must have got there somehow during the time the two lots of policemen were searching my house and the front door was open and while we were upstairs).

Then, as I went to the front door to see if I could see this boy my son-in-law had said he saw the police taking out, I saw no boy, but I did see a policeman going through the front gate with my radio cassette. I ran after him and another policeman made as if to trip me up. But I reached the policeman with my radio cassette and grabbed hold of it (both of us were holding on to it then). I said how dare you take my property. He said we are the law and we do what we like. And after that he said he was taking it to the police station. When I then asked him for a receipt he said, 'don't be so f------ stupid, what do you take us for'. Then he went into the car with my radio cassette and then all the other policemen left too.

When I went back into the house and into my sitting room, after that, I found two coats that did not belong to anyone in my family. So, when I later went out to a shop to get some potatoes, I phoned the . . . police station and told them that two coats were left in my house and to come and collect them. But little did I know that while I was out and making that telephone call another seven policemen were searching my house all over again. They stripped every part of my house and left it in a terrible mess; I was disgusted at the state they left it in. They even searched the garden. Also, they insulted my children about the food they eat, making jibes about green bananas and yams. After searching my lodger's room and seeing a black and white television there, they made more remarks: 'look at the poor b------, he's got a black and white one and all those coloured tellys flashing about'. On the landing of my house I have a drawer where tools for jobs around the house are kept. Looking at these, one of the policemen said to my daughter (about me) 'she's got enough tools here for house breaking'. My television is a slot meter one, I have had it four-and-a-half years. Looking at that, a policeman said to my daughter, in front of a friend, 'has your mother found a way of fiddling this yet?' My daughter was annoyed and embarrassed, but replied, 'my mother does not fiddle'.

When I arrived home, around 5.30pm, my daughter told me about the police search which I have just described and the things they said and did. Then there was a knock at the front door and when I opened it there were five plain clothes policemen standing there. They asked me to come down to the police station with them to make a statement and promised to sort out the matter of my radio cassette. When I got outside there was a police van standing there and, when I got in it, I saw four more policemen in it. I was taken to the police station (which is not my local police station). Once inside the police station, a police officer said 'nick this b------ for receiving a television radio cassette which was stolen from _____ Road'. I said, 'what television, what are you talking about, I have no television and never seen no television in my house that doesn't belong to me'. He said, 'well, we will see about that' . . .

At that time I was also concerned about the radio cassette the police had taken from my house. It was my property and I wanted it back. I went to the police station on two occasions and asked for it back, or a receipt for it. I was told I could not have either. After my first court appearance, my barrister asked a police officer why the police were holding my radio cassette. He admitted that it was not stolen, that it formed no part of any charge and that the police had been wrong to take it in the first place from my house. He also said that if I went to the police station I could have it back. I went to the police station three times the next day, Wednesday, and each time I was told that he was not there and that I could not have the radio cassette back. I phoned the police station later in the evening and spoke to him. He said that if I came to the police station the next day, Thursday, I could have it back. But on Thursday it was the same story . . . Finally I did get my property back, the following week, when I went again to the police station with my solicitor. Then there was no trouble, I got my radio cassette back without any argument. But I feel that if I had kept going there alone I would not have got it back to this day''.

Mr P

"I arrived home on the 26th after having spent the weekend with friends and what I saw filled me with total horror. It was as if a destruction company had done their best to demolish my home. I could not get a word out of my 12 year old son, he clinged to me in terror and could not stop crying, he was almost hysterical. I managed to calm him down and was told the following story of what had occurred.

On the 24th July at about 9 o'clock in the morning, my 12 year old son was awaken with a gun pointed at his head. Our dog must have sensed the danger and got the man's arm and my son took the gun and pointed it at the man. When my son called the dog off the man, he managed to tell my son he was a police officer and that he had a warrant for his older brother.

How was my son to know this was the truth? He is fully aware of the fact that people break in and kill people for no reason. He could have pulled the trigger and killed the person in question.

This has done serious damage to my son, he keeps on waking up at night and has nightmares, and has began to walk about in his sleep and when asked what's wrong he keeps saying, there is a man in there trying to kill us or he is seeing things in the mirror.

When I saw my older son, he also told me he was awaken with guns pointed to his head, by at least 8-10 police officers in plain clothes. They had not been admitted into my home by anyone and did not break down the door. How did they get in?

The warrant was for my son's arrest, why did they search my bedroom and the rest of my home and why did they leave my home in total destruction. It took me three days to put it back in reasonable order. I took pictures of the way they left my home. Furthermore they confiscated all my diaries, business and private correspondence, pawn tickets and valuations of my jewellery, all my private photographs, holiday snaps etc, which was in a beauty bag and ornaments which had nothing to do with my son.

My son has his own room and all his belongings are confined to his room, so why did they go through my belongings and confiscate my private things? The warrant for an arrest was not for me or a search warrant for my home. They also came to my son's business, but never produced a search warrant for this, while they took away cheque book, paying in book and correspondence . . . Serious damage has been done to my child and the intrusion and destructive way my home was submitted to should be known to the public and I will take measures to contact the press and submit to them the pictures taken, both here and abroad. I will not stand for guns being used upon children, nor a home being abused and the knowledge the police can enter my home with a key or whatever method it was."

Mrs Z (incident described by adviser)

"Mrs Z telephoned to report that on Tuesday 25 August at about 8.10am three plain clothes policemen burst into her house. She had answered their knocking in her nightdress and they ignored her request to allow her time to change and also refused to let her see a search warrant. Their subsequent behaviour was most aggressive and abusive both to her and her two sons. Her husband was upstairs in bed and is deaf.

She said the policemen said they were searching the house for stolen electrical goods and jewellery. She accuses them of manhandling her sons, grabbing them by the throat and pushing them against the furniture. She says she herself was pushed from one end of the room to the other and that her husband was taunted about his deafness.

She subsequently discovered that the officers were CID and they did have a search warrant that had been issued on the Friday. The reason given for not showing it was that the officers did not want the risk of it being torn up.''

Mrs A (described by her local councillor)

"The above is a constituent of mine who asked to see me a few days ago. I visited her at her home and interviewed her in the presence of her parents. The reason she asked to see me was to complain of the treatment she alleges she received from members of the Metropolitan Police.

At about 7.45am on 17 March 1981 various police vehicles drew up at her home and about 14 plain clothes officers entered her home. Asked to show any authority or warrant for their entry, a 'piece of paper' was waved before her but she was not allowed to read it. An officer said to her 'you're nicked; get dressed'.

At 8.00am my constituent was taken to a police station where she was interviewed and asked to give answers to questions such as her own name and address, and how many people lived at the address. At 2.15pm she was returned to her cell and at 2.45pm she was told there would be no charges against her and all her property, including jewellery removed from her person, would be returned to her. She was asked if she wished to telephone her father to come to collect her, but she chose to telephone for a taxi to take her home.

Upon her return home she discovered that her room had been searched after her arrest and transport to the police station, and that many items of toiletries and bed-linen had been taken away by the officers concerned.

On 19 March 1981, the goods removed from her home were returned by the officers concerned. She and her parents allege that they were returned – so far as the toiletries go – in a totally unusable condition.

While with my constituent and her parents I personally examined no fewer than 11 goods – and there may have been more in the disgusting plastic carrier bag in which the property was returned with police identification property labels.''

Mr and Mrs B (described by a local councillor)

"Mr and Mrs B reside at D_____. In June at 6.45am Mrs B went to the front door to find out what was happening, and was surprised to see police at the door. She was shocked and somewhat disturbed. The police showed her what appears to have been their identification. She does not think it was a warrant, but could not in the circumstances be certain. She let the officers in, because they threatened to knock down the door. One asked her questions. The other officer began to search the house. The officer searching the house entered their bedroom. Mr B, who happened to be on late duty, was in bed. The officer pushed open the bedroom door, made no comment, and continued what he was doing. Mr B got up, and overheard a police officer asking his wife questions in the sitting room.

Mr B on entering the sitting room was somewhat angry, and asked 'what is all this questioning about?' The officer replied, 'I can do without your insults'. Mr B asked him for a warrant. He replied, 'I have already showed your wife. People like you make my job difficult'. Mrs B was about to say something and was told to shut up. The officer then said to them, 'if you have any complaints go to Scotland Yard'.'

Commenting on this case, I would say that it would be difficult in the circumstances which I have described for Mrs B to know whether they had a warrant or not. The attitude of the police, in this case they were in private clothes (although Mr B thinks the uniformed men were near), was one which explains why there is such trouble in Brixton.''

9. Arrests

Although the definition of "arrestable offences" in the Bill was similar to the existing law[1] the power to arrest without warrant was extended to cover not just "arrestable" offences but *all* offences, however trivial, if certain conditions were fulfilled.[2] These proposed new powers were given very little exposure in the press but were among the most worrying aspects of the Bill in terms of police/community relations. Any extension of arrest powers and encouragement to police to arrest people, particularly young people, could exacerbate the potential for criminalisation.

The new powers were to arrest someone if a police officer reasonably suspected that *any* offence had been, was been or was about to be committed or attempted and one of the following conditions applied:

"(a) that the name and address of the person whom the constable suspected was unknown to, and cannot be ascertained by, the constable;

(b) that the constable had reasonable grounds for doubting:
    (i) whether a name and address furnished by that person as his name and address were his real name and address; or
    (ii) whether that person would be at an address furnished by him for a sufficiently long period for it to be possible to serve him with a summons;

(c) that the constable had reasonable grounds for believing that arrest was necessary to prevent a person causing:
    (i) physical harm to himself or any other person;
    (ii) loss of or damage to property;
    (iii) an affront to public decency; or
    (iv) an obstruction of the highway;

(d) that the constable had reasonable grounds for believing that arrest was necessary to protect a child or other vulnerable person from the person to be arrested."[3]

The Bill did not follow the Royal Commission's proposal that all offences carrying a potential sentence of imprisonment should be made "arrestable". However what it did do was much worse. It conferred a general power of arrest exercisable in relation to *any* offence if one of the "arrest conditions" was satisfied. It meant that anyone could be arrested for very minor offences, such as traffic offences or littering, on the basis of doubt as to the name and address furnished by them or if they were of no fixed abode or were obstructing the highway.

This did not meet the criticisms of those who were concerned that many minor offences which could be prosecuted on summons still resulted in unnecessary arrests (the figures quoted by the Royal Commission showed enormous discrepancies in practices among different police areas).[4] Moreover the Bill entirely removed any obligation on the police to relate the use of power to deprive the suspect of liberty to the offence of which they were suspected.

This slackening of criteria requiring a connection to be made between use of police powers and reasonable suspicion of a particular offence was, as we have seen, one of the most alarming features of the Bill. It might amount to a *carte blanche* for powers of arrest and would give the police powers hugely in excess of what they have enjoyed before.

The new powers of arrest in the Bill had not been the subject of any prior consultation. They were not in the Report of the Royal Commission on Criminal Procedure nor even in the Consultative Memorandum issued by the Home Office shortly before publication of the Bill.[5] Possibly they were suggested by the police. This may have been what Patrick Mayhew MP meant when he said:

"In this case we did not set out proposals in our consultative document in 1981. We asked a number of questions. The clause as drafted is a distillation of what we think is right, having regard to the answers received to those questions."[6]

The "arrest conditions" set out by the Royal Commission were intended as *added* safeguards to ensure that arrest was necessary, not as a means to enlarge without limit the category of arrestable offences.[7] The arrest conditions should therefore have been related to "arrestable offences" only. In the debates in Standing Committee J, the then Minister of State, Patrick Mayhew MP, admitted to "restructuring" the law on arrest[8] and said he was not prepared to confine the arrest conditions in clause 17 only to imprisonable offences because:

". . . the need to imprison has no necessary relationship with the sort
of *firebrigade action* that is contemplated under clause 17."⁹

The new powers would thus give parliamentary approval to what is
often termed "fire brigade policing". This refers to the police
tendency in dealing with tense situations to rely on pressing a panic
button and summoning instant response (or district support) units in
transit vans. Instead of being encouraged to defuse difficult
situations and calm people down, police would be given even more
powers to rush in large numbers and to arrest people at random.
"Difficult situations" often happen when police encounter groups of
young people, who are fooling around or loitering on the streets. The
new powers would therefore exacerbate relations between police and
young people.

In his evidence to the Royal Commission, Sir David McNee asked
for police to be given an absolute power to take names and addresses
from any person.¹⁰ The provisions on arrest would be tantamount to
conceding to this demand. They would be bound to create trouble
between police and young people, who would inevitably refuse to give
names and addresses. They would discriminate against homeless
people. There would also be disturbing overtones of a "pass law"
and the provision could give rise to fears that the power could be used
to collect names and addresses for intelligence purposes.

Patrick Mayhew MP, on behalf of the government, said that the
power to arrest people on this ground would not always be used
because:

"In practice, police officers will radio their headquarters and try to
verify names and addresses and other information that has been
given."¹¹

However Christopher Price MP defended:

". . . the extreme privacy of an address for people who do not want
coppers knocking on the door."¹²

Another disturbing provision would be the arrest condition of "an
affront to public decency". This was not defined in the Bill or
anywhere else and therefore could only be interpreted subjectively. It
constitutes a particular threat to gay people, who are worried that
police would use it as an excuse to arrest them because of their
appearance or sexual preferences.

In addition there were also fears about the arrest condition of "obstructing the highway". Unlike an "affront to public decency" this is already a substantive criminal offence[13] but it is one which is often criticised for its vagueness and the opportunity it affords for police harassment. Complaints are made, for example, about its use against demonstrators, newspaper sellers and (again) groups or young people. A police officer may already arrest without warrant anyone committing the offence defined as:

"If a person without lawful authority or excuse in any way wilfully obstructs the free passage along a highway."[14]

It was not clear therefore why the condition was needed and whether it would be interpreted even more widely than the substantive offence.

Examples of the proposed powers

The following situations could occur if the proposed powers of arrest are incorporated into the new Bill and become law:

(a) Mrs Jones is in a hurry but urgently needs a pint of milk. She parks on a yellow line and dashes inside the supermarket. When she comes out she finds a police constable standing beside her car. He asks her for her name and address and makes a radio check. But the address does not tally with that on the police computer. Mrs Jones remembers that she did not tell the Driver and Vehicle Licensing Centre of her change in address. She is arrested and taken to the police station.

In Standing Committee J debates Patrick Mayhew MP made an unconvincing reply to a description of a similar hypothetic case:

"I do not believe that it would follow. First for such a scenario to get started there would have to be grounds for the officer's reasonably doubting the veracity of the name and address that had been given. That would not arise on many occasions. If it was then discovered that the information did not tally with the licensing authority computer, it would not follow that that could not be explained."[15]

The case of Ms G described in Chapter 10 (p 69) reinforces the scepticism with which the Minister's reply must be regarded.

(b) A group of youths are chatting on the street. They are drinking cans of coke which they have discarded on the street. A policeman approaches. He asks for their names and addresses. They refuse. He arrests all of them for littering; and keeps them in a police cell.

Another new arrest power in the Bill was the power to arrest a person with an offence which would be recorded on national records, on the grounds that they refused to go to the police station to have their fingerprints taken. In Standing Committee J, the government amended it so that it would apply only for a month after the relevant conviction.[16] It was supposed to cover people prosecuted on summons and given a non-custodial sentence, who would never therefore be taken to the police station. Such offences are however likely to be very minor. In parliament the government produced no evidence of the need for this power. Powers to arrest for fingerprinting inevitably have "pass law" overtones, even in such a restricted form.

Unnecessary and provocative arrests create deep seated resentments in a community. A situation can build up where even justifiable arrests result in the instant and spontaneous gathering of protesting people. This establishes a vicious circle whereby the police become nervous and increasingly prone to call for "reinforcements" at the first sign of resistance and the community becomes increasingly tense, unwilling to co-operate with police and prone to misinterpret their every move.

Notes

1. Police and Criminal Evidence Bill (as amended by Standing Committee J) Clause 16.
2. *Ibid* Clause 17.
3. *Ibid*.
4. Royal Commission on Criminal Procedure Report *Op cit* para 3.72.
5. Home Office Consultative Memorandum on the Royal Commission on Criminal Procedure Report, July 1981.
6. *Hansard* Standing Committee J, 8.2.83, Col 568, Patrick Mayhew MP.
7. Royal Commission on Criminal Procedure Report *Op cit* para 3.76.
8. *Hansard* Standing Committee J, 8.2.83, Col 559, Patrick Mayhew MP.
9. *Ibid*, Col 594, Patrick Mayhew MP.
10. Part I of the Written Evidence of the Commissioner of Police of the Metropolis *Op cit* p 23-26.
11. *Hansard* Standing Committee J, 8.2.83, Col 560, Patrick Mayhew MP.
12. *Ibid* Col 561, Christopher Price MP.
13. Highways Act 1980 S 137.
14. *Ibid*.
15. *Hansard* Standing Committee J, 8.2.83, Col 561, Patrick Mayhew MP.
16. Police and Criminal Evidence Bill (as amended by Standing Committee J) Clause 19.

10. Complaints About Arrests*

Mr E

Mr E, a black man of over 50, was returning from work late one evening when he was attacked by skinheads. He was beaten to the ground and kicked. He was helped by two bystanders and directed to a police vehicle nearby. Here he tried to report the incident, but was not assisted either to the hospital or advised that the incident would be investigated. He was told to go away. He tried again to report the incident at a police station but was not helped nor, it seems, were his details recorded. He later attended a hospital receiving treatment for cuts and bruises. At the hospital a policeman took a note of his address and Mr E explained his circumstances.

Four days later at roughly 7.30am in the morning a number of police officers attended his flat, searched it and arrested him. He was taken to the police station, was searched, and locked up for three hours. He insisted that he had been the victim of an attack and was eventually released and a statement taken. He acted as a prosecution witness for the police against a number of skinheads. He sought compensation from a court and was successful. The police claimed they had "mistaken" him for some black youths.

Mr F

"I am writing this letter because I think you should know about the incident of police brutality and actual assault (not to mention racist abuse) that happened to me in January.

This happened in the afternoon. The police story is that I resisted being given a parking ticket (they told my family I was like a mad animal and that I became angry for no reason, used foul language and tried to run a police officer over). I was moving my car off a yellow line as they had asked. As I was doing this three officers came to drag

---

*Accounts given to the GLC or reports in the press of alleged police abuse.

me from my car, pulling my coat and shirt off at the same time. I knew they were going to arrest me so I walked into a nearby cab office to make sure that my brother would mind my 15 month old baby for me.

The next thing I knew police 'reinforcements' came into the cab office and I was handcuffed and taken in a police Rover with four policemen. I was put in the back with an officer either side of me and two in the front. None of these were the police who had given me the parking ticket.

Their racist abuse started as soon as I was put in the car, ie 'you black b------' etc, etc, then the officer on my left spat in my face. I was really angry by now because I'd done nothing wrong and had been handcuffed, insulted and spat at.''

Ms G

"It was mid-afternoon when Ms G told her elderly mother that she was popping out to the supermarket for a few minutes. As she was going to be very quick she risked leaving her oyster-red Ford Granada behind a line of cars parked in a lay-by. She knew this would prevent them from reversing out, but she planned to nip in and out of the supermarket at top speed. When she returned to the Granada a policeman approached and asked if the car belonged to her.

And then began the most explosive chain of events that she had ever experienced. But what happened in the next half hour has led her to bring a civil action against the police in the High Court exactly a year later.

She claims that as she returned to her car carrying a bag of groceries a police officer suggested the car was stolen. She says she offered to produce the bill of sale, which was at her home about two and a half miles away at Woodford Bridge, Essex. She claims that the policeman dragged her from her car, held her and summoned assistance which arrived in the form of seven constables and a woman police officer. Then she alleges she was taken to a police station, about 100 yards away, and dragged from the car into the building. There she says she was searched and her left arm twisted behind her back by a policeman and a woman police constable.

As a result Ms G claims her arm was broken. She also says she was forcibly restrained for 30 minutes before being put in a cell and was refused leave to contact her mother. As well as suffering a broken arm she claims bruising and says she had to have her left arm in plaster for some weeks and is still taking pain-killing drugs" (*Sunday Express* 12.12.82).

Mr H

(This is a case where the person was not arrested under existing law but might well have been under the new law).

"I am 75 years old, living alone at the above address. I suffer from angina pectoris and ulcerated colitis. Nevertheless, I perform all my own household duties and do my own shopping each Tuesday and Friday morning. I run a small car, and because of my infirmities, have a disability disc which permits me to park on a yellow line, except under well-defined and displayed conditions. I am unable to shop unless I can park in close proximity to the point of supply. A distance of 100 yards with a heavy shopping bag is a journey I cannot contemplate.

This morning at about 11.30am I was about to park on the southern side of the road on a single yellow line to the first parking meter, a distance of about 100 ft, taking the place of a very large van that had been parked to the immediate rear of the first parking meter and was about to leave it. My front wheels would then have been about 100ft from the corner of the roads. I was prevented from doing so by the constable, who asked me to move on. I pointed out (politely) that I was entitled to park there because of my disablement licence, but he said I was a risk to the oncoming traffic. This is quite untrue, as the position is regularly occupied every shopping morning by disabled drivers, in accordance with the regulations governing the licence and, indeeed, never questioned by the wardens. The constable insisted that I park 100 yards or so further on down the road. I again explained I could not possibly walk the distance, and told him why. He became more intractable, domineering and menacing. I obtained his name and number and moved on. When I passed the spot a few minutes later, the spot was occupied by a disabled driver . . . The harassment of old people by individual constables is a disgrace to the country."

D. New Powers in the Police Station
11. The Detention of Suspects

The Police Bill contained a list of "detention conditions" which governed whether or not a suspect could be detained, either before or after being charged. Some conditions applied only to detention after charge; others could be used to justify detention before charge. The drafting was very confused and in the Standing Committee debates opposition members constantly complained that it would be impossible for most people looking at the Bill to see which condition applied when.[1]

Detention After Charge

Detention after charge was to be allowed for adults:

1) if their name and address could not be ascertained or if there were reasonable grounds for doubting the one supplied;
2) if it was reasonably believed to be necessary to prevent harm to person or property or for their own protection;
3) if it was reasonably believed they would fail to appear in court or that detention was necessary to prevent interference with witnesses or obstruction of the course of justice.

In the case of a juvenile it would be necessary to show in addition to one of the above grounds that there were reasonable grounds for believing he or she ought in their own interests to be detained.[2]

It is instructive to compare these detention conditions with the criteria in the Bail Act 1976 whereby a person should or should not be granted bail by a court before their case is heard. These are if the court is satisfied that there are substantial grounds for believing that the defendant if released on bail would:

a) fail to surrender to custody, or;

b) commit an offence while on bail, or;
c) interfere with witnesses, or obstruct the course of justice.

Alternatively bail can be refused if it is considered necessary that the defendant be kept in custody for their own protection.[3]

Thus the Bail Act does not require a permanent address to be supplied if there is no reason to think the person will fail to surrender to custody. This raises the question of whether the first detention condition requiring verification of name and address is necessary. It seems inconsistent that stricter criteria should apply *before* being brought to court than after, quite apart from the other problems of the first detention condition – that it discriminated against homeless people, those in temporary accommodation and gypsies or travellers. Lack of a fixed abode was clearly to be a reason on its own for keeping a person in custody. That is not the case in the Bail Act and therefore need not have been in the Bill.[4]

Detention Without Charge

The most controversial provisions of the Police Bill concerned detention *without* charge. Firstly, detention without charge was to be possible if there were reasonable grounds for believing it to be necessary to prevent harm to person or property or for the suspect's own protection *and* if the person arrested was not in a fit state to be charged.[5]

This provision would enable police to keep drunks and drug addicts overnight in cells before charge. It should however be questioned whether police stations should be used in this way. It is arguable that a person who has been arrested, but is not in a fit state to be charged through the influence of drink, drugs or because of bad health, should not be kept in a police cell. A person who is in such a state of intoxication, depression or ill health should be taken to hospital, or at least to a detoxification centre with proper facilities for treatment. Increasing numbers of deaths of drunks and drug addicts in police custody are occurring because of the lack of action of the authorities in relation to this problem. A Home Office Statistical Bulletin noted that the total number of deaths in custody due to "misadventure" or accident rose from 17 in 1981 to 30 in 1982. A third of these misadventures were said to be due to alcohol and/or drugs.[6]

This detention condition could be used to keep in custody someone who was really ill and not simply happy to get a bed for the night. It is interesting that the Minister of State, Patrick Mayhew MP, constantly overlooked this condition when he claimed in Standing Committee that detention for questioning and to secure/obtain evidence was the *only* ground of detention without charge.[7] It is true that the Bill placed a maximum time limit of 24 hours detention without charge on this basis, but most deaths in police custody occur within 24 hours of the suspect first being detained.

Secondly, and most importantly, detention without charge was to be allowed if there were reasonable grounds for believing that it was necessary "to secure or preserve evidence of or relating to the offence for which he (the suspect) was arrested or to obtain such evidence by questioning him".[8] Thus the Bill allowed a suspect to be held without charge purely for the purpose of questioning – an attack on the right to silence which has long been a fundamental principle of English criminal law. As Pauline Morris said in her review of literature on police interrogation for the Royal Commission on Criminal Procedure:

> "The right to silence is the concrete and visible assertion of the fundamental principle that the prosecution must prove their case and that no obligation lies on the accused to prove his or her innocence".[9]

Research has showed that the psychological pressures on persons kept in custody to talk are very strong. After a relatively short period a detainee develops a strong desire to please his or her questioners.[10] This may result in an untrue confession statement or in confused and contradictory statements being made.

The disorientation which results from a long detention has been recognised by judges.[11] The Royal Commission on Criminal Procedure also recognised it, but instead of concluding that detention without charge could not be justified, recommended that it should also be recognised that no statement made in custody could be voluntary.[12] The provisions in the Bill follow proposals over a period of years to curtail the right to silence. Thus the Eleventh Report of the Criminal Law Revision Committee proposed not only that detention for questioning should be allowed but also that juries should be allowed to draw adverse inferences from any failure to answer questions.[13] Although not all of the Report's recommendations have been implemented many of the Bill's provisions were based on them.[14]

In cases of serious arrestable offences detention before charge was to be allowed under the Bill for up to 96 hours (four days) for the purpose of questioning the suspect or obtaining other evidence. This time would run from the arrest of the suspect and their detention in the police station. Time spent transferring the suspect to the police station responsible for investigating the offence in question could however add on up to 24 hours (making five days).[15]

Another clause could even delay the time of detention *indefinitely*. This permitted the police to delay taking an arrested person to a police station if "the presence of that person elsewhere is necessary for the effective investigation of an offence".[16] No time limits were set whatsoever. Geraldine Van Bueren has suggested this provision would be in breach of the European Convention on Human Rights' requirement that detention should be speedily decided by a court. She commented:

> "The power extends to any offence no matter how trivial, without limit on the type of place to which a person could be taken. In Latin America such a power has chilling consequences".[17]

The existing law on detention without charge is confused and uncertain. The normal rule is that a person should be brought to a court within 24 hours. However, in exceptional circumstances and for serious offences, longer periods are said to be permissible. In a 1981 case, the divisional court criticised the apparent open-endedness of this exception and said that detention for more than 48 hours could not be justified.[18] But this decision has been criticised in subsequent cases where the Court of Appeal said there was no rigid rule on the maximum period allowed.[19]

Undoubtedly the police do detain many people for longer periods although the figures may not reveal the extent of such practices. A Home Office Memorandum on this part of the Bill referred to a survey of cases in the Metropolitan Police District over three months in 1982 which revealed only three instances of detention for 96 hours.[20] This figure was suspiciously small, as were figures produced for the Royal Commission showing detention beyond six hours only in a quarter of cases and beyond three days only in a tiny percentage.[21]

A community police monitoring group in Tower Hamlets (the Community Alliance for Police Accountability) included a table (opposite) of lengths of detention in its 1982 Annual Report.[22]

Once again the significance of the Bill's provisions in this area would be to legitimise current police abuse of power and, in so doing, to attack basic principles of the criminal law whereby the liberties of the individual are protected. Under the current law there is no specific

Examples of lengths of detention in police stations in Tower Hamlets

Leman Street	Limehouse	Bethnal Green
9 hours	6½ hours (2 people)	7 hours (3 people)
20 hours (2 people)	8 hours	8 hours (2 people)
22 hours	10 hours	12 hours[2]
24 hours	11½ hours[1]	16 hours[3]
2 days	19 hours	20 hours
	19½ hours	23 hours[4]
	22 hours (3 people)	24 hours
	overnights (many)	25 hours[3]
	30 hours (2 people)	28 hours[3]
		80 hours
		overnights (2 people, 1 not charged)
		day and a half

[1] with Shepherds Bush police   [3] with Romford police
[2] with Derby police   [4] with Ilford police

provision allowing detention without charge for long periods. As Alex Lyon MP said during the Standing Committee debate:

"What is proposed by the Royal Commission and accepted by the Government is that people can be detained in police stations against their will, without charge, for substantial periods. That is such a breach of all that the English common law has set down as a principle that not only we, but many who read the Royal Commission report, were shocked".[23]

The proposed provisions were related to an increasing tendency by the police to use arrest and detention in the hope of extracting confessions from suspects. It would have been open to the Royal Commission on Criminal Procedure to criticise such practices and to demand restrictions on detention without charge. However the Commission specifically validated arrest for the purpose of detaining someone in order to question them:

"Finally, the criterion of having reasonable grounds for suspicion sufficent to justify arrest is not necessarily sufficient to justify a charge: hearsay evidence, for example, may be sufficient grounds for reasonable suspicion, but it is not sufficient for a person to be charged, since it will not be admissible as evidence at trial. Accordingly, the period of detention may be used to dispel or confirm that reasonable suspicion by questioning the suspect or seeking further material evidence with his assistance. This has not always been the law or practice but now seems to be well established as one of the primary purposes of detention upon arrest".[24]

Provisions in the Bill implemented the Royal Commission's recommendations by allowing detention for questioning. Extension of the powers of arrest was a logical and necessary corollary to increased reliance on detention. In the meantime, even before provisions like those in the Police Bill have been enacted, the Court of Appeal has relied on the passage quoted above from the Royal Commission Report in deciding that an arrest was lawful even though its only purpose was to put pressure on someone to confess, and the person could equally well have been questioned under caution without being arrested.

The case of *Mohammed-Holgate v Duke* concerned a woman who was lodging at premises from which jewellery was burgled. The jewellery appeared in a local shop window and the jeweller gave police a description of the person who sold it to him which tallied with that of the woman. Police arrested and detained the woman solely in order to question her. Subsequently she was found to be innocent and was never charged.[25] The decision appeared to conflict with an earlier decision that:

"To give power to arrest on reasonable suspicion does not mean that it is always or even ordinarily to be exercised".[26]

However the court found that the purpose of extracting a confession was perfectly proper and adequate to justify exercise of the power of arrest. The case would almost appear to be a judicial implementation of the provisions of the Police Bill on detention for questioning before they are made law. The court failed to consider the position in Scottish law where confession evidence is regarded very sceptically, and until recently, detention for questioning was not possible at all (the Criminal Justice (Scotland) Act 1982 gave the Scottish police power to hold suspects for questioning for up to only *six* hours).

After 24 hours of detention the Bill provided for a review by a senior police officer who would decide whether or not the detention should continue. After 36 hours the police would then have to apply to a magistrates court sitting in private for a "warrant of further detention" up to a total of 96 hours. Both the officer approving continued detention and the magistrates court would have to be satisfied that the investigation was being conducted "diligently and expeditiously".[27] Legal aid would be available.

These proposals differed from those in the Bill as originally drafted which had provided for review by a single magistrate (not sitting in court with the benefit of a legally qualified clerk) after 24 hours and by a full court after 48 hours. The original provisions were dropped because of objections by magistrates and their clerks. The effect would have been to extend the period of detention before an independent review takes place from 24 to 36 hours.

"Serious Arrestable Offence"

Another factor which was changed during the course of the Bill was the definition of a "serious arrestable offence". Under the Bill only people suspected of serious arrestable offences could be detained without charge for longer than 24 hours.[28] However the Bill contained no list of those offences which could be defined as "serious arrestable", as the Royal Commission on Criminal Procedure had recommended in its original proposal for "grave offences".[29] The Bill simply defined a "serious arrestable" offence as an arrestable offence which the person contemplating the exercise of the power (ie, the magistrate or police officer) *thinks* to be one.[30]

After protests from opposition MPs at this circular definition, the government introduced an amendment that the person contemplating the exercise of the power must have *reason* to believe the arrestable offence to be sufficiently serious to justify his or her exercising it, having regard to a number of factors (see box on p 78).

A mere recital of these factors is sufficient to demonstrate how very wide they were. They were more likely to suggest ways of defining an offence as "serious" than to restrict the ambit of the definition. Particularly worrying were (g) and (h), dealing with harm to the state and the prevalence of similar offences respectively. The first would be likely to encompass even minor Official Secrets Act breaches and new offences of riot and affray proposed by the Law Commission. The second would include petty theft, taking and driving away and burglary offences. Under the Bill suspects for such minor offences would be able to be detained without charge for up to four days, wholly legally. Whatever the confusion in the present system, the police do at the moment detain suspected petty thieves for shorter periods than suspected murderers and rapists. Quite clearly the wide definition of "serious arrestable offence" would substantially extend police powers to detain without charge in respect of lesser offences.

A **serious arrestable offence** was defined in the Bill, as amended, as an offence that the person contemplating the exercise of the power has reason to believe is sufficiently serious to justify his or her exercising it having regard to the following factors:
(a) the nature of the offence;
(b) the scale;
(c) the degree of organisation;
(d) the degree of violence used or likely to be used;
(e) the gain derived or likely to be derived;
(f) the harm caused or likely to be caused to persons;
(g) the harm caused or likely to be caused to the security of the state, the administration of justice or public order;
(h) the prevalence of similar offences (Clause 74)

Detentions Under the Prevention of Terrorism Act

The Bill had excluded from its provisions on the detention and treatment of suspects persons detained under the Prevention of Terrorism (Temporary Provisions) Act 1976. Lord Jellicoe's review of the PTA, which was published on 9 February 1983, recommended that the provisions of this Act be made permanent and that the special arrest and detention powers of the PTA be extended to cover persons suspected of connections with terrorist offences anywhere, not just Northern Ireland.[32] As part of a process of "normalisation"[33] of the PTA, it also recommended that the protection of the Codes of Practice issued under the Police Bill (see Chapter 14) be extended to PTA detainees.

The government wasted no time in implementing Lord Jellicoe's recommendations and the Prevention of Terrorism Bill was published on 8 July 1983. This would allow persons arrested under its provisions to be detained for up to *seven days* without charge. After 48 hours the Secretary of State must grant any extension of the detention for a further period not exceeding a further five days. Although presumably the new Police Bill will allow PTA detainees access to legal advice after 36 hours (subject to the very wide exceptions explained on p 93) the initial period of PTA detention has remained 48 hours.[34]

The effect of "normalising" the PTA will be to change its character to a special discriminatory law applying to those suspected of terrorism instead of, as previously, "emergency" legislation aimed at the situation in Northern Ireland. The transformation is significant both for its own sake and as a precedent and example in the criminal law. In itself it may well be illogical since, as with "serious arrestable offences", persons suspected of the grave offence of terrorism have more, not less, need of the safeguards in the Police Bill. As the *Guardian* commented:

> "One of the most alarming aspects of the Jellicoe Report is the frequent reference to the Police Bill as a norm to which the PTA should aspire – an example, surely, of an insidious circular process in which draconian law softens us up for similar laws which then become the desired standard for further measures".[35]

This circular process can be seen at work also when in Parliamentary debates, new powers in the Police Bill were justified by reference to terrorist suspects.[36]

There was in fact little evidence produced by Jellicoe for his contention that London is turning into an international playground for terrorists thus requiring the extension of the PTA. He produced no analysis or tables of international terrorist activity and only three examples.[37] Meanwhile the then Home Secretary stated in 1982 in a Parliamentary answer concerning London that:

> "There does not appear to have been an increase in crimes connected with terrorism in this period." (10 years).[38]

Policing London reported that it was the evidence given by the Association of Chief Police Officers to Jellicoe that was the deciding factor in his recommendation to extend the Act.[39] This provokes comparisons with the equally influential police input to the Police Bill (see Chapter 1). It is not yet clear whether the extension will result in a widening of the meaning of terrorism to cover domestic sedition or subversion.[40]

The threat to civil liberties posed by the PTA has been well documented. The National Council for Civil Liberties has argued that even for those charged with offences the Act makes no contribution to catching those involved in carrying or planting explosives.[41] J Sim and P Thomas have pointed out that:

> "What does emerge from the official statistics is that the Act's powers

do not produce a successful prosecution level which would be acceptable for other legislation; that they tell us nothing about the preventative nature of the Act but do indicate that the powers under the Act are used for the purpose of information gathering and the suppression of legitimate but critical debate on the Irish question".[42]

By extending dramatically standards for acceptable policing and regulation of detention of suspects, the Police Bill may be said to have paved the way for the extension of the PTA. This extension will mean it could affect a far wider category of people and will make permanent provisions which discriminate on grounds which may be spurious.

Immigration Act Detentions

Similar discrimination already exists with regard to black people in immigration law and would have been continued by the Bill, which also excluded suspects detained under the 1971 Immigration Act from limitations on detention.[43] Persons detained for removal as illegal entrants or deportation may be kept in custody for long periods.[44] The discriminatory nature of the immigration laws may also be said to buttress the discriminatory application of other laws to black people.

Notes

1. For example *Hansard* Standing Committee J, 22.2.83, Col 823, Roy Hattersley MP.
2. Police and Criminal Evidence Bill (as amended by Standing Committee J) Clause 25(2).
3. Bail Act 1976 Schedule I.
4. Clause 37(2) of the Bill also provided that where a person was released on bail because no detention condition applied, the magistrates court before which they were to appear could bail them to appear at an appointed time and enlarge the required surety. This should have been adequate provision for homeless people.
5. Police and Criminal Evidence Bill (as amended by Standing Committee J) Clause 27(4).
6. *Home Office Statistical Bulletin on Deaths in Police Custody* (9/83) 2 June 1983.
7. For example *Hansard* Standing Committee J, 22.2.83, Col 832, Patrick Mayhew MP.
8. Police and Criminal Evidence Bill (as amended by Standing Committee J) Clause 25(2).
9. *Royal Commission on Criminal Procedure: Police Interrogation Review of Literature* Research Study No 3 by Pauline Morris (HMSO April 1980) p 30.

0. *Royal Commission on Criminal Procedure: An Observational Study in Four Police Stations* Research Study No 4 by Paul Softley (HMSO April 1980).
1. R v Reid (1982) Crim LR 514.
2. Royal Commission on Criminal Procedure *Op cit* para 4.73.
3. Eleventh Report of the Criminal Law Revision Committee *Op cit* para 28 *et seq.*
4. See Chapter 1.
5. Police and Criminal Evidence Bill (as amended by Standing Committee J) Clause 31(2).
6. *Ibid* Clause 22(2).
7. *Once more unto Strasbourg* by Geraldine Van Bueren *Legal Action Group Bulletin* May 1983.
8. *Re* Sherman v Apps (1981) 2 ALL ER 612.
9. For example R v Nycander *Times Law Report* 9.12.82.
0. Home Office Memorandum on Police and Criminal Evidence Bill *op cit.*
1. Royal Commission on Criminal Procedure *Op cit* para 3.99.
2. CAPA Annual Report December 1982 (Oxford House, Derbyshire Street, London E2).
3. *Hansard* Standing Committee J, 22,2,83, col 824.
4. Royal Commission on Criminal Procedure *Op cit* para 3.66.
5. Mohammed-Holgate v Duke *Times Law Report* 16.7.83.
6. Hussein v Kahn (1970) AC 942-4.
7. Police and Criminal Evidence Bill (as amended by Standing Committee J) Clauses 32-3.
8. *Ibid.*
9. Royal Commission on Criminal Procedure Report *Op cit* para 3.5-3.9.
0. Police and Criminal Evidence Bill (as amended by Standing Committee J) Clause 74.
1. *Ibid.*
2. *Review of the Operation of the Prevention of Terrorism (Temporary Provisions) Act 1976* The Jellicoe Report 1983 (Cmnd 8803).
3. See *The Prevention of Terrorism Act: Normalising the Politics of Repression* by Joe Sim and Philip A Thomas (Journal of Law and Society Vol 10 No 1 Summer 1983).
4. Prevention of Terrorism Bill Clause 12(3).
5. *The Guardian* 10.2.83.
6. See for example *Hansard* 25.1.83 Col 228-9, Eldon Griffiths MP.
7. J Sim and P Thomas *Op cit.*
8. *Hansard* 24.6.82 Col 417.
9. *Policing London* No 7 April/May 1983.
0. See J Sim and P Thomas *Op cit* for a discussion of this.
1. *The Prevention of Terrorism Act: the Case for Repeal* by Catherine Scorer and Patricia Hewitt (NCCL 1981).
2. *Op cit.*
3. Police and Criminal Evidence Bill (As amended by Standing Committee J)
4. *Illegal Entrants* by Andrew Nicol (Joint Council for Welfare of Immigrants 1981).

12. The Admissibility of Confession Evidence

The provisions legitimising detention without charge were not the only ones in the Bill which would enable the police to rely more on extracting confessions from suspects in order to make a case against them. The Bill also created new tests governing the admissibility of confession statements into evidence at a trial. But the position on admissibility of other evidence (statements from witnesses and the results of searches) remained largely unchanged (see Chapter 14). The Bill proposed to exclude confession statements from being admitted into evidence, firstly if they were obtained "by oppression of the person who made it", or secondly "in consequence of anything said or done which was likely, in the circumstances existing at the time, to render *unreliable* any confession which might be made by him in consequence thereof".[1] "Oppression" was defined to include torture, inhuman or degrading treatment, and the use or threat of violence (whether or not amounting to torture).[2] This would have replaced the present "voluntariness" test, which has been described as follows:

> "It is a fundamental condition of the admissibility in evidence against any person, equally of any oral answer given by that person to a question put by a police officer, that it shall have been voluntary, in the sense that it had not been obtained from him by fear or prejudice or hope of advantage, exercised or held out by a person in authority, or by oppression".[3]

The Eleventh Report of the Criminal Law Revision Committee first recommended restricting the "voluntariness" test to those cases where threats or inducements made the confession *unreliable*. They criticised the broad ambit of the voluntariness test, referring to one case where a police officer's promise to a suspect to take other offences into consideration was held to be an inducement invalidating the subsequent confession.[4] The CLRC's proposals in this area accompanied their proposals to abolish the right of silence (see Chapter 1). They were followed by the Royal Commission on Criminal Procedure which developed their earlier criticisms of the voluntariness tests and recommended simply that:

". . . it should be left to the jury and magistrates to assess the reliability of confession evidence upon the facts presented to them".[5]

The Commission stated its belief that "reliability" would be better ensured by:

"workable and enforceable guidelines for the police, criteria that the courts can apply without a feat of the imagination that sometimes defies belief, and a clear and enforceable statement of the rights and safeguards for the suspect in custody".[5]

In rejecting the voluntariness test the Royal Commission were in part reacting to their own decision to validate detention for questioning. They pointed out that the mere fact of being in custody effectively removed "voluntariness" and therefore the psychological and legal tests of voluntariness did not match. The conclusion they drew was therefore that "voluntariness" was too strict a test, *not* that detention without charge threatened the right to silence.[6]

Reliability

Although the words "voluntary" and "reliable" would appear to be equally vague, the main effect of the substitution of a "reliability" test would be likely to be a substantial reduction in the number of confessions excluded. The CLRC certainly made it clear that this was their intention:

"The essential feature of this test is that it applies not to the confession which the accused in fact made, but to any confession which he might have made in consequence of the threat or inducement. On this scheme the judge should imagine that he was present at the interrogation and heard the threat or inducement. In the light of all the evidence given he will consider whether, at the point when the threat was uttered or the inducement offered, any confession which the accused might make as a result of it would be likely to be unreliable. If so the confession would be inadmissible".[7]

This would seem to suggest that the test will not be whether the suspect in question made a reliable statement, but whether the inevitable "reasonable person" would have made a reliable statement in the circumstances prevailing at the time. An article in the *Law Society Gazette* has exposed the dangers of this approach in relation to confessions:

> "Under the existing regime, the judge's function in determining causation (ie was the statement voluntary or was it obtained through fear of prejudice or hope of advantage?) is a difficult enough task to perform as it is. The proposed rule, on the other hand, will demand of him a journey into the realm of conjecture which it would be quite unreasonable of us to expect him to have to make . . . judges are, by and large, robust and rigorous individuals who, although well versed in the ways of criminal justice, are not principally appointed for their imaginative facilities. It is inevitable, perhaps, that instead of trying to imagine what it was like to be a defendant, the average judge would simply put himself in the defendant's shoes and conjecture his own reaction as a judge to the extraordinary circumstances of being suspected of a crime of which he was innocent. In psychological terms this is projection as distinct from empathy. As a judge, he would keep his wits about him, assert his authority, maintain his sense of proportion, and perhaps even revel in the new experience of what to anyone else would be a stressful ordeal. Certainly, he would treat any inducement from a menial policeman with lofty contempt and would never dream of making a false confession. The reality, by contrast, is that many suspects, resilient enough at their own hearth, become knock-kneed sheep susceptible to the mildest of pressures when carried off to the police station".[8]

The Draft Codes of Conduct issued by the Home Office to accompany the Police Bill would have further changed the position. These were intended to be brought into force under the provisions of the Bill as "secondary" legislation ie, legislation which can be changed without a full discussion in Parliament. The Draft Code on treatment and questioning of persons in police custody suggested that inducements offered to the suspect by the police which were "proper and warranted" actions would not lead to any exclusion of subsequent confession evidence.[9]This would presumably include offers of bail or release from the police station, where such a course of action would be "proper and warranted". At present an offer of bail which substantially induces a suspect to make a confession will lead to it being excluded from evidence. Making promises and/or threats is the most effective way to secure a confession from a suspect. A person kept in isolation in custody for any length of time is likely to be substantially swayed by suggestion of that sort. As Nick Blake has written:

> "Interrogation in a police station can be compared to a bizarre commercial transaction. A confession is valuable to a police officer. It may amount to sufficient evidence to conclude an investigation upon which he can only spend a limited amount of time. The suspect, similarly, wants his/her liberty, or at least the end of the uncertain period of pressure and compulsion that begins with the arrest. Even without improper behaviour or express inducements by a police officer the suspect is made aware that co-operation will result in various forms of benefits. The policeman has control over the conditions of custody — access to solicitors and visitors, length of interrogation, etc and can substantially affect the prospects of bail, or lenient disposal by the way the case is presented to the judge. Apart from implicating others the confession may be the only thing that the suspect can offer in return for these favours".[10]

Oppression

The Bill adopted the criterion of "oppression" as well as reliability. However the definition of oppression was very weak. It was similar to that used in the Northern Ireland (Emergency Provisions) Act 1973 and Article 3 of the European Convention on Human Rights ie "torture, inhuman or degrading treatment". It merely added on to these violence and the threat of violence. The standard laid down by the Convention was, however, only a minimum standard. A judgement in Northern Ireland by Lord Justice McGonigal made this clear:

> "Treatment to come within Article 3 must be treatment of a gross nature. It appears to accept a degree of physical violence which could never be tolerated by the courts under the common law test . . . it leaves open to an interviewer to use a moderate degree of maltreatment for the purpose of inducing a person to make a statement".[11]

As Paddy Hilliard has commented on the Royal Commission proposals:

> "By adding violence and the threat of violence the Commission has extended the minimum standard only a little. Threats, inducements or oppressive techniques designed to disorientate the subjects, all of which are at present illegal, will be permitted under this proposal. In effect, licence is being given to the police to use any form of psychological pressure as well as threats such as 'I will arrest your mother unless you

confess' or 'We will keep you here for three days unless you sign a confession'."[12]

The Truth of a Confession

Another disturbing aspect of this part of the Bill was that it allowed the "truth" of a confession statement to be taken into account in assessing its reliability. If this provision is repeated in the new Bill, it will undermine even more seriously the basis on which confession statements can be challenged. Hitherto the basis of such a challenge has always been to look at the circumstances surrounding the obtaining of the confession and to disregard the actual content of it. The Bill, however, allowed evidence of the content of the statement to be admitted in deciding on its "reliability" in three situations:

1) if the accused gave evidence, he or she could be questioned on whether the statement was *true;*
2) evidence of any relevant fact discovered as a result of a confession (eg hidden stolen goods discovered in the place specified in the confession) can be admitted to corroborate it;
3) evidence not obtained as a result of the confession but tending to confirm the guilt of the accused can be admitted.

Strangely enough the CLRC had voiced some objections to the judge deciding on the truth of a statement as part of a determination on whether it should be admitted as evidence. They said:

"We are opposed to any general provision for admissibility of evidence of statements contained in a confession on the ground that the truth of the statement is confirmed by the discovery of facts as a result of it for this would mean that the judge, for the purpose of ruling on admissibility would have to decide whether the confession, or the part in question, seemed to him likely to be true; and even though the judge's opinion would be provisional and would not be binding on the jury, it would probably be difficult for the jury not to be impressed by it".[13]

But the dangers of the Bill's approach were most forcefully exposed in the briefing by the National Council for Civil Liberties:

"Because the alleged truth of the confession is allowed to affect the question of whether it was obtained by oppression or in circumstances rendering it unreliable, there must be a considerable danger that a judge who has accepted evidence tending to confirm the truth of the confession will conclude that, therefore, it was *not* in fact obtained by oppression or in unreliable circumstances. It will be argued that methods which lead to a confession which the judge accepts to be true cannot have amounted to oppression or circumstances likely to make statements unreliable . . . By allowing the judge to consider evidence as to the truth of the statement allegedly obtained by oppression, this Bill invites the judge to conclude that because the statement was true the treatment through which it was obtained was not in fact oppression. *Thus the Bill does not even provide a clear and certain sanction against the use of the most obviously objectionable forms of interrogation''*[14] (our emphasis).

Notes

1. Police and Criminal Evidence Bill (as amended by Standing Committee J) Clause 59(2).
2. *Ibid* Clause 59(8).
3. Para (e) of the Preamble to the Judges' Rules reaffirmed in R v Rennie (1982) 1 WLR 64 Lord Lane.
4. Eleventh Report of the Criminal Law Revision Committee *Op cit* para 57.
5. Royal Commission on Criminal Procedure *Op cit* para 4.75.
6. *Ibid* para 4.73.
7. Eleventh Report of the Criminal Law Revision Committee *Op cit* para 65.
8. *A New Regime for Confessions* by Wolchover (*Law Society Gazette* 22.2.83).
9. *Draft Code of Practice for the Questioning of Persons Suspected of Crime and their Treatment if in Police Custody,* Revised Draft April 1983 (Home Office) para 12.2.
10. *The Police, the Law and the People, Op cit* p 29.
11. R v McCormick (1977) Northern Ireland Reports 105.
12. *From Belfast to Britain: Some critical comments on the Royal Commission on Criminal Procedure* by Paddy Hilliard *Politics and Power* 4 (1981) (Routledge and Kegan Paul).
13. Eleventh Report of the Criminal Law Revision Committee *Op cit* para 69.
14. *Clause 60: Confession Statements and the Right of Silence* by Patricia Hewitt and Paddy O'Connor (NCCL, March 1983) para 36.

13. The Treatment of Suspects in the Police Station

Search

The Police Bill contained new police powers of searching and taking fingerprints and samples from suspects detained in police stations as well as provisions governing access to a lawyer.

Searches, other than "intimate searches", were to be carried out at the total discretion of the police without the giving of any reason. The sole criterion was to be whether the custody officer "considers it necessary to do so in order that the record required by subsection (1) (record of suspect's property) be complete".[1] This would include **strip searches**, ie where suspects are required to take off all their clothes. There are many complaints that strip searches are already carried out unnecessarily, purely as a means of intimidation (see below). Women who are strip searched also complain that it is done in the presence of male police officers. The Bill, as it was drafted, would do nothing to alleviate these fears or provide any safeguards against random use of the strip search. Indeed it specifically legitimised random strip searches.

In addition, the Bill created an entirely new power to carry out what it called euphemistically "intimate searches".[2] What this actually meant was an internal examination of the parts of the body (vaginas and anuses), which had probably never before been understood to be included in the term "search". It would involve the penetration of delicate body membranes and, as the British Medical Association pointed out, could be extremely dangerous if done otherwise than by a doctor. The proposals in the Bill would allow "intimate searches" to be carried out by force and by police officers of the same sex as the suspect as an alternative to a doctor.[3] This could be argued to be wholly unacceptable in any society. It might also be "degrading treatment" contrary to the European Convention on Human Rights, as Geraldine van Bueren pointed out in the *Legal Action Group Bulletin*.[4] The British Medical Association said that doctors would refuse to carry out "intimate searches" against the will of the suspect.[5]

In Standing Committee the then Minister of State, Patrick Mayhew MP said that suspects would be given a "choice" either to "consent" to the intimate body search and have it carried out by a doctor, or to withhold consent and have it carried out by a police officer of the same sex.[6] "Intimate searches" were only to be carried out if an officer of at least the rank of superintendent authorised them. That officer could only give such authorisation if s/he considered that the offence for which the person was detained was a serious arrestable offence; and if s/he reasonably believed that a search would produce evidence relevant to that offence; or that a search would be necessary to establish that the suspect did not have on them any article which could be used to cause injury to themselves or to others.[7] Thus the grounds for intimate body searches were very wide and, as has already been discussed, the requirement that the offence in question be a serious arrestable one would appear to provide little protection.[8]

Strip Searches

By not including provisions in the Bill requiring reasons for strip searches the government apparently ignored comments previously made by the Police Complaints Board. In the case of *Lindley v Rutter* 1980 the divisional court had decided that a woman police officer was not entitled to remove a woman suspect's bra without good reason to do so.[9] In their Triennial Report of 1980 the Police Complaints Board referred to the number of complaints about strip searches they received and said that they should not be carried out in enquiries which were only routine. They said:

> "We are left with the impression that the procedure is sometimes followed with an element of vindictiveness where a prisoner has given the arresting officers a bad time".[10]

The Royal Commission on Criminal Procedure also expressed concern about strip searches:

> "An extreme and manifestly disagreeable form of search is that for illegal drugs, colloquially called 'strip search'. We recognise that such searches may be necessary if the law, for example in relation to the importation and supply of prohibited drugs, is to be effectively imposed. We consider that strip searches should take place only at a police station, so that they are supervised and monitored. If they

police station, so that they are supervised and monitored. If they involve examination of intimate parts of the body they should be carried out only by a medical practitioner, and only in respect of the most serious offences. We would suggest that such searches should be confined to grave offences. The nature of the places of concealment will limit the range of such offences in respect of which intimate searches will be necessary. One consequence of this approach is that search of body cavities for drugs will be permitted when the offence suspected is one of supplying, importing or exporting drugs".[11]

The case of Ms Brazil quoted on p 113 shows that the courts believe reasons should be given for carrying out strip searches.

Intimate Searches

The Royal Commission was responsible for the provisions in the Bill to the extent that it apparently confused strip searches and "intimate searches". But the power to search body orifices (vaginas and anuses) would probably be new. It is doubtful whether "search" would be interpreted by a court to include probes into internal body parts, although the point has never been tested. Certainly the medical profession clearly consider that such probes should only be done by medical examination. In Standing Committee the then Minister of State, Patrick Mayhew MP, did attempt to claim that the power was not a new one, but could not support this with evidence.[12]

Even Deputy Assistant Commissioner Powis in his training manual is clear that consent has to be obtained in however dubious a manner:

"Watch for the methods of the dishonest pickpocket prostitute who steals from the pockets of semi-drunk clients. A thorough search of the body orifices unpleasant as this is, may be necessary. If a mature and sensible woman officer, or matron, suspects deep interior concealment have the divisional surgeon called (leaving the matron, or officer, with her until he arrives) for a proper examination, *with consent of course*. When such a prisoner sees your determination to get medical evidence she may see the inevitability of detection and cease her deceit, voluntarily producing the hidden money".[13]

The quote is worrying because it suggests that "intimate searches" would be carried out routinely on prostitutes. Similar fears have also been expressed in relation to searches of men suspected of homosexual offences.

In Committee Eldon Griffiths, MP, relied on concealment of drugs and "explosive tampons" as reasons justifying intimate searches.[14] But clearly if the police were to use the power on every cannabis user, this too would be a highly obnoxious practice. In fact there is no evidence that the police, or customs and excise, are asking for this power. Indeed an editorial in *Police Review* actually said that the police themselves do *not* want it:

> "Clause 43 permits a police officer to make a physical examination of a prisoner's bodily orifices without his or her consent. Quite bluntly, the clause permits a police officer to poke fingers into the vagina or anus of an unconvicted suspect. Who on earth wants such a power?
>
> There are roughly three classes of person to whom the provisions of Clause 43 might apply. Prostitutes who calculate that the possession of banknotes and contraceptives might increase the possibility of conviction have been known to conceal both items in either place. But this is hardly the type of offence that warrants such drastic powers. Drug couriers swallow or insert into their bodies cocaine or other illegal substances sealed in plastic. However, drug squads have facilities for isolating such suspects until the packages have been naturally passed. There have been a few cases in which prisoners have concealed knives, matches, or other instruments within their bodies so they can harm themselves or injure others.
>
> Police officers face a continuing dilemma over how thoroughly a prisoner should be searched. The mildest man may cause a fire with a concealed match; neurotics of both sexes have secreted razor blades to make late attempts of slashing their wrists; and the depressed, deprived of belt and shoe laces, have hanged themselves with shirts or tights. But to give police officers power to make the most intimate of body searches or obtain evidence or remove the means of injury in exceptional cases is to license further the handful of bullies who presently use strip searches to intimidate or humiliate prisoners. The honest and professional officer neither wants nor needs this power.
>
> Are we to antagonise the whole of the public for the sake of the ·01 per cent of officers who will not object to being ordered to conduct such searches? Let us hope Parliament has the foresight to reject an indignity that its committee has ignored".[15]

On the whole the police deal with concealment of drugs perfectly adequately by placing grids on lavatories in police stations and with voluntary co-operation. Moreover a common method of concealing drugs in contraceptive sheaths which are swallowed would not necessarily be revealed by an "intimate search" eg a typical press report on the detection of a drugs smuggler stated that: "Customs officers kept 'X' at the airport until the sheaths passed through his system".[16]

It is to be hoped that there will be some government recognition of the protests that these proposals are likely to inspire if reintroduced in the same form. The wisest course of action would be for the government to drop altogether the proposals to create a new power of "intimate search". In any event proper safeguards should be placed on the carrying out of "strip searches".

Fingerprints and Body Samples

The Bill authorised for the first time the taking of non-intimate samples and fingerprints by force from suspects, even from children aged 10 and over. Even the Royal Commission were uncertain about compulsory fingerprinting of children:

> "Some of us feel the case for fingerprinting 10-13 year olds has not been made out. The lack of power to fingerprint offenders in this age group does not appear to lead to difficulties for the police in investigating crime; nor will it often be necessary to fingerprint such offenders for identification purposes. Those of us who take this view also believe that it is wrong in principle to make offenders aged under 14 the subject of this type of formal criminal record and thus to mark them out as criminals. They do not consider that they should be subjected to the indignity of being fingerprinted".[17]

At present fingerprints can only be taken without consent if a magistrate's warrant is obtained first. Although it is very rare indeed for warrants to be withheld, it does mean that if the suspect objects, fingerprints are then taken at the magistrates court and there is no struggle between police and a resisting suspect.

The Bill would allow fingerprints to be taken by force in the police station without recourse to a magistrate. It also divided other "body samples" into two categories - "intimate samples" and "non-intimate samples". An intimate sample was defined in the Bill as a sample of blood , semen, pubic hair, urine or saliva or a swab of a part of a person's body other than the hand. Non-intimate samples were defined as all other swabs, footprints and other body impressions.[18] Intimate samples could only be taken with the consent of the suspect and by a doctor but there was again a new power to take non-intimate samples by force.

The Bill thus attempted to distinguish between taking intimate *samples*, which would require medical examination and the suspect's consent, and "intimate searches" which would not. The distinction would obviously be very dubious and the power to carry out by force "intimate searches" would mean that the requirements to be satisfied for taking intimate body samples would be meaningless. The confusion created by the artificial distinctions in the Bill was illustrated when a police officer erroneously told a public meeting in Bristol in June 1983 that the Bill permitted samples of blood or semen to be taken compulsorily from suspected rapists.

If provisions similar to those in the Bill became law there could be a danger that struggles between suspect and police and the use of force in the police station could be validated by the necessity to take fingerprints and samples by force. The Law Society has stated that it:

> "does not approve of any provision which entitles a police officer to assault a suspect and that the powers to take fingerprints and body samples without consent are therefore objectionable in principle".[19]

Juveniles

The Bill contained special provision for children and young persons who are arrested. However, their additional "rights" turned out to be only that a parent or guardian was to be informed of the detention "as soon as reasonably practicable".[20] It was still not to be an absolute requirement that an independent adult, preferably the parent or guardian, be present at the questioning of children. Although the Draft Codes of Practice (see Chapter 14) contained a provision to this effect, there were exceptions if "the delay in contacting such a person will involve an immediate risk of harm to persons or serious loss of or damage to property".[21]

There was also no provision in the Bill giving protection to mentally handicapped persons. A provision in the Codes is discussed on p 103, but it was no answer for the government to say that the appropriate protection was in the Codes of Practice. Like the Judges' Rules, the Codes are bound to be seen as vague guidelines and, in any event, would be as we shall see, almost wholly unenforceable.

Access to a Solicitor

One of the biggest problems with the Bill was its failure to provide a proper right for suspects to have access to a solicitor. The Bill provided that a person should be entitled, if they so requested, to consult a solicitor privately, and stated that after a person had made a request they were to be permitted to consult the solicitor "*as soon as is practicable*".[22] The real significance of this loophole became apparent in a subsequent clause which stated that:

> "In any case he must be permitted to consult a solicitor within 36 hours from the time when the police first detained him".[23]

The wording of the Bill left it wide open to abuse. It meant that in the majority of cases, the police would continue to find it "impracticable" to allow consultation with a solicitor before questioning. The overall time limit of 36 hours would be ludicrously long and might suggest that the objective was to enable the police to conduct questioning without a solicitor's presence. The Bill permitted yet further delay in the case of "serious arrestable offences", if an officer of at least the rank of superintendent authorised it on one of the following grounds: that access to a solicitor would lead to interference with evidence or person; to the alerting of suspects; or would hinder the recovery of any property.[24]

The present situation, whereby the police constantly deny suspects access to a lawyer, is well documented. A study by Baldwin and McConville found that more than three quarters of defendants in Birmingham who stated they had asked to see a solicitor reported that their requests were turned down by the police.[25] Another survey by Michael Zander had broadly the same findings.[26] The Royal Commission suggested that failure to ask for a solicitor was as much of a problem as police refusals to let suspects see a solicitor and that, ".... it is not known why so few suspects make a request to see a solicitor".[27]

It would seem highly likely that the reason why so few people request a solicitor is that most realise that there is little chance of the police permitting them to see one.

The Draft Codes of Practice dealt with requests to have a solicitor present at interview, but stated that such a request would not be granted if:

> "a police officer of the rank of superintendent, or above, has reasonable grounds to believe that to delay interviewing him involves a risk of harm to persons or serious loss of or damage to property; or that awaiting the arrival of a solicitor would cause unreasonable delay to the processes of investigation (having regard to the time limit for lawful detention that applies)".[28]

This was an improvement on the earlier Draft Code of Practice produced by the Home Office which had simply stated that a request could be refused on the grounds that it would interfere with the conduct of the interview.[29] And the new Draft Code of Practice also explicitly stated that access to a solicitor may not be denied or delayed on the grounds that s/he will advise the suspect not to answer questions.[30] However, the second ground, that awaiting the arrival of a solicitor would cause "unreasonable delay", may still be widely interpreted and open to abuse.

In the official inquiry report on the Confait Case, Sir Henry Fisher said:

> "The right to consult a solicitor is so important and fundamental a right that I should expect such discretionary exclusion to follow automatically in the event of a breach. If there is any doubt whether it will, I favour a change in the law making exclusion an automatic consequence of a breach of the principle".[31]

The Confait Case became notorious because the confessions of three young defendants were shown to have been false. But every day suspects held in police stations, on minor and serious charges alike, are denied access to lawyers. It seems likely that the police will continue to deny access if legislation does not enforce it. As Judge McKenna said in *R v Allen*:

> "If the police are allowed to use in court evidence which they have obtained from suspects to whom they have wrongly denied the right to legal advice, they will be encouraged to continue this illegal practice. If the police know the answers to their questions will not be admitted if they have refused, without good reason, to allow their prisoner to see a solicitor ... there will, I think be fewer complaints about the denial of this right".[32]

The Royal Commission on Criminal Procedure recommended that there should be an absolute right to see a solicitor in private and to have them present at questioning. However, they paved the way for the weak proposals in the Bill by making an exception of grave offences where it was considered that giving access to a legal adviser might lead to interference with evidence or witnesses, the alerting of suspects or would hinder the recovery of property.[33] The Royal Commission therefore appeared to validate Sir Robert Mark's views about "bent lawyers".[34]

In a briefing paper on the Bill the Law Society stated that it was concerned that:

"The operation of sub-clause (7) may give rise to complaints that solicitors are being prevented from seeing their clients when they should not be. The clause gives scope for the exclusion of solicitors who, though entirely reputable, are not popular with a particular police station".[35]

It also pointed out that those held on suspicion of serious offences would have the most need of access to legal advice. It is certainly arguable that, if it really is necessary to stop access to particular solicitors, the suspect should at least be given the opportunity to name an alternative solicitor from a duty solicitor rota. Opposition amendments to this effect were inevitably rejected by the government in relation to the old Bill.[36]

The Bill also provided for a right to have someone informed of one's arrest. This was largely a re-enactment of the existing "right" under S62 Criminal Law Act 1977. Under the Bill this right could also be delayed where the offence was a "serious arrestable offence" and if the police reasonably thought there was likely to be interference to evidence, alerting of other suspects or hindering of the recovery of property.[37]

The right to have someone informed is obviously very important to anyone with a family, particularly women with children. This provision was again criticised on the grounds that the category, "serious arrestable offence", was far too wide. In Standing Committee the government undertook to bring forward amendments to place a time limit of 24 hours on police compliance and to provide a right for an alternative acceptable person to be named, if the first person specified was unacceptable.[38] These were not in the batch of amendments tabled by the government at Report Stage, however, and may therefore need to be argued for again, in relation to the new Bill.[39]

Generally the provisions in the Bill giving the police new powers over suspects detained in the police station would be an attack on another longstanding legal principle; that suspects should not be obliged to incriminate themselves. There would be a significant shift towards refusing the suspect basic rights, even though they had not been charged with any offence, let alone convicted of one. A substantial degree of force could also be used by police against the suspect, as this would be necessary to enforce the new powers.

Notes

1. Police and Criminal Evidence Bill (as amended by Standing Committee J) Clause 42(2).
2. Police and Criminal Evidence Bill (as amended by Standing Committee J) Clause 42.
3. *Ibid* Clause 42(6).
4. *Legal Action Group Bulletin* May 1983.
5. Letter in *The Times* 17.2.83 from the Secretary of the British Medical Association and the Secretary-General of the Law Society. It said that, "medical practitioners are prevented on ethical grounds from carrying out operations on patients without their informed consent" and also that the BMA may have to advise its members, including police surgeons, not to carry out "intimate searches" without the "informed" consent of the suspect, ie given after access to legal advice (which under the Bill can be delayed for up to 36 hours or longer).
6. *Hansard* Standing Committee J, 17.2.83, Col 720-1.
7. Police and Criminal Evidence Bill (as amended by Standing Committee J) Clause 42(9).
8. Police and Criminal Evidence Bill (as amended by Standing Committee J) Clause 74.
9. Lindley v Rutter (1981) QB 128.
10. Police Complaints Board *Triennial Review* Report 1980 (HMSO Cmnd 7966) para 48.
11. Royal Commission on Criminal Procedure *Op cit* para 3.118.
12. *Hansard* Standing Committee J, 15.2.83, Col 681.
13. *The Signs of Crime* by David Powis *Op cit* p 75.
14. *Hansard* Standing Committee J, 17.2.83, Col 706-7.
15. *Police Review* 25.2.83.
16. *South London Press* 8.7.83.
17. Royal Commission on Criminal Procedure *Op cit* para 3.132.
18. Police and Criminal Evidence Bill (as amended by Standing Committee J) Clause 50.
19. *Briefing memorandum on the Police and Criminal Evidence Bill* -The Law Society.
20. Police and Criminal Evidence Bill (as amended by Standing Committee J) Clause 44.
21. *Draft Code of Practice for the Questioning of Persons Suspected of Crime and their Treatment if in Police Custody* (Home Office April 1983) para 15.4.
22. Police and Criminal Evidence Bill (as amended by Standing Committee J) Clause 45(1) and 45(3).
23. *Ibid* Clause 45(4).
24. *Ibid* Clause 45(7).

25. *Police Interrogation and the Right to see a Solicitor (Criminal Law Review* 1979 145-152).

26. *Access to a Solicitor in the Police Station (Criminal Law Review* 1972 342-350).

27. Royal Commission on Criminal Procedure Report *Op cit* para 4.83.

28. Draft Code of Practice *Op cit* para 5.3.

29. *Ibid* November 1982.

30. *Ibid* April 1983 para 5.2.

31. Report of an Inquiry by the Hon. Sir Henry Fisher *Op cit* para 2.20.

32. R v Allen (1977) CLR 163.

33. Royal Commission on Criminal Procedure *Op cit* para 4.91.

34. See Chapter 1 page 11.

35. *Police and Criminal Evidence Bill - Detailed Memorandum on Clauses 43-51* Law Society, February 1983, p 3.

36. *Hansard* Standing Committee J, 17.2.83.

37. Police and Criminal Evidence Bill (as amended by Standing Committee J) Clause 43(9).

38. *Hansard* Standing Committee J, 17.2.83, Col 736 and 751, Patrick Mayhew MP.

39. Statistics are published on the operation of Section 62 of the Criminal Law Act 1977, but appear to be unsatisfactory (see *Home Office Statistical Bulletin* 8/82). According to the *New Law Journal* the statistics do not indicate how many out of the one and a half million persons arrested in 1981 failed to exercise their rights because they were not aware of them. No indication is given of the number of arrested persons whose requests that their detention should be notified to a person of their choice were not dealt with at all. Such a request is regarded as "dealt with" if there is "an attempt" to make contact with the person named, even though the attempt is unsuccessful. If it fails "it appears the police are under no obligation to try to contact a second nominee, even though such a nominee may be readily contactable" (*New Law Journal* 20.5.82).

14. The Judges' Rules, the Codes of Practice and Exclusion of Evidence

Judges' Rules

At present there is no Act of Parliament which regulates the conduct of the police towards the suspect who is being arrested and interrogated. However, in 1912 and 1918 some non-statutory regulations, the Judges' Rules, were formulated which were revised in 1964 and are still the only general statement of police powers. They govern such matters as the form of caution to be given to a suspect, rights of access to a lawyer, the necessity for statements to be "voluntary", the point at which a suspect should be charged and the prohibition on questioning after charge. They have been added to by a series of Home Office circulars on matters such as identification procedures and the questioning of children and young persons.[1] However, they do not have statutory force and there is no direct sanction against the police breaking them. Moreover many of them contain wide exclusions which have generally rendered them ineffective eg, access to a solicitor can be refused a suspect in detention if the police consider it would cause "unreasonable delay or hindrance" to the processes of investigation or the administration of justice.[2]

In 1977 the report of the judicial inquiry into the Maxwell Confait case by Sir Henry Fisher found that breaches of the Judges' Rules had been perpetrated by senior police officers without adverse comment from higher ranking police officers, the officers of the Director of Public Prosecutions, treasury counsel, defending counsel, or from the judge at the trial.[3] The Report also found that:

> "Some of the Rules and Directions do not seem to be known to police officers and members of the legal profession. Others are misunderstood by some police officers and members of the legal

profession. Others are misunderstood by some police officers and are not given their proper effect".[4]

The Royal Commission on Criminal Procedure was set up in the wake of the revelations by the Fisher Report of police ignorance and contempt for the Rules. They made the following recommendations:

"For the actual conduct of questioning we need to replace the vagueness of the Judges' Rules with a set of instructions which provide strengthened safeguards to the suspect and clear and workable guidelines for the police. We call this a code of practice for the regulation of interviews and recommend that it should be contained in subordinate legislation subject to affirmative resolution of Parliament and made by the Home Secretary after consultation with the police, the judiciary and persons with the relevant expert medical and psychological experience. The code of practice will be part of the general provisions governing the treatment of persons in custody that we have been developing . . . and it should be aimed at producing conditions of interview that minimise the risk of unreliable statements. Its provisions will also amount to a statement of what is viewed as acceptable practice when the police have to interview those who are reasonably suspected in connection with an offence. So, as well as the sanctions attached to its breach it will carry an element of social and moral imperative".[5]

Codes of Practice

In July 1982 the Home Office issued two sets of draft Codes for consultation; one on the interrogation of suspects and their treatment in police custody and one on identification parades and procedures. These Codes were published in revised form in April 1983 and the comments refer to the revised editions.[6]

When the Bill was published in October 1982, it placed a duty on the "custody officer" (the station officer made responsible for the detention of a suspect) to ensure that the suspect was treated in accordance with the provisions of the Bill and the Codes of Practice.[7] As we shall see, however, the duty was only to be enforceable through internal discipline, as were the provisions in the Bill itself.

The division of subject matter between the Bill itself and the Codes was not particularly clear or logical. For example, as we have seen (p 93), rights of access to a solicitor were included in the Bill but the question of whether a solicitor should be present during questioning was in the Codes. Even more notably, provisions dealing with questioning of children and young persons were in the Bill, whereas those dealing with the question of the mentally ill or mentally handicapped were in the Codes. Generally the Codes did contain more detailed instructions, eg on matters to be included in the custody record, but in some cases were repetitive of provisions in the Bill.[9] Extremely important subjects crucial to suspects were in the Codes but not in the Bill, such as access to medical attention and identification parade procedures.

There was little in the Codes that would help to prevent the increasing numbers of deaths in police custody.[10] Despite evidence of overcrowded and inhuman conditions in police cells (eg prisoners sharing tiny cells without natural daylight) there were no standards of space, ventilation, or lighting for cells set out in the Codes. The Royal Commission had recommended the setting of such standards for interview rooms but not for cells, which seemed illogical.[11] In the case of a man who hanged himself in a police cell in a West London police station last year, it was revealed that his cell, which was not ventilated, had a temperature of 82 degrees Fahrenheit at the time.[12] In another case in Brixton police station, a detainee who died from the effects of alcohol was sharing a tiny cell. At the police station that night there were 16 prisoners held in five cells and two detention rooms.[13]

Another factor which can be important in preventing deaths in custody is easy access to a doctor. The Codes did contain some instructions on summoning doctors which could be a slight improvement on those operating at present, eg a doctor would be called if a suspect was unable to appreciate the nature of the proceedings or was "incoherent or somnolent" *and* if the custody officer was in any doubt about the circumstances of his/her condition.[14] But too much was still left to police discretion and neither the Codes, nor the Bill, gave the suspect an absolute right to see their own doctor instead of a police surgeon, except possibly if they alleged assault by the police.[15] A suspect's own doctor would of course have access to more information about their medical condition, as well as being independent of the police. The case of James Ruddock who died at Kensington Police Station on 15.3.83 illustrated the importance of prompt medical attention. Ruddock who was incoherent and somnolent saw no doctor for twelve hours and died of hypothermia.[13]

The Codes also dealt with cautioning, but contained only minor alterations to the form of cautioning before questioning.

The caution is required to be delivered as soon as a police officer has reasonable grounds for suspecting that a person has committed an offence. The present form is:

"You are not obliged to say anything unless you wish to do so, but what you say may be put into writing and given in evidence".

The form recommended by the Codes was:

"You do not have to say anything unless you wish to do so, but what you say may be given in evidence."[16]

It was no improvement on the original, although Sir Henry Fisher had previously drawn attention to the ambiguity of the wording:

"The second half of the caution . . . assumes that the person does talk and may well seem to a simple person to negate the first part, especially when followed by a question or an invitation to speak".[17]

A revised form of caution might read:

"You do not have to say anything unless you wish to do so, but if you do decide to say anything this will be written down and given in evidence".

The provisions in the Codes were often so weak that even if they were made properly enforceable, they might still be of little use to the suspect. Thus a provision requiring refreshments at two hourly intervals (apart from mealtimes) was marred by a wide exception:

"if the interviewing officer considers that the delay caused by such a break may:
  (i)   involve a risk of harm to persons or serious loss or damage to property, or
  (ii) delay unnecessarily the person's release from custody, or
  (iii) otherwise prejudice the investigation".[18]

Another cause for concern in the Codes was the provision for a third party present at the interview to sign the record of it or a written statement.[19] Increasingly social workers, members of the clergy and relatives are being allowed access to suspects held in police stations for the limited purpose of witnessing a statement or record of an interview. This was done, for example, in the Confait case where parents countersigned statements made by their children. Such persons should be asked to sign statements *only* if they have been present throughout all the interviews and have sufficient knowledge of the suspect to know that their statement was voluntary.

There was no provision in the Bill dealing with the questioning of mentally ill or mentally handicapped persons. This was despite the criticisms of Sir Henry Fisher in his inquiry into the Confait case that a mentally handicapped person (Colin Lattimore) was interviewed without an independent person present and in an "unfair and an aggressive" manner.[20] Under the Codes parents or guardians of mentally ill or handicapped persons were to be informed of their detention and if a police officer had suspicion of mental illness or disorder, they were to call a police surgeon.[21] With regard to mental illness and handicap the Codes provided that:

> "If an officer has any suspicion that a person, who may be questioned, whether or not in custody, may be mentally ill or mentally handicapped or there are reasonable grounds for doubting that the person understands or is capable of understanding the significance of questions put to him and his replies, the person shall not, subject to paragraph 14.3, be interviewed save in the presence of a parent or other person in whose care, custody, or control he is, or, in their absence, of some responsible person (where possible a person with experience of the treatment of mental disorder) who is not a police officer".[22]

and that

> "A mentally ill or mentally handicapped person may be interviewed in the absence of such an adult only if the police officer concerned reasonably believes that the delay in contacting such a person will involve a risk of harm to persons or serious loss of or damage to property. Any decision to interview a person who appears to be mentally ill or handicapped in such circumstances shall be taken by an officer of the rank of Superintendent or above and the reason for the decision recorded on the custody record where the person is in custody".[23]

The exception in the second part of this provision would be similar to that concerning the interviewing of children and young persons. Like that provision it made no reference to the wishes of the suspect, so that a parent, guardian, or other responsible person could be contacted *against* the wishes of the mentally handicapped person. But a major difficulty was that the Codes failed to provide any real definition of mental handicap or to distinguish between it and mental illness. To leave the decision as to whether a person is or is not so handicapped to the subjective opinion of a police officer (the test is not even one of "reasonableness") seems wholly wrong and it is doubtful whether these provisions would do much to prevent mentally handicapped people being interviewed without an independent person present in the future.

The Royal Commission had recommended that special attention be given to the problems surrounding the taking of statements from children and the mentally handicapped.[24] Both groups are likely to be susceptible to suggestion even if there is no misconduct on the part of police officers, as the draft Code acknowledges.[25] The case of Mr D in 1982 (see p 112) illustrated this problem.

The provisions in the Codes relating to identification parades and procedures were similarly unsatisfactory. Their worst defect was that they failed to guarantee the suspect access to legal advice before deciding whether or not to consent to an identification parade.[26] The use of identification parades as evidence is a highly technical matter and only those suspects versed in police station procedures could be expected to appreciate the implications. Under the Codes the suspect would be entitled to have a solicitor present only provided that this can be arranged "without causing unreasonable delay having regard to the lawful period of detention".[27] The presence of parents or guardians (rather than a solicitor) was also to be allowed to validate parades involving children despite the fact that they would usually not be familiar with the procedure.[28]

Other serious defects in these procedures included: failure to provide for any right of challenge as to the membership of the parade by the suspect or his or her lawyer; provisions allowing two suspects to be paraded together;[29] and parades in prisons to be composed wholly of prisoners.[30]

The Codes also provided for an identification procedure which, although not an identity parade, conformed to one so far as possible.[31] Difficulties often arise in holding parades of black people because black members of the public cannot be persuaded to take part. This has led to the practice of, for example, Brixton Police Station conducting a facsimile identity parade on a tube escalator or elsewhere with unsuspecting members of the public. Since such procedures are fair neither to the suspect nor the members of the public (who may be wrongly picked out) their inclusion in the Codes was regrettable. In 1982, one MP unsuccessfully asked the Home Secretary to prohibit this practice.[32] If a parade is not possible or the suspect does not consent, identification should be on the basis of a one-to-one confrontation.

Enforcement

The most crucial question in relation to the Codes is that of enforcement. The present situation illustrates perfectly the problems of lack of enforceability.

A series of cases has established that breach of the Judges' Rules need not of itself lead to exclusion of evidence.[33] There is some confusion about whether there is a discretion on the part of a judge to exclude because of breach. Some commentators have argued that the only test which should be applied is whether or not the evidence in question was obtained "voluntarily".[34] Court judgements have contained statements that illegally obtained evidence should generally be admitted unless obtained by a trick.[35] But in one case in 1977 a confession was excluded because it was obtained after the defendant had asked to speak to a solicitor and been refused.[36] This case was subsequently much criticised and in 1979 the House of Lords decided that judges only had a discretion in relation to the voluntariness of confessions but not in relation to other evidence:

"It is no part of a judge's function to exercise disciplinary powers over the police or prosecution as respects the way in which evidence to be used at the trial is obtained by them. If it was obtained illegally there will be a remedy in civil law; if it was obtained legally, but in breach of the rules of conduct for the police, this is a matter for the appropriate disciplinary authority of the police to deal with".[37]

The Bill followed the approach of the Royal Commission on Criminal Procedure by relying on internal police discipline to prevent breaches of the Codes or the Bill, instead of exclusion of evidence provisions. Michael Zander has pointed out some of the defects:

"The trouble with this approach is that police disciplinary proceedings are held in secret and no one outside the force has any knowledge of what goes on. There is no published information about the extent to which breaches of the Judges' Rules lead to disciplinary charges being brought or, if so, of the penalties imposed.

The annual reports of Chief Constables and of HM Inspector of the Constabulary carry global figures about the numbers of cases in which police officers are disciplined and of the punishments meted out. But no detail is given and there is therefore no way of knowing to what extent breaking the Judges' Rules is treated as a serious matter by the police."[38]

One view is that internal discipline will never be sufficient to enforce police compliance with rules of behaviour. According to this the police motivation to secure convictions is so strong that the whole police organisation will connive at rule breaking. If that happens (and it is certainly happening now in relation to observance of the Judges' Rules) internal disciplinary sanctions enforced by the organisation itself cannot be relied on. A National Council for Civil Liberties briefing on the Bill stated:

> "When NCCL asked the Metropolitan Police solicitor when a police officer had last been disciplined for breach of Rules, he was unable to remember a single instance".[39]

The view of the GLC and NCCL is that the only effective means of enforcement would be that which operates in the USA and other countries, namely the exclusion of evidence rule. This would mean that evidence obtained in breach of provisions in the Bill or the Codes would not be admitted into evidence in court. In English civil law there is a legal doctrine, picturesquely described as "the fruit of the poisoned vine", which prohibits reliance on evidence which has been wrongfully obtained. The exclusion of evidence rule would be an extension of the same principle to criminal law.

The Royal Commission rejected exclusion of evidence as a means of enforcement firstly because they decided that it had little or no deterrent effect, secondly because they said that there would be an increase in disputes about the admissibility of evidence (with consequent trial delays) and thirdly because they said it would lead to criminals going free because of police blunders.[40] Their views on the lack of deterrent effect were based on some US research.[41] But as J Driscoll has pointed out, the research in question was old and concerned only with a relatively restricted area of law enforcement involving mainly illegal searches concerned with gambling, narcotics and weapons' offences. Driscoll drew attention to other research which contradicted the conclusions of the US study, relied upon by the Commission. He commented:

> "America has its divisions between federal and State Law and, compared with England and Wales, greater complexity of criminal procedure and police organisation with a separation between the police and prosecuting authorities. The Royal Commission correctly recognised the differences but then made a double error: first its inadequate consideration of the published research resulted in a failure to take into account the way specifically American factors affected the implementation of the rule; and second the Commission made the

unjustified assumption that it was only the differences between the systems which made the exclusionary rule necessary in the United States and, by corollary, unnecessary here.

Instead a fuller review suggests that the factors which led Americans to the exclusionary rule are very similar to those which faced the Royal Commission and that England and Wales with a unified legal system, relatively homogenous police organisation and greater police commitment to the outcome of prosecutions may well provide a more fertile environment for the rule than the United States''.[42]

He also pointed out that the exclusionary rule in the USA was not automatic and that illegally obtained evidence may be admitted if it will not substantially prejudice the defendant's case – the so-called "harmless error" doctrine. A similar provision could be incorporated in any legislation in this country.

In the end the question may come down to whether it would be better to deter police abuse and run the risk of letting a few guilty people go free, or whether obtaining high conviction rates is an overriding objective. But it should be pointed out that even if one takes the latter view, the reports of police abuse generally may well be bringing the police into disrepute and encouraging juries to disbelieve police evidence and acquit more people. Thus again there must be doubts as to whether unfettered police powers will bring greater police efficiency, quite apart from the implications for civil liberties.

Notes

1. These are all contained in Home Office Circular No 89/1978 reproduced as Appendix 12 to the Law and Procedure volume of the Royal Commission on Criminal Procedure *Op cit*.
2. *Ibid* preamble to the Judges' Rules.
3. *Report of an Inquiry by the Hon Sir Henry Fisher, Op cit* para 15.6.
4. *Ibid* para 2.17.
5. Royal Commission on Criminal Procedure Report *Op cit* paras 4.109-4.110.
6. *Draft Codes of Practice for the Treatment, Questioning and Identification of Persons Suspected of Crime* Revised Draft (Home Office April 1983).
7. Police and Criminal Evidence Bill (as amended by Standing Committee J) Clause 29(l).
8. eg Consulting a solicitor; *Draft Code of Practice for the Questioning of Persons Suspected of Crime and their Treatment if in Police Custody, Op cit* para 5.2; Police and Criminal Evidence Bill (as amended by Standing Committee J) Clause 45.
9. *Draft Code of Practice for the Questioning . . . , Op cit* paras 9.1-10. 4; *Draft Code of Practice for the Identification of Persons Suspected of Crime, Op cit*, paras 2.1-2.25.

10.   For evidence of increasing deaths see p 72.
11.   Royal Commission on Criminal Procedure Report *Op cit* para 4.111.
12.   Inquest on Douglas Coverdale reported in *Policing London* No 4 November 1982.
13.   Reports on Thomas Connor and James Ruddock by Inquest (22-8 Underwood Road, London E1 5AW).
14.   *Draft Code of Practice for the Questioning . . ., Op cit* para 9.2.
15.   *Ibid* para 9.3 (this conferred an obligation on the police to ask the suspect if they wished to see their own doctor if assault by the police had been alleged).
16.   *Ibid* para 10.2.
17.   *Report of an Inquiry by the Hon Sir Henry Fisher, Op cit,* para 18.1.
18.   *Draft Code of Practice for Questioning . . ., Op cit* para 11.7.
19.   *Ibid* para 13.6.
20.   *Report of an Inquiry by the Hon Sir Henry Fisher, Op cit,* para 2.13.
21.   *Draft Code of Practice for Questioning . . ., Op cit* para 14.1.
22.   *Ibid* para 14.2.
23.   *Ibid* para 14.3.
24.   Royal Commission on Criminal Procedure Report *Op cit* para 4.107.
25.   *Draft Code of Practice for Questioning . . .* para 14.2.
26.   *Draft Code of Practice for the Identification . . ., Op cit* paras 2.4-2.6.
27.   *Ibid* para 2.6.
28.   *Ibid* para 2.7.
29.   *Ibid* para 2.17.
30.   *Ibid* para 2.12.
31.   *Ibid* para 3.1.
32.   The request of Arthur Lewis MP was refused by Christopher Mayhew for the Home Secretary (*Police Review* 5.3.82).
33.   For example R v Prager (1972) 1 WLR 260, CA R v Lemtasef (1977) 2 ALL ER 835, R v Haughton (1978) 68 Cr App R197.
34.   For example *Voluntariness, Discretion and the Judges' Rules* by K W Lidstone (*New Law Journal* 8.11.82).
35.   See for example Jeffrey v Black 3 WLR 895.
36.   R v Allen (1977) CLR 163.
37.   R v Sang (1979) 3 WLR 236.
38.   *The Guardian* 11.10.82.
39.   *NCCL Briefing on the Police and Criminal Evidence Bill* Clause 60; Confession Statements and the Right to Silence *Op cit* para 41.
40.   Royal Commission on Criminal Procedure Report *Op cit* paras 4.123-4.130.
41.   *Studying the Exclusionary Rule in Search and Seizure* by Dallin H Oaks (*University of Chicago Law Review* 39,665).
42.   *Legal Action Group Bulletin* June 1981.

15. Complaints About the Detention and Treatment of Suspects*

Detention Without Charge

"A 17 year old black youth was homeless because his parents split up and didn't want him. He slept in various places, including floors, park benches, a vicarage in South London and a hostel. He was befriended by an old lady who let him sleep in her council flat sometimes. However, she took up with a man who didn't like the youth and stopped him coming to the flat. Some time later the old lady was brutally murdered. Her man friend suggested to the police that the youth might have done it. The youth had never been in trouble with the police and they had no evidence against him except the woman's friend's.

The police arrested the youth and kept him in custody in order to question him for five days. He was not allowed access to a solicitor in private, on the grounds that this would "obstruct justice". He was questioned over and over again about his movements two to three weeks before and made constantly contradictory statements. Police threatened his solicitor (whom he did not know) when she tried to advise him of his right of silence. He was very confused and frightened. He could not remember whether he had spent one particular night on a park bench, in a vicarage or with a friend. The police kept checking on what he said and then accusing him of lying.

The old woman had been sexually assaulted. The youth was traumatised by the police asking him questions about whether he had kissed the old lady. He only found out about the sexual assault because of the questions.

---

*Accounts given to the GLC or reports in the press of alleged wrongful detentions or police abuse.

The police searched the flat of a friend of the youth and took samples from his clothes. They had a doctor examine him medically. Eventually after five whole days of questioning they let the youth go. He was upset and confused. His solicitor had been threatening to apply for *habeas corpus*, but had done nothing out of fear that this would precipitate a charge against him.

The story does not end there because the experience devastated the youth. From that time on he began to get into trouble with the police. At first it was just minor things – obstructing the highway and assaulting a shop assistant. But then he broke into a school with friends. He was sent to the Crown Court for sentencing. While on remand in Wormwood Scrubs Prison, the gentle youth of a year before was threatening to 'kill all police officers'. He was sent to Borstal.'' (Account given to the GLC)

Wrongful Confessions
The Confait Case

"Early in the morning of 22 April 1972 the fire brigade was called to a house in Catford, in South London. When the fire had been put out, the brigade found the body of a man, later identified as Maxwell Confait, who had been murdered. Two days later the police arrested and interviewed three young men: Colin Lattimore, aged 18, but severely mentally subnormal; Ronald Leighton, aged 15; and Ahmet Salih, aged 14. On the basis of confession statements made in the absence of parents or solicitors and later repeated when their parents arrived at the police station, the three boys were charged with arson, and Lattimore and Leighton with the murder of Maxwell Confait.

At the trial in November, at which the three pleaded not guilty, Lattimore was convicted of manslaughter on the grounds of diminished responsibility, Leighton of murder and all three of arson. Salih was ordered to be detained for four years, Leighton to be detained during Her Majesty's Pleasure and Lattimore to be detained at Rampton Hospital for an indefinite period. Their applications for leave to appeal were refused. But subsequent examination of the evidence by a leading forensic pathologist (who was brought into the case by the National Council for Civil Liberties at the request of Lattimore's parents) revealed that the Home Office pathologist, whose evidence had been accepted by the trial court, had misjudged the effect of the fire upon the cooling of the dead man's body, thus misleading the court about the likely time of the murder. This must in fact have taken place much earlier in the evening, at a time for which

Lattimore had a firm alibi. It was not until October 1975, however, and only after a sustained campaign led by the boys' MP, Christopher Price, that the Home Office referred the case back to the Court of Appeal, which quashed all the convictions. And it was not until 1981 that the boys were offered by the Home Office compensation of £65,000 between them for the three years they had wrongly spent in detention.'' (NCCL *Briefing on the Police Bill*)

NCCL Cases

"In our evidence to the Royal Commission on Criminal Procedure, we quoted the case of a young man employed as a garage forecourt attendant who was accused of theft from his employer. He was taken to the police station, interrogated, and finally confessed to stealing the money. In the meantime, the employer had discovered that the money had never in fact been stolen at all! The case of **Errol Madden** is a vivid reminder of the pressures which can be placed on a suspect at a police station. Madden, a 17 year old black student, was arrested on suspicion of theft late one night as he was walking home from the cinema. After several hours questioning, he signed a statement written for him by the police officers, 'admitting' the theft of two model toys which had been found in his bag. If the police had searched more thoroughly, they would have found the receipt for at least one of the toys, both of which had been purchased by Madden with his own money a few days earlier.'' (NCCL *op cit*)

Mr G

"A London man was wrongly sentenced to 25 years' imprisonment after Scotland Yard's robbery squad had unlawfully arrested him, held him incommunicado for *eight days*, and extracted unreliable confessions from him, an appeal judge said. He added that Mr G, aged 52, of Cheshunt, had started a hunger strike in protest at his treatment: he had fainted during one police interview. The behaviour of the robbery squad officers had been a breach of the Judges' Rules on arrests and interviews. In a reserved judgment on Mr G's appeal, Lord Justice O'Connor said: 'It seems to us that it is quite unsafe to say that Mr G's will was not overborne by the treatment to which he had been subjected'.

Mr G was gaoled for 25 years in July 1979 on three counts of armed robbery and one of conspiracy to rob. He appealed and in October 1981 the convictions were quashed. . . . Lord Justice O'Connor said that Mr G was one of several suspects arrested in the early hours of

November 8, 1977 by a robbery squad which had been set up under the command of Detective Chief Inspector Tony Lundy to investigate attacks on security vans. Mr Lundy had ordered his men to refuse the suspects access to anyone, including their solicitors.

A clerk for Mr G's solicitors had repeatedly tried to see him and had been refused. The solicitors had decided after six days to apply for a writ of *habeas corpus*. Later, officers had admitted that their strategy was designed to 'get G to crack'. The arrest itself had been unlawful since Mr G was not told that he was being arrested, or what offences were supposed to be involved, but this had not by itself put pressure on him. Lord Justice O'Connor said that Mr G should have been brought before a magistrates' court by November 10 at the latest. He had finally appeared on November 16. He should have been charged on the evidence by November 13: he had not been charged until November 15. At his trial, the prosecution had relied on the evidence of informers and three admissions which Mr G was said to have made during his eight days in custody. Mr G had always denied making any admissions." (*Guardian* 19.6.82)

Wrongful Confession by a Mentally Handicapped Person

"Police who obtained a confession to murder by a 31 year-old mentally handicapped man will not be the subject of an inquiry . . . The officers involved have been given the 'strongest possible admonishment' for their conduct, but no further action has been taken. Lord Renton, the chairman of MENCAP, the Royal Society for Mentally Handicapped Children and Adults, called for the inquiry because he believed that the alleged confession amounted to a forgery and positive action was needed to prevent the same thing happening again.

The confession was obtained from Mr D during three days he was held in custody by police in Greater Manchester. He was arrested at _____ Community School in February, 1981 for the murder of _____ and taken to _____ police station. Three people contacted the police station during that day and evening to inform the police that Mr D was mentally handicapped, among them Mr Kevin Hunt a local councillor who works for MENCAP.

Mr Hunt saw Mr D's family and found that he had been in bed at the time of the murder, sharing a room with his brother. Police told Mr Hunt to come to the police station the following day. Next day when Mr Hunt saw Mr D in the cells he discovered he had already signed a confession to the murder. Mr D could not read or write, although he could sign his name. He said he had signed the confession because he was pressured into it.

Mr D's mother waited eight hours at the police station and was not allowed to see him. A solicitor was allowed to see Mr D after waiting two hours at the police station and was told his client was to be charged with stealing a pair of boots from a milk float. He had signed a confession to this as well, although again in circumstances contrary to Judges' Rules. The following day it was discovered that a man called Mr K, who had been in custody at the same time as Mr D, had made a confession to the murder . . .

The Police Complaints Board Chairman, Sir Cyril Phillips, told MENCAP that the officers did not feel that Mr D was mentally handicapped, although he was educationally backward. The Deputy Chief Constable had come to the conclusion that the police officers had made a serious error of judgment, but that there was no wilful disobedience to police instruction. He intended to administer the strongest possible admonishment and told the Board that consideration would be given to removing all the offending officers from CID. The Complaints Board decided that the action was correct and decided to do nothing more.

MENCAP objects to this decision and says police went far beyond a 'serious error of judgement'. It is also deeply disturbed that there was no mention of the false statement of confession allegedly made just before someone else admitted he was guilty. Later the Police Complaints Board wrote to MENCAP again saying what caused Mr D to confess was unexplained. The confession had been written by a police officer on the basis of what Mr D had said.'' (*Guardian* 23.4.82)

Strip Searches

"A 19 year old girl who was forcibly strip-searched by police without a proper reason being given was cleared by High Court judges in London of assaulting police officers in the execution of their duty. Lord Justice Robert Goff said that Miss Brazil's case raised an important question on police powers to search people in custody in police stations. He said: 'In this country a person is entitled to his freedom. To require someone to submit to a personal search is to impose a restraint on that freedom and, generally speaking, a person should not be required to submit without a plain reason being given'. Miss Brazil . . . was arrested after she had refused to leave a public house on New Year's Eve, 1981, and taken to Guildford police station. When told by a police constable that she would be searched 'for her own safety', Miss Brazil hit the officer with her handbag. She assaulted a second woman police constable while the search was being carried out. Lord Justice Goff allowed Miss Brazil's appeal against her conviction by Guildford magistrates. She had been fined £50 on each of the two assaults.

The appeal judges sent the case back to the magistrates, with a direction that Miss Brazil should be convicted of the less serious offence of common assault for the handbag incident. Before hitting the WPC in the face with her handbag Miss Brazil was told that she would be searched because 'everybody brought into the station must be searched for their own safety'. But such a blanket rule could not be upheld, the appeal judges said. The police officer should have considered whether in the particular circumstances it was sensible to search Miss Brazil. When the girl refused to co-operate the station's acting inspector was brought in. He ordered a forcible search because he suspected that Miss Brazil might be in possession of drugs. Miss Brazil was not informed of his suspicions.'' (*Guardian* 30.3.83)

E. Police Powers and Police Methods

16. Stereotyping – How Do Police Identify "Criminal Types"?

The Royal Commission on Criminal Procedure stated that, in relation to powers of stop and search, "the principal safeguard must be found in the requirement for and stricter application of the criterion of reasonable suspicion". However, they went on to find that it was "impracticable" to define "reasonable suspicion".[1]

The inherent illogicalities in the legal position were similarly shirked by the Home Office Advisory Committee on Drug Dependency in their Report, *Powers of Arrest and Search in Relation to Drug Offences* (1970). Despite expressions of concern about the basis of determining reasonable suspicion, they rejected a proposal by Professor Glanville Williams that a police officer who searched a person merely because they were "young, dressed unconventionally, carrying a case and out late at night" would be acting illegally. But they did recommend that it should be standard police practice to require reasons for search other than dress or hairstyle.[2]

Criminologists have long argued that stereotyping by police has an important influence in deciding how police resources should be deployed and in determining the response of individual police officers to particular incidents. For black people, stereotyping means frequent and unjustified stop and search and is a manifestation of a society that denies their identity. Derek Humphry in *Police Power and Black People* remarked that:

"Black people rightly assume that to the majority of policemen one black man is as good as another and 'they all look the same anyway'.

One other factor which has made resentment of the police and expectations of police maltreatment so universally felt among the black community is that, as policemen themselves admit, they have no way of distinguishing 'potential criminal types' among black people. In other words any black man could be expected to fit the description of the man the police are interested in. The police stop and search black people indiscriminately for drug offences, carrying offensive weapons, being in possession of stolen property in a way that they will never in normal policing run the risk of doing in the white community".[3]

The stereotyping of blacks by police was put to Commander B K Fairbairn at the Scarman inquiry.

"*Mr Woodley (Counsel)*: Commander Adams has said that he associates mugging and robbery with the blacks. You agree with that, do you? That is their crime stereotype.
Commander Fairbairn: If he says that in evidence, yes, I would go along with that".[4]

"*Lord Scarman*: A young white policeman, let us take a probationer or one shortly out of probation, not very experienced in his dealings or in his relations with West Indians, or people of the West Indian ethnic group, has difficulty does he not, as a white person who has not had much contact, for instance, with a West Indian ethnic group, in identifying individuals; he is accustomed to identifying one white face from another, but he does have difficulty does he not, until he knows his area well in distinguishing one black face from another.
Commander Fairbairn: Yes, I think that is fair to say. That happens to all of us, my Lord. I found it difficult when I first went to Harlesden.
Lord Scarman: I think it is a real difficulty which is not often discussed. It should be faced. Take the absurd analogy that I cannot identify one sheep from another in a flock of sheep, but the shepherd can.
Commander Fairbairn: Yes.
Lord Scarman: White people, not accustomed to mixing with an ethnic group different from theirs of a different coloured skin will have difficulty until they are experienced, will they not?
Commander Fairbairn: At the outset, yes.
Lord Scarman: This is something which senior policemen who are responsible for policing multi-racial areas have got to bear in mind, have they not?
Commander Fairbairn: Yes, indeed.
Lord Scarman: It can lead to trouble if this means that young blacks are being wrongly identified very much more than young whites, could it not?
Commander Fairbairn: Yes.
Lord Scarman: Thank you".[5]

The racism reflected in incidents of harassment is not just a question of the prejudice of individual officers, but of the way police priorities are established and particular practices institutionalised. Research has indicated that the "culture" of the police station is the strongest influence on police behaviour. Maureen Cain has documented the existence of values which have a crucial impact on police responses to individuals:

> "City policemen tend to divide society into the police and the rest, the public. And the public, too, was broadly sub-divided into the 'rough" and the 'respectable', and within these categories by race and sex. The respectable were alternatively referred to as being 'a nice class of people'. This was descriptive of their behaviour patterns rather than their socio-economic group, relationship to the means of production, or any other sociological definition of class. The division of the public into these categories enhances the possibility of police violence. Identification and therefore empathy is with certain categories only; the corresponding distancing of the other categories could enhance their vulnerability to rough treatment".[6]

Since stereotyping is first and foremost a matter of attitudes some of the most potent evidence comes from the police themselves. A training manual for police by Deputy Assistant Commissioner David Powis systematically analyses how to identify "criminal types" on the basis of their appearance. He contends that:

> "The first fundamental is to learn to distinguish between normal and abnormal conduct of members of the community. This aquired knowledge will sink into the subconscious mind and, when unusual conduct is observed, suspicion will rapidly register without conscious rationalisation of cause and effect".[7]

The manual instances such as examples of abnormal conduct, in cases where "conscious rationalisation" is notably lacking: women without handbags are to be automatically suspect; the "athlete" dressed in a track suit is also to be watched as a likely "homosexual nuisance". The manual continues:

> "Watch for the possession of 'these are your rights' cards or pamphlets on loiterers generally ... Obviously, they will be carried by persons who consider it at least possible that they will break the law and be interrogated by police. Thus they are carried by male homosexuals, by industrial and other agitators, by 'Angry Brigade' inadequates and

similar amateur criminals, but rarely by the shrewd and hardheaded professional thieves".[8]

Again young people driving new cars or mechanics with dirty hands are suspicious:

"There is a general tendency for thieves not to be over-fastidious with cleanliness, whereas an honest mechanic, so often a family man, will purchase and use chemical cleansers, for he has to be clean at family meals".[9]

In case anyone should think that the manual's premise is in any way questioned by the police establishment, they should reflect on the fact that Sir Robert Mark, then Commissioner of the Metropolitan Police, wrote a foreword specifically commending it and pointing out that it was unusual for a Commissioner to endorse a training manual. Moreover, David Powis himself is of course still Deputy Assistant Commissioner at Scotland Yard in charge of all CID operations.

If the police consider the identification of "criminal types" to be a valid and essential part of the police armoury, on whom does their suspicion fall? Undoubtedly the socially deprived are a first and obvious target. James Anderton, Chief Constable of Greater Manchester, has described the targets of modern policing as "social nonconformists, malingerers, idlers, parasites, spongers, frauds, cheats and unrepentant criminals".[10] In a speech given to a joint Conference of the Association of Metropolitan Authorities and Association of Chief Police Officers in 1979 Mr Laugharne (now Deputy Commissioner of the Met and one of the most senior police officers at Scotland Yard) said:

"Violent crime is nearly always domestic and therefore locally based. The drunken rioter, the user of illicit drugs, the rapist, the indecent assaulter, the genital exhibitionist, the vandal, *and the socially deprived* - particularly the young - who turn to crime in despair for kicks, are more often than not seized of their impulses when close enough to home to seek sanctuary in it afterwards"[11] (our emphasis).

Until recently however police acknowledged less openly that they were prone to identify black people as criminal "types". For example, David Powis's book barely mentions race as a factor. However this stereotyping of blacks has always been disproportionate to their inclusion in the treatment meted out to the "socially

Policing By Coercion

p.8   Vague points

P17/8   Police stereotyping

Good.   & p.122

p201.   Tape recording of police
         Interviews....

deprived''. This has been documented in the Lambeth Council Working Party Report[12] and the evidence of the Institute of Race Relations to the Royal Commission.[13] More recently a Home Office research study on stop and search has shown that black people are two to three times more likely to be stopped than white people.[14]

A significant recent development is what appears to be almost a planned attempt by the police establishment to validate police stereotyping of blacks. It began in 1972 when the media, led by the police, first started the "mugging" scare. The "moral panic" that ensued and its impact on the black community and the police has been extensively documented.[15] In March 1982, as a direct counter-offensive to the Scarman Report, the Metropolitan Police issued criminal statistics of supposed "mugging" offences, broken down according to race and purporting to show that black people were disproportionately involved in them. The selective leaking of these statistics to papers such as the *Daily Mail* before they were officially released demonstrated the extent to which they were part of a planned propaganda drive.

The way in which the statistics were presented gave a totally misleading impression. "Mugging" is not a category made in law or by statistics and the "robbery and other violent theft" category into which it falls also includes, for example, burglaries from off-licences.[16] Pronouncements from Scotland Yard revealed a tendency to use the terms "robbery" and "theft" almost interchangeably in an unscientific manner. The resultant blurring of the degree of violence involved in these rather different crimes has the effect of increasing rather than reducing public fears of crime.

A study of "mugging" by Dr Michael Pratt - a senior civilian employee at Scotland Yard - made the point that fewer victims of robbery in the open are subjected to violence than is commonly supposed: 58% of Pratt's sample received no injury whatsoever, and a further 37% received injuries which were described as slight. Pratt's study also revealed that 81% of the victims were male, a fact at odds with the popular conception of this issue, as is the finding that 14% of victims in the 1981 figures were over 60 years old, whereas 53% of victims were between 17 and 40.[17] This picture of the victim as typically young and male was subsequently borne out in the British Crime Survey.[18]

In a far-reaching critique of criminal statistics Louis Blom-Cooper and Richard Drabble explained the high rates for "mugging" offences in 'L' district (Lambeth) by looking in detail at the manner in which theft-related offences are recorded by the police. Their article shed important light on the discretion which police bring to bear on the categorisation of crimes and, in particular, how changes in the way crimes are catalogued can engineer what appear to be "crime waves".[19] The authors focused on what Sir Robert Mark has called the "blurred" distinction between robbery and theft. They pointed out that a uniquely high level of street robberies in Brixton was not only the reason for Operation "Swamp 81" but also the justification for a local policing policy which stressed the requirement to combat "muggings". They challenged the statistical basis of this view of crime, pointing out that the unusually high level of "robbery and other violent theft" is matched by an unusually low level of "simple theft and handling" offences during the same period. A total of 836 fewer offences of the latter were recorded in 1981 than in 1976, whereas there were 773 more offences of "robbery and other violent theft". The authors also noted that though the levels for each category of offence were uncharacteristic of the Met district as a whole, their combined total conforms to the pattern of theft related offences found elsewhere in London. They suggested that:

"Crimes which are, in districts of the Metropolitan Police other than 'L' district, being categorised merely as theft from the person (eg pickpocketing) are being categorised by young officers in the Brixton force as snatches and placed in the 'other violent theft' category".[19]

Blom-Cooper and Drabble supported the view that the recording of robbery and theft offences is, in itself, a significant factor in determining the eventual rate of these crimes. Their argument also questioned the validity of the compound categories used to present crime rates to the public. These, though they have no relation to the legal categories of crime, are the sole basis on which Londoners are expected to judge the issues of "mugging" and "street crime". The authors conclude that:

"The whole Brixton experience demonstrates that the perception by police officers of Brixton as a 'unique' area was part of the problem and could well have been, partially and statistically, a self-fulfilling prophecy".[19]

In another critical response, the Lord Chief Justice, Lord Lane, told the Lords:

"So far as the (police) statistics are concerned, I propose to say nothing, except that they are mostly misleading and very largely unintelligible".[20]

During the Scarman enquiry it was established that only 27% of total crime in Lambeth was known to have been committed by black people. The so-called "foot pad" offences (robbery and violent theft) were 1,945 out of 31,000 serious crimes in 1980.[21] The police deliberately focused attention on what is only a minute fraction of recorded crime and attempted to show disproportionate involvement of young blacks by a misleading presentation of the figures. The exercise was repeated in 1983 following a series of parliamentary questions from Harvey Proctor MP.[22]

In consequence of this vilification of black people, "mugging" has become a term with overt racial overtones. This suggests that the police have deliberately attempted to pass on their own stereotyped attitudes to the rest of the white population.

It is not necessary to recite a catalogue of incidents of police harassment of black people to know that racism exists at all levels of the Metropolitan Police Force, as this has been done elsewhere.[23] As recently as July 1983 a police constable asserted confidently in court that he started watching some black people on the street, because: "the vast majority of street crime which takes place in the West End is committed by black people".[24]

There are also allegations that the Criminal Attempts Act of 1981 is being used in a similar way to the old "sus" law. A solicitor's clerk was reported as saying:

"Our firm has up to 20 attempted theft cases where two police officers allege they saw young black men doing things like looking at women's handbags. The alleged victim is not produced in court and the police evidence is the only evidence".[25]

A letter received by the GLC Police Committee put the situation powerfully from the point of view of a black person:

"Well, if this is the way police treat black people, I can well imagine why the recent riots have taken place, by causing the tension, considering all of us are working that anyone black, red or white would not tollerate (sic) this kind of behaviour for long, because if the colour of your skin can tell the content of your character, then I wish I were never born. I know police have a job to do, but it seems like it is becoming one law for one, and another law for another. I only hope you can help us before it gets out of hand".

It is of course not only black people who suffer from stereotyping. Young working class and gay people are also affected. Letters received by the GLC Police Comittee have described the experiences of gay people at the hands of the police. These have also been extensively documented by Paul Crane in his book which shows that police stop gay people on the street simply because of their appearance and raid gay clubs, discos and parties randomly and in a manner suggesting harassment.[26]

Policing by stereotyping necessarily involves harassment because of its irrational approach. Even this has been justified by some police officers. Inspector Basil Griffiths, speaking to a fringe meeting of the Monday Club at the 1982 Tory Party Conference, said:

"In every urban area there is a large minority of people who are not fit for salvage. The only way in which police can protect society is quite frankly by harassing these people".[27]

The police hope to minimise the potential for conflict arising from random police harassment by preceding and controlling it with surveillance techniques wherever possible. These techniques and their relationship to the Police Bill are examined in chapter 19.

Notes

1. Royal Commission on Criminal Procedure *Op cit* para 3.25.
2. *Op cit* para 155(v).
3. *Police Power and Black People* by Derek Humphry (Panther 1972) p 223.
4. Transcript *Op cit* volume 11 p 98.
5. *Ibid* volume 11 p 99-100.
6. *Society and the Policeman's Role* by Maureen E Cain (Routledge and Kegan Paul 1973) p 81-2.
7. *The Signs of Crime* by David Powis *Op cit*, p 1.
8. *Ibid*, p 92.
9. *Ibid*, p 95.
10. Quoted in *The Powers of Policing* by Martin Kettle *Op cit* p 43.
11. Speech given by Mr A Laugharne, QPM, at a Joint Association of Metropolitan Authorities and Association of Chief Police Officers Conference in 1979.
12. *Final Report of the Working Party into Community/Police Relations in Lambeth* (London Borough of Lambeth January 1981).

13. *Police Against Black People* Race and Class pamphlet No 6 (Institute of Race Relations 1979).
14. *The Use, Effectiveness and Impact of Police Stop and Search Powers* by Carol F Willis *Op cit*.
15. *Policing the Crisis: Mugging, the State, and Law and Order* by Stuart Hall, Chas Critcher, Tony Jefferson, John Clarke and Brian Roberts (Macmillan Press 1978).
16. See GLC Committee Report PC 23 which shows how the 1982 statistics may give a false impression.
17. *Mugging: a social problem* by Michael Pratt (Routledge & Kegan Paul 1981).
18. *British Crime Survey* Home Office Research Study no 76, 1983.
19. *The British Journal of Criminology* April 1982.
20. *Hansard* Lords 24.3.82.
21. Scarman Inquiry Transcript *Op cit* Vol 11 p 17; vol 19 p 53.
22. *Hansard* 22.3.83, 28.3.83, 31.3.83.
23. See for example *White Law* by Paul Gordon (Pluto Press 1983).
24. *Guardian* 4.7.83.
25. *Ibid*.
26. *Gays and the Law* by Paul Crane (Pluto Press 1982).
27. *City Limits* No 60 (26.11 - 2.12.82).

17. Community Policing, Crime Prevention and Social Control

"Community policing" is still understood by most people to mean simply putting more uniformed officers back on the beat, patrolling the streets and estates by foot. It is counterposed to what is called "fire brigade"policing involving the use of paramilitary style special units (the SPG and the District Support Units), riot trained and using riot equipment. However although current police thinking does involve putting more (but some would say, not enough) officers back on the beat, the issues surrounding "community policing" are far more complex than this.

Community policing and fire brigade policing are not counterposed in practice. The GLC's response to the Scarman Report pointed out that ever-increasing numbers of ordinary police are being trained in techniques of riot control and then expected to go back to ordinary policing duties.[1] As will be seen in the next chapter the new policing strategies announced by Sir Kenneth Newman, the Metropolitan Police Commissioner, place more emphasis on the work to be done by special squads and units, including the SPG, than they do on increasing beat police.

The disturbing thing about the wider meaning of community policing is that it can actually be used to reinforce and direct fire brigade policing. Thus the concept of community policing has been expanded into areas of multi-agency co-operation and a new "crime prevention" role.

Multi-agency Policing

Multi-agency policing has been most enthusiastically propounded by John Alderson the ex-Chief Constable of Devon and Cornwall, who also called it "pro-active" policing to distinguish it from preventive policing:

"Whereas preventive policing tends to put the system on the defensive, pro-active policing reaches out to penetrate the community in a multitude of ways. Unlike reactive policing and to some extent preventive policing, pro-active policing envisages a more pervasive effect. It seeks to reinforce social discipline and mutual trust in communities, while having due regard for legal discipline as it always must".[2]

The strategy involves liaison between police and social welfare agencies such as probation, social services, schools and education welfare officers. Inter-agency committees are set up on subjects such as juvenile crime. For example in Exeter a joint juvenile bureau/social services office has been established where police and social services review cases together and decide what action should be taken.

The concept of multi-agency co-operation is of course neither new nor confined to policing initiatives. But since about 1977 it has been promoted as a new approach to crime prevention by both the police and the government. The government's circular on intermediate treatment for juveniles in 1977 advocated co-operation between agencies and in 1978 the Ditchley Park Conference of senior police officers and representatives of other social and education services was held. In September 1982 a seminar on crime prevention at the Police Staff College at Bramshill involved representatives of local government, Department of Health and Social Security and the Home Office. More recently in July 1983 the Home Office issued for consultation a draft circular on crime prevention which advocates the establishment in each area of regular "core" meetings of the police, the magistracy, the social and probation services and local government officers responsible for education, housing, highways, planning and leisure provision.[3]

Multi-agency co-operation may of course mean simple and essential communication between one organisation and the other. What may be changing its character – and the nature of the demands being placed on the police – is the transformation of the role of agencies other than the police, due to government policies and their effect on the welfare state. As originally conceived the main policy objective of agencies such as the National Health Service, DHSS and local authority housing and social services departments was to restore the balance in favour of the unemployed, sick or disadvantaged persons. The rationale was however not one of "charity"; benefits were paid for out of earnings and some were directly earnings-related.

But social security claimants, council housing occupants and other recipients of welfare state services have become increasingly stigmatised and receipt of benefits is now often seen not as a right but as a welfare hand-out.[4] Moreover, the present government is determined to expand the private sector and to contract out and withdraw public provision. Paradoxically more and more people are also losing their jobs and having recourse to that provision. Inevitably the agencies which were once primarily oriented towards providing services are now increasingly pressurised into denying and limiting their operations, and assuming a policing function to ensure this. The result has been the establishment and development of fraud departments in social security offices and in policing functions developing in other agencies too eg housing departments and hospitals demanding passports from their users.

Some agencies have always had a policing role, whether incidental or central to their functions. The immigration service is a self-contained and autonomous policing agency, while increasing stress is being laid on the policing and supervisory roles of probation officers and social workers, as opposed to their caring and supportive functions. The change in emphasis is partly due to the "law and order" lobby's enthusiasm for punishment and partly because of an increasing dependence by the courts on reports from agencies to recommend appropriate sentences for offenders.

Clause 10 of the Police Bill would have turned the other agencies into open sources of police information (see also p 148).

In his first Annual Report as Commissioner, Sir Kenneth Newman said:

> "Crime control is just one aspect of social control. In that wider context, crime statistics are as much a reflection of the performance of other social agencies as they are of police performance. Critics who ignore this more rounded approach to crime control are working against the public interest by obscuring the role that other agencies must play if we are to secure an improvement in the overall situation".[5]

But the police do not just see themselves as one of many agencies working towards the same aims. What multi-agency policing means is co-operation directed and controlled *by* the police. Thus social control becomes police directed. John Brown, Director of the Cranfield Institute of Technology and one of the main advocates of "community policing", referred approvingly to the view that an nnovatory police role in local social policy:

> "is not only socially imperative but also the *right* of a service that all too often has to take the can back for failures and omissions in social policy and urban planning"[6] (our emphasis).

The primacy of the police in multi-agency co-operation strategies is being assured by a redefinition of the concept of "crime prevention". Previously crime prevention consisted of the police giving advice on 'nuts and bolts" ie the way in which environmental factors can be changed to minimise the impact of crime. The obvious example is simple advice on door locks and security, but police insights on street lighting, estate layout and general planning matters can also be useful. Provided the liaison is subject to public scrutiny and the police view is one of a number of views taken into account, inter-agency co-operation such as this is helpful to all concerned. However the new crime prevention strategies involve far more than this.

The draft Home Office circular of July 1983 says crime prevention measures should include those "aiming to limit or remove the opportunities for crime as well as *those that aim to reduce the motivation of people to engage in crime*"[7] (our emphasis). In relation to the latter measures (which are called the "social approach" to crime prevention) the circular suggests increasing the role of Education Welfare Officers to deal with truancy from schools, inter-agency committees to deal with juveniles offending and that:

> "The scope for contributions by education authorities may be particularly wide, centring on the schools' concern with the development of responsible behaviour and self discipline in children and extending to aspects of the design, maintenance and care of education buildings and steps to facilitate the use of school facilities by the community outside school hours".[8]

The draft Home Office circular does not explain who will lead the new crime prevention strategies. But the plans envisage support for the initiatives being sought from crime prevention panels, 'Scarman"-type consultative committees and inter-agency juvenile crime committees, all of which are police controlled.

Sir Kenneth Newman's new policing strategy, for example, involves consultative committees being "utilised as a vehicle" for directing crime prevention schemes by co-ordinating the police, public and local agencies.[9] On 8 March 1983 Newman told the chief executives of London boroughs that the police were only prepared to take part in consultative arrangements as "free and equal partners".[10] Background papers on a new neighbourhood policing project in London involving multi-agency co-operation stated:

> "The police policy formulated must be expanded to acknowledge and influence policy decisions made by all other agencies who provide any kind of service to the communities. Where the policies are incompatible the police must make forcible attempts to convince the other parties as to the value of a co-ordinated approach".[11]

Newman has set out the police priorities in developing crime prevention as:

> "Close contact with other statutory and voluntary agencies, neighbourhood watch schemes, co-operating with other agencies in priority estates projects and community liaison".[12]

The contact with other agencies has been most marked in determined police efforts to establish liaison with schools and youth clubs, particularly those in deprived areas. The police involvement in schools has taken the form of talks on road safety, quizzes, disco-dancing competitions, football matches, proposals to set up police cadet units on the lines of army cadet corps and "citizenship training". These schemes while being welcomed by some teachers have been criticised by others as propaganda. One disturbing effect is the informal links which the police may have built up and the use to which these links may be put.[13]

Chief Inspector W Peden of Lothian and Borders has described the aims of schools liaison thus:

> "We try to follow pupils as they go through primary school and on to high school. However, although this is an admirable aim, it is not always easy to achieve . . . The formal structure of high school administration makes it harder for an officer to drop in for an informal chat with the head teacher than it is in a primary school – and informal visits are one of the keystones to successful schools liaison".[14]

In 1982 there was a furore in the press when the National Union of Teachers' branches in Hackney and Lambeth decided to oppose police being in schools. They were worried about their pupils' civil liberties as well as the appropriateness of police liaison.[15] The infringement of civil liberties which may arise out of a close relationship between the police and local schools is illustrated by an incident which occurred in Waltham Forest in 1983. Teachers provided intelligence to the police about the physical appearance, names and addresses of schoolchildren (without their parents' knowledge) resulting in the police arresting outside the school an innocent 11 year old and holding him in the police station.[16] Other similar cases have also been reported, in which parents have also expressed fears that school records may contain information about supposed criminal activities, as a result of the school's liaison with the police.[17]

Neighbourhood Watch

Neighbourhood watch schemes are being enthusiastically promoted by the police, having been set up throughout London from September 1983. The idea comes from the USA where such schemes are often barely concealed vigilante style patrols, although the police here have maintained that this is not what they are proposing. The idea is for members of the scheme to collect all "suspicious" information and for the warden in charge of the scheme covering the street or estate to systematically notify it to the police. In South Wales schemes have been in operation for some time and there are said to be over 1,600 street wardens covering 37,500 dwellings.[18] Their function is said to be, "to report even seemingly trivial incidents . . . a strange car going up a cul-de-sac is worth noting".

In Mollington, near Chester, the neighbourhood watch scheme was told to inform police about "undesirables hanging around schools and other public buildings".[20]

On the other hand an article in *Police Review* about the South Wales scheme noted that the "higher echelons" of the police were having difficulty in persuading the "grass roots of the force" that such trivial information was worthwhile.[21]

Such schemes are not without their problems. Apart from internal difficulties in getting police officers to appreciate the value of the intelligence being provided, the membership can also be hard to control. Attitudes of street wardens in South Wales were described thus by one police officer:

> "Some street wardens felt they were joining some sort of vigilante group. One gentleman felt people should tell him all their problems and he would take it all on his shoulders. Another felt we couldn't cope and needed a hand".[22]

However, it was suggested of participants in the Chester scheme that:

". . . provided the correct initial approach is taken by the police, (they) may even feel they are being given specialist police training, thus ensuring an even greater degree of active participation".[23]

Although the enthusiasm for the schemes tends to come more from the middle class areas, in London the police are actively promoting them on estates in deprived areas and persuading tenants' associations to adopt them. The initiative to create the schemes forms a new aspect of multi-agency policing, involving the police in actually *creating* agencies to supply them with information as well as encouraging existing bodies to give it to them. The *New Statesman* made the following comments on Newman's proposals:

"Again drawing on his Ulster experience, Newman's view of community policing seems to be that of 'corporate policing' of society by itself as unpaid auxiliaries to the police. The phrases about liaising with the statutory and voluntary agencies, with teachers and social workers, carry with them very real dangers of the rapid erosion of basic civil liberties and rights of privacy - particularly when combined with expansion of police and other computerised data banks".[24]

The Police and the DHSS

Multi-agency policing encourages the creation of criminal stereo-types based on take-up of welfare provision. The word "scrounger" has acquired a mythology of its own which is as powerful as that associated with "mugging" (see p 119).

Joint operations between DHSS fraud departments and the police are increasingly common. One in Newham in February 1983, aimed at allegedly fraudulent claims for social security, resulted in people being arrested outside the local DHSS office and placed in transit vans to go to the police station.

Information about individual social security frauds may come from anonymous information. A DHSS fraud officer was quoted as saying of such reports, "A lot of that arises from ended marriages, neighbour disputes, that sort of thing".[25]

Detailed information about claimants is stored on DHSS computers, which are used to detect fraudulent claims. It seems likely that the police have access to the information collected also.

The most notorious of the joint police/DHSS operations was however on 2 September 1982 when there was a mass arrest of homeless people in Oxford for alleged fraud in claiming rent allowances for lodging houses in which they were not living. The operation involved the mass and indiscriminate arrest of 283 people on the basis of their social status (ie their homelessness). Of these, 104 people were released without charge, after being held for many hours in cramped and uncomfortable conditions. Detainees subsequently released without charge received no assurance that their particulars, photographs, fingerprints and the video film taken of arrests, and while they were in custody, would not be stored in police files and used against them in future.

The multi-agency approach involving the police, DHSS and magistrates did not extend to defence lawyers and the probation service, who were not notified in advance. Ros Franey commented:

> "The harsh and punitive attitude towards claimants generally, and the equation of 'claimant' with 'criminal' was implicit in the arresting of every claimant who entered the fake benefit office. This, reinforced by information fed by the police and the DHSS to the press both at the press conference and subsequently, made the whole operation look like a campaign against those on benefit".[26]

The report on the operation submitted to the Police Authority by Peter Imbert, the Chief Constable of Thames Valley Police, relied heavily on criminal stereotypes to justify the police treatment of those involved. It constantly cited previous criminal histories of the people arrested and even when they had not been charged with anything:

> "Thus it can be seen that the picture to emerge is somewhat different from that at first imagined by the statistics of 142 apparently homeless individuals making false claims. In reality it is a mixture of *travelling fraudsmen and unemployed itinerants.* Even amongst those released without charge some failed to supply their correct address even whilst on police bail for criminal offences elsewhere, as evidenced by the case of a man who at the time was already on bail for an offence of aggravated burglary in his home county, Warwickshire, and for which he is now serving a lengthy term of imprisonment. It can therefore be said with some positive justification that in reality many of those arrested as a result of the operation could be best described as *active travelling and local criminals.* The description 'criminal' is intended to indicate a person with a number of previous convictions for various or persistent crime and not minor theft charges"[27] (our emphasis).

The report by Imbert also contained details of police intelligence about some of the people who were not charged and speculation about its significance, for example allegations about fraudulent identities. It concluded with a series of questionable moral judgements:

> "It can be said that the purpose of law is to promote the general good of the community. Any action taken to the possible detriment of the minority can only be morally excused on the grounds of being far outweighed by the general good. The law is the boundary which marks the limit of our authority and to step beyond it is to invite stern rebuke. The action taken was, in my view, clearly for the general good, and will be judged to be so by all reasonable men. One can only speculate what the situation might now be in Oxford if such action had not been taken. Sympathy must be expressed for all under-privileged or unemployed persons throughout the country but their individual plight should never be allowed to cloud the values of honesty, as the firm basis of all good government is justice not pity. Operation Major disclosed widespread criminality by fraudulent claimants for whom no amount of rhetoric can defend, for to do so would be a total injustice to the thousands of totally honest citizens who in spite of their own restricted circumstances would never commit crime or seek to abuse the welfare state".[28]

The Police and the Immigration Service

Black people are particularly affected by multi-agency policing because of an expanding system of internal immigration controls. Thus access to hospitals, housing, school and welfare services is increasingly being made conditional on production of passports. This is, *inter alia,* on the basis that many immigrants are prohibited by immigration regulations from "having recourse to public funds", because of the charges for health services made to visitors to the country and because of a definition of "intentional homelessness" which embodies immigration considerations.[29]

As Paul Gordon has pointed out, the shift in emphasis of immigration control from the operation of control at the point of entry to control *after* entry means that the enforcement of such controls has increasingly become a function of the police.[30] Thus the Special Branch undertake vetting of nationality enquiries and collect intelligence on immigrants. The Illegal Immigration Intelligence Unit based at Scotland Yard had 24 officers assisted by two civilians in 1980 and keeps its own records on the controversial Met police "C" department computer.

The police work closely with the immigration service on searches for illegal entrants, collecting all kinds of intelligence on black people resident in the country, sometimes long after they or their families have been accepted for permanent residence. The opportunity for taking action against long-term residents has been facilitated by the way in which the definition of "illegal entrant" has been extended by the courts to include persons who did not declare "material" facts at the time of entry.[31]

As with social security fraud allegations, the system encourages the giving of malicious information anonymously against neighbours, relatives or friends. For example: an immigration unit based in Deptford Police Station regularly visits homes to follow up such "information". Black people may also be subjected to demands for passports and questioning about their immigration status in the course of routine contact with the police on other matters, for example in reporting burglaries in their own home. *Policing London* No. 5 noted a case in which a family in Walthamstow who reported a burglary were subjected to intimidatory demands to see their passports. In addition since 1979 the immigration notices refusing extensions of stay to overstayers have been served by the police, a practice suggested by the Association of Chief Police Officers.

This insidious system of internal controls depends very heavily on multi-agency co-operation and as elsewhere this is increasingly controlled by the police. For example, in March 1980 a Spaniard who had been in the UK for two years applied to Ealing Council's homeless families unit for himself and his family and on being asked for his passport said that he had lost it. The unit then phoned the Home Office to attempt to ascertain his immigration status and in the process gave his name and address (he was living in a squat). The police went to the address and arrested him as an illegal entrant.[32]

Most notable are the raids carried out by the police and the immigration service; "passport raids" are made on workplaces where it is known that large numbers of black people are employed. One company which employs Nigerian students as early morning cleaners (at extremely low rates of pay) is regularly raided, as the students work in breach of passport conditions forbidding paid employment. The raids are based on general intelligence about workplaces where people without national insurance cards obtain low paid and casual employment. Wholly innocent black people at those workplaces are often detained for long periods before being released without charges and the raids have been shown to be little more than "fishing expeditions". After protests in December 1980 the Home Office reviewed the procedures and issued new guidelines requiring more effort to be made in identifying specific suspects.[33] But these guidelines have made little difference and further similar raids have been carried out since. As Paul Gordon has said:

"In effect the review restated that the police and immigration service had a right to carry out raids and demand to see passports. It still required a person suspected of an immigration offence to prove his or her innocence, reversing the normal procedure".[34]

Notes

1. *The Policing Aspects of Lord Scarman's Report on the Brixton Disorders* GLC 9.3.82.
2. Ditchley Conference on Preventive Policing, March 1978.
3. Home Office Draft Circular on Crime Prevention July 1983.
4. See eg *Women and the Welfare State* by Elizabeth Wilson (Tavistock Publications, London, 1977); *Manifesto, A Radical Strategy for Britain's Future* by Francis Cripps and Others (Pan Books 1981) p 59-63.
5. *Report of the Commissioner of Police of the Metropolis for the year 1982* (HMSO Cmnd 8928) p 10.
6. *The Primary Object of an Efficient Police* in the *Cranfield Papers on the Prevention of Crime in Europe* (Peel Press 1978).
7. *Op cit* para 12.
8. *Ibid* para 23.
9. Report of the Commissioner of Police of the Metropolis to the Home Secretary; *Summary of a Preliminary Assessment of Problems and Priorities* Jan 1983 reprinted as Appendix 31 to the *Report of the Commissioner 1982, Op cit* para 10.
10. Minutes of the meeting of the Association of Chief Executives of London Boroughs held on 8.3.83 p 3.
11. *Labour Weekly* 6.8.82.
12. Report of the Commissioner of Police of the Metropolis to the Home Secretary *Op cit* para 13.
13. *Policing London* No 2.
14. *Police Review* 1.7.83.
15. *Policing London, Op cit.*
16. Case reported to the GLC.
17. *Where to Find Out More About Education* (July/August 1983) p 8-14 quotes several cases.
18. *Police Review* 17.6.83.
19. *Ibid.*
20. *Police Review* 13.5.83.
21. *Police Review* 17.6.83.
22. *Ibid.*
23. *Police Review* 13.5.83.
24. Editorial in *New Statesman* 28.1.83.
25. *South London Press* 19.8.83.

26. *Poor Law* by Ros Franey (Campaign for Single Homeless People, Child Poverty Action Group, Claimants Defence Committee, National Association of Probation Officers and National Council for Civil Liberties 1983) p 23-4.
27. *Operation Major* Peter Imbert, Chief Constable Thames Valley Police, June 1983 p 31.
28. *Ibid* p 44-5.
29. See *Passport Raids and Checks: Britain's Internal Immigration Controls* by Paul Gordon (The Runnymede Trust June 1981).
30. *Ibid* p 26.
31. The definition of illegal entrant which was so dramatically widened by *R v Secretary of State for the Home Department Ex Parte Zamir* (1980 AC 930) has now been somewhat restricted by *Bonar Singh Khera v Secretary of State for the Home Department* and *Salamet Ullah Khawaja v Secretary of State for the Home Department* House of Lords reported in *The Times* 14.2.83. There is now no duty of *uberrima fides* to reveal all relevant facts but it was held that "deception might arise from silence as to material fact in some circumstances".
32. Paul Gordon *Op cit* p 73.
33. Home Office Circular 131/1980.
34. Paul Gordon *Op cit* p 42.

18. The Policing Strategies of Sir Kenneth Newman

Although he has been in office as Metropolitan Police Commissioner for only a short period of time, Sir Kenneth Newman is already implementing important changes in the policing of London. The new strategies are likely to be adopted elsewhere, if successful, and can be connected with the new powers it is proposed to give the police in the Police Bill.

The Northern Ireland Background

Newman's background is important in understanding his approach. From 1976 to 1979 he was Chief Constable of the Royal Ulster Constabulary in Northern Ireland. He therefore inherited and extended a sophisticated intelligence system involving close co-ordination between the police and the army applying the counter insurgency tactics put forward by General Kitson.[1] One commentator has said that these tactics:

> "entailed saturation and harassment of the ghettos on a massive scale, alternating with selective intervention in a district, a street, a house, a family or an individual . . . Harassment took various forms: raids officially designed to uncover weapons, or activists 'on the run' but whose widespread, repeated and systematic use served also to harass and terrorise the population and to collect 'low intensity' intelligence; screening, arrest and detention without charge, from between several hours up to seven days; curfews or ringing round an area, district or set of streets . . . targeting or zeroing-in, which amount to techniques of dispersed information and data-gathering with computers to draw up a routine profile of alleged members of an illegal organisation, but more generally of a whole community."[2]

In Northern Ireland Newman controlled a police force operating in conditions of war. His period in office coincided with the government's determination to "reassert the primacy of the police" over the army in security matters. His aim was to work for the removal of the barricades round the ghetto areas and to establish police control over the Republican areas, where previously only the army ventured. Newman achieved this not (as is sometimes claimed) by enlightened "soft" policing but by selective hard hitting interventions. He introduced regional crime squads and acquired fleets of new armoured vehicles. It has been claimed that he set up a comprehensive intelligence service with access to army and Scotland Yard computer records and a completely revamped fingerprints branch.[3] Gradually the RUC began to take over the army role, starting off with the "listening watch" and progressing to forays into the ghettos.[4] These forays, based on the intelligence collected, resulted in a record number of arrests from the Catholic population. As early as the end of 1976 Newman proudly revealed that charges against IRA suspects had more than doubled in a year.[5]

Although he had stopped some of the blanket harassment of the Catholic population carried out by the army, Newman's selective raids resulted in more arrests. He has recently been quoted as saying of that period:

> "The RUC was not clear about its mission. The implication was that the army would be there for ever. The RUC was painfully conscious of the need to project an impartial image but had to deal effectively with the IRA. This meant a high capability, sensitively applied".[6]

Sensitive application meant the use of policing strategies called "targeting" by Newman. The basis of the approach was selective use of "heavy" policing methods such as searches combined with increased use of technology. Newman himself was later to draw parallels:

> "Some of the problems of Northern Ireland, he says, are similar to those which he faces in London: the selective and accurate targeting of criminals, trying to isolate them from their host community. In West Belfast if you got the right man, there was no difficulty. It was only if you picked the wrong man that there was trouble".[7]

Newman's period of office in Northern Ireland was most notorious for allegations that suspects were being maltreated in custody, leading to the Bennett Enquiry into police procedures during interrogation. The publication of the Bennett Report, which led to international protests from organisations such as Amnesty, identified cases of maltreatment of and assaults on suspects.[8]

While in Northern Ireland, Newman had already formulated a "sociological" approach to policing which he was to develop after becoming head of the Police Staff College at Bramshill in 1979, teaching what he described as "order maintenance"[9] and incorporating the multi-agency approach to policing in the inner city, also advocated by John Alderson, then Chief Constable of Devon and Cornwall. During his time at Bramshill, Newman studied other models of policing, particularly management techniques practised in the United States.

One of the new ideas he introduced was "investigation" by teams of senior officers into the problems of "ethnic flashpoint" areas. The investigations were said to be looking particularly at whether there were potential conflicts between the police and other agencies dealing with social services, housing, education, employment and other local community services and whether these could be resolved. Each group was to spend a week in its area, with individual officers linking up with the heads of the other agencies. They were to investigate what the problems of each area were, what the local response to the problems was, and then evaluate them.[10]

The Newman Plan for London

After being appointed Commissioner in October 1982, Newman first revealed how he would apply this experience to London in a press release issued by Scotland Yard in January 1983.[11] He had presented the Home Secretary with a report but the public were not allowed to see the full text. Instead the press release purported to summarise the main points of the report.

The release stated that there appeared to be a widespread feeling that the police "are losing the battle against street crime and burglaries" which "points to the need for a programme to educate the public that the 'battle' analogy is inappropriate". It said that future strategy would have two main thrusts; crime prevention and crime detection.

Crime detection would concentrate on "improved information gathering, analysis and targeted action, backed up by better management of the detective function". Measures proposed to carry out these roles were to include redeployment of manpower to more "ground cover" and its allocation to areas on the basis of "high incidence, moderate incidence, and low incidence of street robberies, street disorder and burglaries". Areas of "special difficulty" would receive highest priority.

On public order Newman proposed "a redefinition of the role and responsibilities of Instant Response Units by giving them specific and continuing roles in Districts on standby". They would carry out, "anti-burglary patrols, rowdyism patrols, stop and searches, roadblocks, observations and execution of warrants" and were renamed District Support Units. In addition the Special Patrol Group would be retained to concentrate on "anti-burglary patrols". Thus both the SPG and the new local SPG-style units were given a permanent role in relation to the detection of crime as well as to riot control. It is not, however, clear what was meant by anti-burglary and rowdyism patrols other than random forays by transit vans into residential areas and roads outside pubs. But the searches and roadblocks they are carrying out are a clear preparation for the new powers in the Police Bill and the most obvious indication of how they link into Newman's plans.

Newman then singled out street crime and burglary from other crimes on the grounds that they are, "random and opportunist in character and often offer little opportunity for detection after the event". He proposed "better information, better analysis and better targeting of those who commit these crimes". In order to provide this, Analytical and Targeting Units were to be established in each Metropolitan area, appropriately equipped with "technical support". In addition Divisional Crime Squads would be reorganised on a District basis and a "screening system" would be introduced, so that some of the relevant crimes would be deemed insoluble and investigated only by a uniformed officer rather than by CID.

Redefining Crime

Newman has effectively redefined police responsibilities in relation to "crime detection" and related them to a new "pro-active" crime prevention role described in the last chapter. He started from the premise that police cannot solve crimes such as burglary and "street crime" by traditional detection.

The screening system, introduced throughout London in September 1983, ensures that the CID's time is not wasted by following up cases of burglary where there is little chance of detection. The vast majority of burglaries are to be classified as "insoluble" by means of a points system, and only dealt with by beat officers.

A detective chief inspector at Ealing, where this system was tested, explains how it worked:

> "Each burglary attracted a number of points for pluses, such as possible fingerprints, a suspect car, and very identifiable property. A certain total of points means that the whole investigation would be taken over by the CID".

Fewer points meant that it would be left to the home beat officer to deal with the case.[12] Crime detection will be able instead to concentrate on catching offenders by "targeting and surveillance" techniques.

Targeting and Surveillance

Targeting is of course a strategy that is used in relation to traditional crime detection eg, looking for a man with red hair driving a blue car because the victim saw a man answering this description driving away from the scene of the crime. The disturbing thing about the new "targeting" is that it relies on and reinforces police stereotypes rather than using specific detection to challenge them.[13]

Thus Newman does not advocate improved targeting by reference to known facts about specific crimes. As explained, many burglaries will not really be investigated at all but simply handed over to uniformed officers who will cope with the victim (the system could also be extended to other "insoluble" cases). Instead Newman proposes targeting – and subsequent surveillance – by reference to the systematic collection of intelligence on the streets.

The techniques used are similar to those he introduced in West Belfast in targeting members of the IRA. Senior officers at Scotland Yard have been quoted as saying that the new strategies are directly attributable to Newman's experience in Northern Ireland. The *Observer* commented:

> "In Ulster it is used to identify key members of terrorist groups who are then watched surreptitiously to build up a picture of their organisation and activities. Even if no prosecution results the information is still valuable".[14]

The first of the new intelligence and surveillance units to be set up is operating out of East Dulwich police station and covers South London, particularly of course, Brixton. Officers from Scotland

Yard crime squads, including the Anti-Terrorist Squad, the Central Drugs Squad and the Criminal Intelligence Branch, have been imported to staff this Centre which will combat "street crime" in particular. They are reported to be using techniques practised by the Flying Squad to track down and gather intelligence on professional criminals. A senior officer explained:

> "We have been targeting bank robbers, major burglars, drug dealers and other top criminals for many years . . . But it is the first time we have used these techniques to track down muggers. We are determined to put an end to street crimes particularly muggings".[15]

Chief Superintendent Tony Speed of Brixton Division has said, "We identify known muggers and burglars and then use surveillance techniques to find out what they are up to".[16] The *Observer* said of the work of the Unit, that:

> "Its role is to use a variety of techniques to identify criminals who are then placed under surveillance *in the hope* that this will produce evidence which will convict them".[17]

This suggests that identification of the criminal precedes identification of the crime.

Targeting and surveillance methods seem likely to combine the techniques of "hard" or "fire brigade" policing with the new multi-agency "community policing" approach. Newman purports to be applying a "sociological" theory of policy, claiming that it is possible to analyse patterns of crime, predict where crimes are going to be committed and by whom, identify potential criminals from local intelligence and make arrests after surveillance. The process is to rely on intelligence supplied by welfare agencies and the new neighbourhood watch schemes. But it will also incorporate heavy policing tactics, such as the use of special squads and stop and searches on selected "targets", as well as more surveillance and intelligence gathering methods.

Newman's own acceptance of the fact that crime clear up rates in London are unlikely to improve is a powerful indication of the nature of his strategies.[18] However in the initial phase of their implementation, the police are claiming some success in terms of reducing certain crime figures in Lambeth.[19] It would be wrong to deny that there may be persistent offenders who will be apprehended as a result of the new tactics. There may also be a short-term deterrent effect on a particular area, although this may simply shift crime to another area and may not affect clear-up rates. But the more long-term effects of the strategies on both police and public must also be considered.

The strategies assume that there are a limited number of "criminals" or "public order offenders" who can be identified and locked up or dealt with. Once that happens, the population is then supposed to return to "normality". But there is in reality no "underworld" of petty thieves which can be infiltrated – only the lives of ordinary people. The approach ignores the importance of "criminalisation", particularly on youth, and the extent to which "heavy" policing tactics actually *create* crime. In practice it involves seeing policing as a form of social control rather than a method of crime detection, as Newman acknowledged in his Annual Report (see p 126).

New police powers are needed not to detect crime but to assert control over the streets, firstly by surveillance (police record-keeping, roadblocks, searching homes), and secondly by actual interventions (stop and search, roadblocks, detention without charge). Newman needs the powers in the Police Bill to enable him to carry out this strategy without reference to the commission of specific crimes.

"Symbolic" Areas

A major part of Newman's plan is the identification of priority areas or areas of "special difficulty", apparently on the basis of the incidence of street robberies, street disorder and burglaries. The use of criminal statistics to pin point "high crime" areas has been identified by the Home Office as an unreliable measure of crime because police activity *itself* creates higher statistics.[20] As *Policing London* pointed out:

> "Newman's identification of street disorder with street crime suggests he accepts that the problem for the police in those areas is not just criminal activity in itself but the possibility of violent reaction to the police. Thus the maintenance of order becomes the highest priority".[21]

The true significance of the priority areas became more apparent in a press release launching Sir Kenneth's first Annual Report as the new Commissioner. In that he refers to "symbolic locations", which he lists as: Railton Road, Brixton; All Saints Road, Notting Hill; the Broadwater Farm Estate, Tottenham; and the Finsbury Park area. These are all areas where there have been confrontations between police Instant Response Units and black people escalating to public disorder. It is in *this* respect, rather than in an unusually high incidence of burglary or thefts/robberies on the street, that they are all symbolic.

The new powers of arrest in the Police Bill will help the control of such "symbolic" areas. But all the other powers may also be used randomly against the people in those areas – roadblocks, stop and searches and searches of homes. Meanwhile Sir Kenneth Newman is encouraging officers from the lowest level upwards to build up crime profiles of areas and "patterns of crime" and to develop justifications for special input into particular communities.

The New Strategies and Police Powers

Newman's ideas are certainly not new. The issues behind his strategies were examined by the Royal Commission on Criminal Procedure before Newman propounded them in London. David Steer of the Police Staff College was employed by the Royal Commission to do research on policing, and produced a Research Study on the police role.[22] The study provided the Royal Commission with an analysis of the theory of policing which laid the foundation for their recommendations on police powers. It started by examining the work of criminologists on the stereotyping of "deviants" by the police. One criminological approach distinguishes between police investigations which start at the offence itself and those where direct investigation of the circumstances of the offence is unimportant and the main strategy is to search for a culprit among those known to the police.[23]

Steer criticised the view that the latter approach was widely used by police and necessarily entailed police harassment of persons known to them. He maintained that a particular form of police strategy had been elevated on the basis of very little evidence to that of the major police strategy in the general run of cases.[24]

The contention of the Research Study that there was no evidence to support the importance of such strategies, particularly in the investigation of crimes such as burglary, looks odd now, in the light of Sir Kenneth Newman's overt commitment to "targeting and surveillance" on the basis of "criminal types". That developments in this direction were already taking place before Newman's arrival is revealed in a passage in the Research Study. This referred to the establishment of an "Experimental Burglary Squad" in Bromley (reported in an unpublished Metropolitan Police Management

Services Department Report of 1976), which applied techniques of "targeting and surveillance" used by Regional Crime Squads on professional criminals to the tracking down of burglars.[25] The importance of this as a new strategy was however dismissed by the Research Study:

> "A clear distinction must be drawn between the strategies that may have been adopted at various times and those that actually succeeded, for in the latter case less may have been changed than at first meets the eye. Thus in the Bromley burglary squad experiment one of the main reasons for an increase in the detection rate was that more time was spent by detectives on the squad interviewing persons coming into police custody!"[26]

Of course the observations about the reasons for increase in detection in Bromley may well be true, but that is no argument against the harassment that is likely to accompany the overt adoption of these strategies.

The greatest irony of all is that one of the Research Study's main defences of the traditional crime detection role in policing would be totally invalidated by the new provisions in the Police Bill. It maintained that the "targeting and surveillance" strategies cannot be of importance in everyday policing, as the criminologists claim, because the law would not allow it. It said the criminologists showed an almost total disregard for legal constraints on the police.

> "It is – on occasion – almost as if the legal definitions of offences, powers of arrest and search, simply did not exist, or at least could be conveniently ignored as soon as the suspect was identified as fitting the police stereotype or was less than co-operative in his attitude when approached".[27]

and again, it asked of "stereotyped" suspects:

> "what evidence is it envisaged that police officers will offer to connect their suspect with the crime?"[28]

The answer to such strictures is to be found in the pages of the Police Bill. Stop and search provisions would, as we have seen, amount to a requirement that suspects "stereotyped" by police justify to them the possession of articles carried in their pockets. The exercise of these powers would be unconnected to detection of specific crimes (see Chapter 2). The connection between suspicion of specific offences and the powers of arrest would be substantially weakened by allowing arrest for the most trivial of offences (see Chapter 9). Provisions allowing search of premises would completely remove any requirement that the occupier be suspected of a specific criminal offence (see Chapter 6). Roadblocks would be set up simply by reference to a "pattern of crime" (see Chapter 4). And finally, in reply to the Research Study's last question, the evidence used to convict the suspects identified by the police could be confession evidence obtained after long periods of detention without charge allowed by the Bill (see Chapter 15).

Ironically the original research carried out by David Steer for the Royal Commission led him to find that:

> "There are no obvious powers which police might be given that would greatly enhance their effectiveness in the detection of crime".[29]

This was a finding which the Royal Commission chose to ignore when it went on to propose new powers. Nevertheless that finding would have had more force if the Research Study had admitted that the existing powers of the police are not clearly enough defined and that the police "stereotyping" of suspects is already a significant and disturbing part of policing strategies. Meanwhile what distinguishes Newman's plans from past practices is their overt promotion by the police and the link up with the legitimisation of the powers needed by the police to carry them out, proposed in the Police Bill.

Notes

1. *Low Intensity Operations; Subversion, Insurgency and Counter Insurgency* by Frank Kitson (Faber and Faber London 1971).
2. *Britain's Military Strategy in Ireland. The Kitson Experiment* by Roger Faligot (Zed Press 1983) p 118.
3. *Guardian* 19.4.82.
4. *Observer* 18.6.78.
5. *Guardian* 19.4.82.
6. *Observer* 3.10.82.
7. *The Standard* 3.12.82.
8. Discussed in *Ten Years on in Northern Ireland. The Legal Control of Political Violence* by Kevin Boyle, Tom Hadden and Paddy Hilliard (The Cobden Trust 1980).
9. *Labour Weekly* 14.5.82.
10. *Sunday Telegraph* 4.4.82.
11. *Report of the Commissioner of Police of the Metropolis to the Home Secretary* January 1983 *Op cit.*

12. *Police Review* 1.7.83.
13. *Marxism Today* May 1983.
14. *Observer* 21.8.83.
15. *Sunday Telegraph* 14.11.82.
16. *Observer* 21.8.83.
17. *Ibid.*
18. See *Policing London* No 8 June/July 1983 on Newman's comments in his first Annual Report that the crime clear-up rate in London is a poor indication of police efficiency, despite the findings of the Home Office Research Unit to the contrary. The Met's rates are compared with those of six other urban forces and shown to be substantially worse. *Policing London* comments, "Newman has been working to gain public acceptance of the fact that the Met cannot solve the majority of crimes".
19. Figures went down in all areas of Lambeth for the first six months of 1983 except Streatham where there was an increase. (*South London Press* 19.8.83).
20. GLC Police Committee Report PC29, 25.3.82.
21. *Policing London* No 6 February/March 1983.
22. *Uncovering Crime. The Police Role* (Royal Commission on Criminal Procedure Research Study No 7).
23. *Becoming Deviant* by David Matza (Prentice Hall 1969).
24. *Op cit* p 13.
25. *Op cit* p 123.
26. *Ibid.*
27. *Ibid* p 18.
28. *Ibid* p 22.
29. *Op cit* p 125.

19. Policing and Surveillance

Alongside the selective input of heavy policing into particular areas there is an input of advanced surveillance equipment into the same areas. But monitoring video equipment or telephone taps is highly labour intensive; police intelligence activities are restricted by the number of staff available to service such equipment.

Newman is tackling this problem in two ways. First he is developing area policing strategies to justify concentrations of effort. Secondly he is setting up intelligence gathering systems which do not rely solely on technology. More use is being made of plain clothes officers in covert surveillance and the systematic analysis and collection of intelligence from beat officers is being encouraged.[1]

The so-called safeguards in the Police Bill will be far more effective as a method of information collection than as protection for members of the public. Ensuring that police officers record every detail of encounters with people on the streets will be of enormous value to police record keeping. The provisions of the Bill will encourage the police to take names and addresses (with power to arrest anyone who refuses for a minor offence). If beat officers, along with patrol cars, are linked into a computerised Command and Control System (see p 150), a comprehensive street control mechanism will have been built up. This may give access to information which is analysed and collected in each police station by the local police collator. Some collators produce "bulletins" containing information and speculation about local suspects. The extent to which speculative and hearsay intelligence is stored differs from area to area.[2]

Data Protection and the Police

The Police Bill was not the only piece of legislation which fell when the 1983 General Election was declared. The Data Protection Bill which was also affected was reintroduced (in July 1983) virtually unchanged. This Bill is the result of pressure on the government to follow the lead of many other European countries in passing similar legislation. However it is seriously defective, particularly in respect of police record keeping. Thus the parts of the Data Protection Bill allowing individuals access to files kept on them and preventing disclosure of data to other bodies will *not* apply where allowing such access or preventing such disclosure would be likely to prejudice any of the following:

> "(a) the prevention or detection of crime
> (b) the apprehension or prosecution of offenders
> (c) the assessment or collection of any tax or duty, or
> (d) the control of immigration".[3]

This means not only that records kept by the police will be exempt from inspection, but also that the police will be able to acquire information without a record on the register of the police having acquired the information. So, for example, the police could acquire a person's record from a credit agency without their knowledge or consent and without any record being made that the information had been passed to the police, and there would be no means of informing the police that the data they were using was incorrect.

The British Medical Association has pointed out that the same would apply to disclosure of medical records by hospital employees (even if the police have no coercive powers of access, there is of course nothing to prevent voluntary disclosure by agencies).[4] It would also apply to immigration control, where permission to enter or stay in this country often hinges on information given to the Home Office or Immigration Service by other agencies.[5]

Rather than preventing the misuse of inaccurate personal data, the Data Protection Bill, by providing a Central Register, will actually make it *easier* for the police to acquire confidential records without the individual's knowledge and consent and without providing any check on the accuracy of the records taken. The Central Register will provide a ready-made list of all agencies keeping information on individuals.[6] Even if the police are not given blanket powers of access to confidential information (clause 10 of the Police Bill) they can still obtain it voluntarily from agencies.

The Data Protection Bill is also seriously defective in that it applies only to computerised data, not to manually stored information. Thus paper files which are indexed through computer will be excluded, even though a computer index vastly increases the accessibility of information stored in this way. Much of the sensitive personal data held by the police, including Special Branch files and national criminal records, are stored in manual files and indexed through computer.[7] There is also a catch-all provision in the Bill whereby the Secretary of State can decide to exempt anything "which appears to him to be of such a nature that its confidentiality ought to be preserved ....".[8]

After the Data Protection Bill becomes law, there will still be no protection for the individual in the area of police records, where the misuse of sensitive personal data could be most harmful, and where there is the greatest danger of unsubstantiated allegations and inaccurate information being stored under the guise of "criminal intelligence".

The Lindop Committee Report on Data Protection, published in 1978, on which the present Bill is supposedly based, expressed particular concern over the kind of information which was stored or would be stored on police and security services computers.[9] In considering the use of computers by the police the Lindop Committee drew an important distinction between criminal *information* (or criminal histories) and criminal *intelligence*. Criminal information was defined as "hard, factual data" which can be verified, such as names, date of birth and previous convictions. Criminal intelligence on the other hand may be "speculative, suppositional, hearsay and unverified such as notes about places frequented, known associates, suspected activities." The Lindop Committee was concerned about the computer systems (eg the multi-factor searching capacity in a free-text retrieval system*) in which information and intelligence could be correlated.

Police Computers

Since Lindop reported, there has been a rapid development in the number and sophistication of computer systems being used by the police. Many of these, including the **Police National Computer (PNC)**, hold criminal intelligence on people, many of whom have never been convicted of any crime. In February 1983 15 police forces outside London were listed as operating or planning a criminal information system, including criminal intelligence.

The PNC holds information, including intelligence, on over five million people and 400,000 vehicles, as well as keeping an up-to-date copy of information held by the Driver Vehicle Licensing Centre in

---

*"Free text retrieval" means the computer can locate all references to a given word, combination of words, or even syllables.

Swansea on 30½ million vehicle owners. The PNC handles over 30 million enquiries from the police a year. It is now technically possible to link local criminal information systems to the PNC, creating a national police computer network.

The Metropolitan Police Force alone has 30 computer systems including the highly secret **"C" Department computer** which handles Special Branch files and immigration intelligence. By 1985 the "C" Department computer is likely to be holding records on over two million people, of whom only under 10% will be in the category of major or other criminals.[10]

The Home Office is also responsible for computer systems used by the **Immigration** Service. The government is planning a network of computers at British ports and airports to monitor people entering and leaving the country, and which could be linked to the Home Office computer in Merseyside which checks on immigration status. This would create a national network of computerised immigration control. In addition the Immigration Service's own intelligence system has been computerised as has the confidential suspects index which is used by the Home Office, Special Branch and MI5 to check the movements of some 18,000 individuals of interest to them. These numbers are likely to expand once the information is on computer.

These are just some of the systems which, under the Data Protection Bill, will be registered in the name of the Home Office. Their combined capacity would easily accommodate information on every member of the British population. Millions of people are already entered on one or other of the systems, and are therefore classified as "suspect" – yet many have no criminal convictions and are there only because of "suspected" criminal associations, political or industrial activities, or completely by accident. Under the proposed legislation, none of this data would be open to scrutiny by either the individual concerned or by an independent authority – yet much of it will be easily accessible to police officers, immigration officials and members of the security services. The potential for misuse has already been demonstrated in cases where police officers have used computer records to find missing relatives for personal reasons or have sold information to security services.[11]

Two new developments in the Met's computer systems will particularly affect the exercise of the new powers in the Police Bill. First the **Command and Control System** now being installed should guarantee "instant responses" to incidents. This type of system was originally designed for military purposes and enables the Information Room at Scotland Yard to link an emergency (999) caller with cars and vans available in the area of the caller. *Policing London* commented:

> "There is a danger that the use of a command and control system will reinforce the practice of 'fire brigade' policing. While rapid response to incidents, such as robberies, burglaries and assaults, is obviously of crucial importance, this may also bring unnecessary and excessive use of force in situations where it is not required".[12]

This danger will be reinforced by the new powers of arrest for trivial offences in the Police Bill, which will make it easier for blanket arrests to take place. Twenty other police forces in England and Wales have or are planning Command and Control systems.

Secondly the Met has well advanced plans to introduce a **Crime Report Information System**. The system will computerise crime reports containing information about crime, location, description, victim, witness etc. But it does not just record reports of crime; it also deals with the processing of investigations including details about suspects interviewed, searches of premises carried out, comments from the investigating officer etc. The dangers of such a system are likely to be compounded by the application of "free text retrieval" which will simplify the retrieval of information. *Policing London* pointed out that computerising the crime reports for 1982 would give access to some three million individual names and addresses, only a fraction of whom would be on record for committing an offence. The plans for the system indicate that it may be linked into command and control terminals so that police officers on duty will also have access to more comphehensive intelligence than that provided by the PNC.

As *Policing London* pointed out the new crime report system will be an important aid to "targeting and surveillance":

> "Police response to individual members of the public will be shaped by instant information on their previous association with crime and whether or not they have ever been convicted of an offence. Police interrogation of suspects using intelligence gathered by computer will play a larger part in the criminal justice process".[13]

C N M Pounder has also highlighted the importance of intelligence gathering for the new strategies:

> "The police hope that by finding out snippets of information on who is spending money and where, or who has received a new video whilst being on the dole, or who has been drinking with whom, that they will

be able to identify a change in an individual's status that would indicate that the 'target' person may be have been involved in crime".[14]

He has argued that the computerisation of the Criminal Information System to make intelligence instantly available at street level reinforces discriminatory policing. A vicious circle is established whereby people of interest to the police become more interesting when stopped again and entries may be made on the computer, even though no offence has been committed. Such people are likely to experience different policing from those about whom there are no "warning flags" on the computer.

New powers in the Police Bill used for intelligence purposes eg, searching houses for "evidence" and checking cars in roadblocks, would boost the collection of information on individuals and communities. Detailed profiles may soon be drawn up of certain areas, particularly the "symbolic" ones. Intelligence provided by neighbourhood watch schemes will also be collected. The Police Bill (clause 54) also contained provisions allowing evidence from computer records to be admitted in court with virtually no safeguards attached.

Not only does the Data Protection Bill contain no safeguarding against the random collection of intelligence by police but the Police Bill also placed no limits on or definition of police powers to video, photograph, record or tap the telephones of suspects. This was despite a recommendation by the Royal Commission on Criminal Procedure that magistrates warrants should be obtained for surveillance devices.[15]

Undercover surveillance is being increased as part of the new strategies. The use of video cameras is already an important part of police surveillance techniques, eg traffic monitoring cameras used for demonstrations. But surveillance is being extended in "symbolic" areas. In Brixton the police have had a camera positioned in a high tower overlooking Railton Road,[16] while in All Saints Road, Notting Hill a detective carried out surveillance for months from the roof of a building.[17]

Collecting evidence by these means is in direct contravention to existing Home Office guidelines, but there is no pressure on the police coming from government or elsewhere to restrict these practices. In January 1983 the Assistant Chief Constable of Kent said on television:

"I do not think one should be hidebound in developing new techniques solely because of an obscure piece of paper brought out five or six years ago".[18]

Quite clearly video cameras and other equipment are being used freely by the new Intelligence and Surveillance Centres, like the one in East Dulwich (see p 140). But it is an interesting reflection on the lack of police accountability that the public does not know, and there has been no public discussion about, the nature of the increased technical equipment being used in Lambeth and elsewhere. When the Lambeth Police Consultative Committee considered a paper by Commander Marnoch informing them of increased police use of surveillance equipment, no specific questions appear to have been put to the police about its use.

Notes

1. See *Policing London* No 6 February/March 1983.
2. See for example the instructions given to constables in Lothian and the Borders to secure the services of an observer in every street (R Baldwin and R Kinsey *Police Powers and Policies* (1982) p 287).
3. Data Protection Bill (HL) 23.6.83 Clause 28(1).
4. This has been a problem in the past. After the Brixton disturbances, police officers approached employees at St. Thomas's Hospital casualty department to ask for information about people with injuries (Letter from the Director of Patient Services at St. Thomas's Hospital to the Community Health Council 24.4.81).
5. See Chapter 18.
6. *Policing London* No 8 June/July 1983.
7. *Data Protection and the Police* by C N M Pounder (*Journal of Law and Society* Volume 10 No 1 Summer 1983).
8. Data Protection Bill (HL) 23.6.83 Clause 33(2).
9. Committee on Data Protection, Report, Sir Norman Lindop 1978 (Cmnd 7341).
10. *Policing London* No 7 April/May 1983.
11. *New Statesman* 23.10.81.
12. *Policing London* No 7 *op cit.*
13. *Ibid.*
14. C N M Pounder *Op cit.*
15. Royal Commission on Criminal Procedure Report *Op cit* para 3.57.
16. *Guardian* 2.2.83.
17. *Sunday Times* 16.8.83.
18. *Just William* TV South 27.1.83, reported in *Policing London* No 6 February/March 1983.

20. Policing and Coercion

An Oxford prison governor, James Horsfall, caused widespread protests when he urged police to "duff up" criminals.[1] One aspect of the Police Bill which has so far received little attention is its permitting the use of force against the person by police officers, in situations where the ordinary citizen would be acting illegally. Yet provisions allowing police to use "reasonable force if necessary" to carry out routine searches of the person signify a departure from the notion of policing by consent, which has at least underpinned the legal theory of police power up to now.

A grandiose passage from the report of a Royal Commission on the Police in 1929 is worth quoting in full:

> "The police of this country have never been recognised either in law or by tradition as a force distinct from the general body of citizens. Despite the imposition of many extraneous duties on the police by legislation or administrative action, the principle remains that a policeman in the view of the common law is only a person paid to perform, as a matter of duty, acts which if he were so minded he might have done voluntarily . . . Indeed a policeman possesses few powers not enjoyed by the ordinary citizen and public opinion, expressed in Parliament and elsewhere, has shown great jealousy of any attempts to give increased authority to the police. This attitude is due we believe not to any distrust of the police as a body, but to an instinctive feeling that, as a matter of principle, they should have as few powers as possible which are not possessed by the ordinary citizen and that their authority should rest on the broad basis of the consent and active co-operation of all law-abiding people."[2]

Since 1929 governments have become successively less "jealous" of police power and specific powers of arrest, entry and seizure have been given to the police in numerous Acts of Parliament.[3] Thus police historians and text books on constitutional law began some time ago to mention the notion of "the citizen in uniform" in a vaguely apologetic manner stating that it no longer really applies.[4] Nevertheless the law as it exists at present gives to a police officer no more power than that given to every other citizen, to use force against a person.

The use of "force" of course can range from a mild restraining action to the firing of a gun to shoot someone and it is here that the concept of "reasonableness" is important. The law as it stands at present is as follows:

> "A person may use such force as is reasonable in the circumstances in the prevention of crime or in effecting or assisting in the lawful arrest of offenders or suspected offenders or of persons unlawfully at large" (S3 Criminal Law Act 1967).

The question of what is "reasonable" is extremely fraught. To date it has not been dealt with in any detail in English courts and in one case it was simply said that, "In the circumstances one did not use a jewellers' scales to measure reasonable force".[5]

The Seventh Report of the Criminal Law Revision Committee, which recommended the existing statutory provision, stated that in determining what force was reasonable the court would take into account all the circumstances, including the nature and degree of the force used, the seriousness of the end to be prevented and the possibility of preventing it by other means.[6] Such guidelines are very general and there appear to be no specific prohibitions eg it was reported that a detainee who died in a struggle in a police station in March 1983 had been restrained by police in an arm grip believed to have been banned in the United States.[7]

The law regarding police use of force has fallen into most disrepute in Northern Ireland. The Royal Ulster Constabulary are also supposedly governed by S3 Criminal Law Act 1967. This is despite the fact that:

> ". . . the constitutional and political basis of the police in Northern Ireland has always been different to that of the police in Britain. While British police forces have grown up within the traditions of local accountability, community consent and political independence, the RUC comes from an imposed and sectarian tradition".[8]

In Northern Ireland allegations of shootings by security forces are frequent. The Police Bill would not apply to Northern Ireland but it may achieve the same effect in England and Wales as the Northern Ireland (Emergency Provisions) Act 1973, has had there.

In relation to the use of firearms, English law is not clear whether a police officer is entitled to shoot an escaping fugitive or, if so, in what circumstances. The main principle that text books seem to agree on is that the degree of force necessary to affect the arrest of the escaping offender would have to be balanced against the one which would follow from failure to prevent the specific crime in question. In deciding this it would be important to remember that under existing law the criteria apply not just to police officers but to *any* citizen. Thus if a police officer shoots and kills a person, it must have been justifiable for anybody to have done the same if it was justifiable for the officer to have done it.

Chief Superintendent Colin Greenwood, a senior officer in the West Yorkshire Police Force, has argued that it would be "reasonable" in some circumstances for a police officer to shoot an escaping person in the back.[9] The two examples he gave were an escaping armed robber and an escaping terrorist. He rejected what he called the view of the "self-defence theorists" and laid great emphasis on the discretion and professionalism of the police officer:

> "The problem really reduces itself to the balancing of two evils. For a police officer to kill is an evil which society must be reluctant to accept; but it would be an even greater evil for a police officer to allow liberty to a man whom he knew to be a serious danger to society, a man whom he believed to be likely to cause death or grievous bodily harm to those members of the public whom the police officer is bound to protect".[10]

He argued that police officers should never be expected to shoot to wound instead of to kill:

> "The correct approach, it is submitted, is to say that there must be no shooting at all unless there is absolutely no alternative, and unless any death which results will clearly amount to justifiable homicide. No shots must be fired until the situation has reached that extreme stage. Once that stage has been reached the officer should simply shoot to stop".[11]

At an inquest into a shooting by police in 1979 the Deputy Chief Constable of Essex, Barry Price, had told the jury:

> "The policy cannot be to wound or maim . . . a policy of shooting to wing or wound is extremely dangerous and it will be a sorry day for this country if it is ever introduced".[12]

By contrast the firearms training of police officers in Sweden requires that they are penalised for aiming to kill.[13]

Superintendent Greenwood's arguments – which may alarm many – rely on a power which applies to all citizens not just the police. But in his book he arrogated to the police special duties of protection, with consequent special powers. This was seen quite clearly in his concentration on the importance of police professional decisions based on what he identified as three points. These were identification of the offender, an "assessment of the offender's willingness or ability to kill or cause further serious danger to the public", and finally an "assessment" of the offender's opportunity to kill or cause serious danger before arrest. According to Greenwood:

> "A great deal of confusion has been caused by those senior police officers who apologise for the existence of police firearms and who refer to them as 'purely defensive' and attempt to define the police role in similar terms. The role of the armed police officer has been clearly defined in Chapter 1 as 'to protect society by neutralising a dangerous offender' ".[14]

The implication of his arguments might be that special duties of protection given to the police may justify the use of extreme force on the basis of "assessments" made by the individual police officers.

Undoubtedly police officers other than Superintendent Greenwood give a wide interpretation to the wording of S3 Criminal Law Act 1967, when it applies to the actions of police officers. Fortunately for them the inconvenient image of the citizen in uniform will soon be demolished by Parliament. The Police Bill would give to a police constable specific power to use "reasonable force if necessary" both in carrying out a stop and search and in detaining a person for that purpose so that the use of force would not, as at present, be related to the prevention of a specific crime or the apprehension of an offender.[15] It would be merely an addendum to special coercive powers given to the police, powers which would be related to the prevention of crime only in a highly speculative manner. It seems clear also that the phrase "if necessary" does not mean that the person being stopped should be resisting in order to justify the use of force. Indeed the Minister of State, Patrick Mayhew, MP, specifically said that forcible "frisking" may be necessary even where there is no resistance.[16]

Apart from the legitimisation of the use of "reasonable force" in stop and searching, the Police Bill would also allow police to carry out strip searches and "intimate searches"[17] (a new power to search suspects' vaginas and anuses) against the consent of the person being searched, as well as to take fingerprints[18] and body samples.[19] These provisions could legitimise assault of suspects by police officers.[20]

There was nothing in the Police Bill about the use of firearms by police, despite growing public concern. On the evening of 15 January 1983 Stephen Waldorf was shot and seriously injured by Metropolitan Police officers. This case led to questions being asked about the circumstances under which guns are issued and can be used. But as *Policing London* pointed out:

> "The difficulty in establishing exactly how many people have been shot by the Met is reinforced by the difficulty in finding out about the force's general policy toward the use of guns in particular circumstances."[21]

Revised guidelines on the use of firearms were issued by the Home Office in March 1983. These propose that the authority of a deputy chief constable or at least of a superintendent normally be required for firearms issue.[22] But the Met's own instructions require only an inspector's authority and the new guidelines are not legally binding. In April 1983 the Chief Constable of Manchester made controversial remarks about the routine arming of his force.[23] Metropolitan Chief Superintendent Hoare has expressed concern at the number of gun issues to the Met in particular.[24] During the last three years the Met have authorised an average of 17% of their officers to use firearms. In 1981 this amounted to 4,274 from an establishment of 25,161. In the same period, over 500 officers have been trained annually in the use of revolvers alone.[25]

According to the *Observer,* London police "carry guns more than twice as often as armed criminals". Guns were carried by criminals either to attack individuals or stage robberies on 2,164 occasions in 1981. But guns were issued to police on 4,983 occasions in 1981. This figure does not include the guns worn regularly by armed specialist bodyguards. The *Observer* also noted that detectives in London carry drawn revolvers far more frequently than uniformed men. About 35% of detectives are authorised to carry guns. Guns were issued "on an average of 18 occasions every day last year in London".[26]

The shooting of a suspect by a police officer, and a slight "duffing up" on the street or in the police station may appear to have little in common. But the principles governing both are the same. It is of little value for the government to make promises to limit police use of firearms if at the same time it is determined to legitimise special coercive powers for the police.

Notes

1. *Guardian* 23.6.83.
2. Royal Commission on the Police 1929.
3. See, for example, Misuse of Drugs Act 1971 s23 and Criminal Damage Act 1971 s6.
4. eg, *Constitutional and Administrative Law* by E C S Wade and G G Phillips 9th ed by A W Bradley (Longman 1977) p 347.
5. Reed v Wastie (1972) *The Times* 10.2.72.
6. Criminal Law Revision Committee 7th Report *Felonies and Misdemeanours* May 1965 (Cmnd 2659) paras 20-23.
7. *Guardian* 16.8.83.
8. *State Research Bulletin* No 26 Oct-Nov 1981.
9. *Police Tactics in Armed Operations* by Colin Greenwood (Paladin Press 1979) p 23.
10. *Ibid* p 26.
11. *Ibid* p 24.
12. *The Times* 5.7.82.
13. *Policing London* No 3, Oct 1982.
14. *Op cit* p 20.
15. Police and Criminal Evidence Bill (as amended by Standing Committee J) Clause 2(5) gave power to use "such reasonable force as is necessary" to detain a person. Before the old Bill fell because of the General Election a government amendment had been tabled to change the wording to refer to use of "reasonable force if necessary" both in carrying out the stop and search and in detaining a person for that purpose.
16. *Hansard* Standing Committee J 21.12.82, col 140.
17. Police and Criminal Evidence Bill (as amended by Standing Committee J) clause 42.
18. *Ibid* Clause 48.
19. *Ibid* Clause 48.
20. See p 93.
21. *Policing London* No 6 February/March 1983.
22. *Sunday Times* 3.4.83.
23. *New Statesman* 15.4.83.
24. Thesis written for an M.Sc degree at Cranfield Institute of Technology Social Policy Unit *The Pattern of Experience in the Use of Firearms by Criminals and the Police Response* by M A Hoare (September 1980).
25. *Policing London No 3* Oct 1982.
26. *Observer* 21.1.83.

F. The Safeguards
21. Records of Reasons for Police Exercise of their Powers

The Bill provided that police officers be required to write down the reasons for the exercise of the powers in it. In relation to stop and searches on the **street**, the suspect would be able to obtain a copy of the written record subsequently and to challenge the exercise of the power in the courts by reference to the record. In relation to powers exercised in the **police station**, a "custody record" was to be kept for each suspect detained in the station which would systematically detail the interrogations and treatment of each suspect. The responsibility for keeping the custody record would fall to the officer designated custody officer at the time in each station, who would not be involved in the investigation of any offence for which any of the suspects under their care had been arrested. There was however no provision for the suspect to obtain a copy of the custody record subsequent to their release prior to any court proceedings.

The proposals in the Bill followed the Royal Commission recommendation that:

> "Decisions, to the extent that it is possible, should be explained to the suspect. They should also be written down, together with a narrative of the events, while a person is in custody. They can then be available for the record for inspection and if need be, challenged by supervisory officers, by the suspect or his legal adviser and by the courts".[1]

Stop and Search in the Street

Under the Bill if a police constable proposed to stop and search a person or a vehicle in the street s/he would have to inform the person or the driver of the vehicle of his or her name, of the purpose of the search and of the grounds for undertaking it. A record in writing would have to be made of the search either at the time or, if that was not reasonably practicable, as soon as was possible afterwards. The person who had been searched or the owner of the vehicle which had been searched would be able to obtain a copy of the record of search after it had taken place. In the Bill as originally drafted there was a time limit on this of three months after the search but, before the Bill fell, the government introduced an amendment to extend it to 12 months after the search.[2]

The criterion of "reasonable suspicion" which was to justify search was not defined in the Bill. It was not therefore clear what sort of information the police officer would be required to write down as "grounds for search". A recent Home Office Research Study stated that police officers often found it extremely difficult to explain their reasons for searching people in the street.[3] In London reasons for stops written out by police were exceptionally brief. Most stops were described as "re movements", a category which had no fixed meaning and which, the Report commented, probably simply covered stops made on grounds which the police could not specify. The Report concluded that the requirements in the Bill for police officers to specify grounds for search would pose problems for them.[4]

In the past there have been proposals for "negative" definitions of reasonable suspicion. A minority view of the Advisory Committee on Drug Dependence, in their Report on *Powers of Arrest and Search in Relation to Drug Offences* (1970) was that there could be such a definition, which Professor Glanville Williams had set out:

"The following circumstances shall not be sufficient in themselves, whether alone or in conjunction with each other, to establish reasonable grounds for suspicion . . .
(a) That the person searched appeared to be the kind of person who is frequently found in possession of drugs,
(b) That he was carrying any article, other than an article commonly associated with the possession of drugs,
(c) That he was found in a locality where drugs were frequently possessed,
(d) That he was found in a public place at night or in the early morning".[5]

Professor Glanville Williams and others who supported this negative definition explained its purpose and effect:
"This proposal would not wholly exclude the four grounds from

consideration but it would require them to be used only as secondary factors, supporting other grounds of suspicion. The effect of the proposal, if it were implemented by statute, would be that a police officer who searched a person merely because he was young, dressed unconventionally, carrying a case and out late at night would be acting illegally. Damages could then be obtained for the illegal search, though the illegality would not affect any subsequent criminal proceedings brought against the person searched if evidence were found against him. Perhaps the most important effect of the proposal would be that it would enter into the instructions given to the police and so would be likely to have a restraining effect upon police searches".[6]

The majority of the Committee rejected this proposal on the grounds that; "The factors influencing a police officer's judgement cannot be reduced to simple formulae".[7]

On the other hand the majority were sufficiently concerned to state that standard police practice should incorporate the principle that dress and hairstyle should never, in themselves or together, constitute reasonable grounds for stop and search.[8]

The word "reasonable" was liberally sprinkled throughout the Bill, and the Standing Committee debating it had several discussions on what particular meanings could be ascribed to it. Lawyers include the word "reasonable" in legislation to denote an objective as opposed to a subjective test. In other words when considering whether or not the exercise of the power was illegal, the courts would have to decide what a "reasonable" view (that of "the man on the Clapham Omnibus") would be. Reliance on this concept is widespread in English law and much of the connection between statute law and the common law (created by precedent in the courts) depends on it. The problem is that when legislation is passed there is often little means of telling how the courts will interpret "reasonableness" in relation to the particular provision.

Few commentators have been very optimistic that the requirements for recording of reasons for search on the street would provide much protection against random searches. Firstly it may be significant that the Bill required grounds for the search, not for the reasonable suspicion, to be given. The courts have already decided that there is a common law requirement to tell a person of the reasons for search, and that failure to do so will mean the search is illegal.[9] The reason for search has however been interpreted as being synonomous with the purpose of the search, ie, to look for stolen goods or drugs. It could be that the added requirement of stating "grounds" for search in the Police Bill would simply mean quoting the relevant section of the Misuse of Drugs Act or the Police and Criminal Evidence Act (as it would be).

It would be understandable if the courts decided that they too, like the Advisory Committee on Drug Dependence and the Royal Commission on Criminal Procedure, were unable to lay down standards of "reasonable suspicion". If this proved to be the case, the requirement for the recording of reasons would simply be an exercise in filling out standard form details which would offer little opportunity for challenge.

Even if the courts did interpret "grounds" as requiring details of the alleged "reasonable suspicion" there would still remain the question of the basis and opportunity for challenge. The standards which would be set for "reasonable suspicion" would be unlikely to be higher and might well be much lower than those which were necessary to prove the old charge of being a suspected person under the Vagrancy Act (now repealed).[10] Clare Demuth has shown the unsatisfactory nature of the evidence in sus cases in a survey of 19 of them.[11] As she pointed out, cases tended to be dismissed on the basis of character references given for the accused rather than because of any rational basis of challenge of police statements of the accused's suspicious behaviour.[12]

One of the key determining factors in the courts' interpretation of the provisions would be likely to be the lack of opportunity for challenge. One ground for refusal of legal aid is that the damages likely to be recovered do not justify the cost of proceeding. This would prevent legal aid grants to challenge any search where there has not been an added factor, such as violence causing injury, for which damages can be claimed. In practice therefore the issue would be most likely to be discussed by the courts as a subsidiary to criminal cases eg, if the person being searched resisted and was charged with obstruction of the police officer, it would be necessary for the court to determine whether or not the search was legal to know whether the police officer was acting "in execution of his or her duty". The result might be that only certain kinds of cases would come before the courts and the impact on the random search of persons who do not resist, and have nothing to hide, would be nil.

It might be argued that even if the individual has insufficient redress through the courts, the provisions would have a deterrent effect in alerting the police to the problems and activating internal checks against abuse of the power. According to this view the complaints system and internal discipline could provide the sanctions missing from the safeguards in law. It also seems clear that the Royal Commission had envisaged the safeguarding as a combination of measures for redress in law and measures for more general accountability. The Report stated that the recording of reasons:

"Should also make possible general oversight of the process by the police authority, by central government through its inspectorate, and ultimately by Parliament. In the nature of things it is not possible for the cell block, charge office and interview rooms of a police station to be open to members of the public to come or go as they please. But the procedures should provide satisfactory means of supervision and review, in order that the suspicions of what goes on behind those closed doors can be diminished".[13]

The Bill (clause 5) provided for statistical records to be kept about numbers of stop and searches, reasons for roadblocks, numbers of persons kept in detention without charge for more than 24 hours and numbers and details of warrants of further detention. These records were to be included in the annual reports submitted by Chief Constables under S12 Police Act 1964 and by the Metropolitan Police Commissioner. But only the records of road checks in Annual Reports were to include the reasons for them being carried out as well as numbers. Stop and search records would not therefore contribute to any definition of the "reasonable suspicion" necessary for a stop and search. It is difficult overall to conclude that these external requirements would add much, even if the general accountability system was stronger.

Finally the idea that internal checks would work is rendered doubtful not only by failures of definition but also by lack of enforceability. If, as discussed previously, the whole police organisation were to connive at rule breaking to allow random stop and searches to take place, only an exclusion of evidence rule would be likely to be an adequate deterrent. Without this the main effect may be an increase in bureaucracy. As Geoffrey Robertson has written of the Bill:

"Its overall effect will be to promote policing by paperwork. If the correct routines are followed, if the right forms are signed by the officer of the appropriate rank, there will be little scope for complaint. Pictures of innocence are unlikely to emerge when detectives are obliged to paint by numbers".[14]

In the Police Station

The position with regard to exercise of powers in the police station would be a little different. The introduction of the "custody record" proposed by the Bill would be really useful to all parties. At present much court time is spent on disputes as to what happened in the police station and record keeping can vary enormously. Defence lawyers have found it increasingly necessary to call for the Occurrence Book or the Movement of Prisoners Book but the required information is not always there.

But the requirement to keep a custody record is only useful to the suspect insofar as proper reasons are required for the exercise of police power. There were some serious omissions from the Bill in this respect. Thus no reason would have to be given for carrying out a strip search. Moreover the suspect's "right" to see a lawyer was far too loosely worded, with exceptions which were too wide.

The Bill also failed to provide for adequate access by the suspect to the record. Firstly it made inadequate provision for the suspect to be notified of the reasons for detention or provided with a copy of the written record. There was a clause which provided that the suspect need not be told which detention condition applied if they were:

"(a) incapable of understanding what is said to him
 (b) violent or likely to become violent
 (c) in urgent need of medical attention" (clause 28(b)).

This was a definite loophole and could lead to the police bartering the explaining of reasons as "a favour" to the suspect. And the reasons given were arguably insufficient to justify not stating the ground of detention. If the suspect's failure to understand was because of language the police should be required to get an interpreter. Moreover persons in urgent need of medical attention should be taken to hospital and not detained.

There was also no right of the suspect to be notified of the grounds for continued detention prior to the hearing of a warrant for further detention in the magistrates court. And even after the suspect had been released there was no requirement for the police to supply him or her with a copy of the custody record to ascertain whether police actions inside the police station could be challenged.

Given the nature of the powers that can be exercised (intimate body searches, taking of samples etc), the principle of access to records should also apply to the custody record, as it was to stop and search records. If these failures were remedied the custody record would go some way towards protecting the suspect. It must however be pointed out that without provisions for access to a lawyer there will still be frequent disputes about the custody record. The same problems of enforcement would also remain in the absence of any exclusionary rule related to the actual rules themselves rather than to some notional concept of either "voluntariness" or "reliability".[15]

Notes

1. Royal Commission on Criminal Procedure Report *Op cit* para 2-20.
2. Police and Criminal Evidence Bill (as Amended by Standing Committee J) Clause 3(9). House of Commons Order Paper 9.5.83 773.
3. *The Use, Effectiveness and Impact of Police Stop and Search Powers* by Carole F Willis *Op cit.*
4. *Ibid* p 15, 24.
5. *Op cit* para 124.
6. *Ibid.*
7. *Ibid* para 126.
8. *Ibid* para 155 (v).
9. McBean v Parker *Times Law Reports* 4.1.83.
10. S4 Vagrancy Act 1824.
11. *Sus: a Report on the Vagrancy Act 1824* by Clare Demuth *Op cit*
12. *Ibid* p 29.
13. Royal Commission on Criminal Procedure Report *Op cit* para 2-20.
14. *Guardian* 9.5.83.
15. See Chapter 14.

22. The Independent Assessor of Police Complaints and Statutory Police Liaison Committees

A small section of the Police Bill (Part VIII – *Police – General*) contained concessions of little value to the growing public concern about police accountability. The provisions in it were purely cosmetic and would have made only minor changes to the existing system.

The existing police complaints system has changed very little since 1908. The Deputy Chief Constable of the force concerned appoints the investigating officer who may or may not be from the same force. When the investigation report has been completed, the Deputy Chief Constable may send it to the Director of Public Prosecutions to decide whether or not there should be charges against police officers. If, however, s/he is satisfied no criminal offence has been committed, s/he has to decide whether or not to bring disciplinary charges.

The Police Act 1976 established the Police Complaints Board for England and Wales. This provides an independent check, but only at a very late stage after the above process has been completed. Thus if the investigation report has not been sent to the DPP, it will be sent to the Board after the Deputy Chief Constable has decided whether or not to bring disciplinary proceedings. The Board has power to overrule and decide that disciplinary charges *should* be brought where the Deputy Chief Constable has declined to do so. In exceptional cases, where an officer denies a disciplinary charge, the Board can also decide that the charges should be heard by a tribunal composed of two members of the Board together with the Deputy Chief Constable, instead of by the Deputy Chief Constable alone.

The Police Bill provided for the Chair or Deputy Chair of the Police Complaints Board to be appointed as an "Independent

Assessor" to supervise the investigation of certain complaints.[1] It was difficult to tell from the Bill exactly what this would involve since it provided only that the procedures would be laid down by regulations.[2] And there were no indications in the Bill that the "Independent Assessor" would be given any staff. The Bill also divided complaints into three instead of two categories, adding a new category of trivial complaints which could be resolved informally by conciliation, as well as complaints involving possible criminal and disciplinary charges.[3] However procedures for the informal resolution of complaints were once again to be provided for in regulations, so there was no indication in the Bill of what precisely would be involved.

The most comprehensive statement of the government's intentions was contained in its Reply to the Fourth Report from the Home Affairs Committee of the House of Commons.[4] After hearing evidence, that Committee had recommended that:

> "A complaints office headed by an Independent Assessor, should be established in every region and every major metropolitan area. Any complaint alleging a serious criminal offence should be reported by the police at the earliest opportunity to the complaints officer, who from that point onwards would assume overall responsibility".[5]

and that:

> "A local complaints officer could also provide a convenient point of contact for members of the public who have reason to feel concerned about the handling of minor or disciplinary charges".[6]

The government however turned down the idea of a comprehensive network of regional offices saying that:

> "It seems better that the possible development of a comprehensive regional presence should be examined in the light of practical experience of the operation of the scheme".[7]

Under the government proposals (contained in Annex A to the Reply) the only Assistant Assessors would be deputies appointed on a broad regional basis who would also be members of the Police Complaints Board. The proposals did however state that a comprehensive regional structure would not be ruled out if experience suggested it was necessary.[8]

The government also proposed that the Independent Assessor

would be involved only in complaints involving serious injury or other serious assault and serious corruption cases. This was narrower than the category, proposed by the Home Affairs Committee, of any complaint alleging a serious offence. Under the government proposals also the decision whether or not to involve the Independent Assessor would be made by the Chief Officer of Police with a residual power of the Assessor to call in a case.[9]

The government proposals on conciliation were also substantially less radical than those of the Home Affairs Committee. The Committee Report had given the "local complaints office" (under the Independent Assessor) an important role either as arbitrator or as an independent lay presence at a conciliation.[10] The government rejected arbitration on the grounds that it would result in procedures which would be too formal and made no proposal for any other involvement by the Independent Assessor. Instead the complainant could choose conciliation, the arrangements for which would be made by an officer of the rank of Inspector or above. The police officer against whom the complaint was made could not be compelled to attend a conciliation meeting but if they did choose to attend, nothing said at the meeting would be admissible in either disciplinary or civil proceedings.

The government did state that the arrangements for such a meeting could include, at the discretion of the police officer in charge, attendance of a lay person, drawn from a panel of people. It suggested that the panel should be maintained by the police authority but did not say what would happen in London. The lay person would have had no previous connection with the complainant or interest in the case. The outcome of the conciliation process would be recorded by the police in a register available for inspection by the police authority and HM Inspector of Constabulary and a complainant could obtain a copy of the entry.[11]

Conciliation (or "informal resolution") would not be available to the complainant, if the complaint concerned either a criminal offence or an offence against the Police Disciplinary Code. In those cases the investigation would be carried out by a police officer from another force (possibly under the Independent Assessor depending on the nature of the case and the Chief Officer's decision). The Chief Officer would receive the investigation report from the officer investigating and would then consider whether it indicated any criminal offence had been committed and, if it had, whether the allegation was too serious for him or her to deal with by preferring disciplinary charges.

If s/he decided it was, the report would be sent, as before, to the DPP. Otherwise s/he would decide whether or not to bring disciplinary charges and send the report to the Police Complaints Board as under the existing system. Also, as at present, separate disciplinary procedures would apply for officers of the rank of superintendent or above, with charges drawn up by a solicitor and the hearing in front of a person nominated by the Lord Chancellor. Other disciplinary procedures would be before the Chief Constable sitting alone, unless the Police Complaints Board recommended (exceptionally) a hearing by tribunal.

As discussed above, government proposals did not even go so far as the majority view of the Home Affairs Committee. They omitted its proposals for a comprehensive network of complaints offices, which might at least have made the "independent" element in the complaints system more accessible to the complainant than at present. In addition the government rejected a proposal of the majority of the Committee for statements taken during the investigation of the complaint to be made available to the complainant's legal adviser for use in any connected prosecution of the complainant. This proposal had been made on grounds of avoidance of wrongful convictions.[12] The government also rejected proposals that the DPP and Independent Assessor should give the complainant reasons for their decision – instead a standard letter would be sent out giving an account of general factors taken into consideration.[13]

The debates in Standing Committee J were ample demonstration that the changes proposed by the Police Bill were likely to satisfy no one. Some of the government backbench MPs were as unhappy as the opposition. One of them, Kenneth Warren MP, had co-authored a Conservative Political Centre pamphlet which had criticised the government proposals and suggested a system based around an independent Ombudsman. The pamphlet comments:

> "The Police Complaints Board comprised of so-called laymen has not allayed the public's fears. That is why what amounts to a re-shuffling of the same pack of cards – another kind of independent assessor – will not produce a satisfactory solution now, any more than it did in 1976. We need a new pack – a fully independent procedure. Semi-independent assessors have failed to command the public's confidence in the past. There is no reason why they should suddenly do so now. We must not make the same mistake again".[14]

Although opposition MPs did not share Kenneth Warren's enthusiasm for an Ombudsman system, many of them were in favour of an independent investigatory system. In a dramatic shift of position this too was the view of the Police Federation, expressed by its Parliamentary spokesman Eldon Griffiths MP. The proposal for a wholly independent system was rejected by the then Minister of State Patrick Mayhew MP who said that at the heart of the government's case for resisting the claim for an independent system:

> "has been a recognition that the Chief Officer is at the head of a disciplined service and that it is difficult to reconcile that important position with a derogation from his supremacy in the bringing of discipline charges".[15]

The government suffered its only defeat in the Standing Committee on the Police Bill during discussion of the complaints procedure, when Eldon Griffiths and another Tory MP voted with the opposition to give police officers the right to legal representation in disciplinary tribunals.[16] It is likely therefore that changes to disciplinary procedures will be incorporated in the new Bill.

Other proposals for changing the police complaints system are examined in the next chapter, as is the operation of the double jeopardy rule which did not feature in the Bill, but was much discussed in the Standing Committee and the House of Commons. Meanwhile the Police Bill made its only other gesture towards police accountability in a provision dealing with police/community liaison.

Liaison Committees

The Bill would have implemented Lord Scarman's recommendation that liaison committees between police and public be put on a statutory basis. Lord Scarman found that the breakdown of police/community liaison had been a significant factor in raising tension in Brixton in 1981. However he rejected any increase in accountability in London by substituting an elected body as police authority instead of the Home Secretary. He believed that the crisis of confidence in the police in Lambeth could be averted by re-establishing voluntary consultation, preferably on a statutory basis.[17] In the face of increasing calls for police accountability, especially in London, the government enthusiastically adopted Lord Scarman's proposals for liaison committees in each borough. The Home Office took the initiative in setting up a consultative committee in Lambeth.

For some time however it was not clear whether these committees would be provided for by act of Parliament.

Statutory liaison is in many ways a nonsensical concept since consultation necessarily depends on voluntary co-operation and, in the absence of any defined power relationship, it is not possible to force people to talk. Another problem was the meaning of the word "community"; especially since the Home Office was anxious to overcome the problem that in Labour boroughs, such as Lambeth, a majority of the elected representatives (the local councillors) did not believe liaison on its own was sufficient to increase police accountability.

The outcome was the short clause in the Police Bill which placed a responsibility to make arrangements for consultation on the police authority in every police area except London. In London the responsibility was placed on the Metropolitan Commissioner (and the City Commissioner for the City of London Police) to make separate arrangements by borough or district. Consultation was defined as:

> "obtaining the views of people in that area about matters concerning the policing of the area and for obtaining their co-operation with the police in preventing crime in the area."[18]

In London the Commissioner was to consult each borough council but there was no provision for the views of the elected representatives to prevail on how consultation should be carried out. There was also of course no requirement for the police to give the liaison committee specific information or to take any notice of its views.

Following protests about the Home Secretary off-loading the entire responsibility for consultation arrangements in London onto the police themselves, the government made an addition to the clause in Standing Committee, allowing the Secretary of State to issue guidance for consultation arrangements which the Commissioner would have to take into account.[19] However in London the situation still remained that the ultimate task of deciding who and how the police should consult in a local area would be given to the police themselves – hardly a convincing indication that statutory liaison/consultation would increase accountability.

In practice the effect of a similar provision in the new Bill is likely to be attempts to by-pass the local councils. Some Labour local authorities have for some time been attempting to establish police/community liaison committees as council sub-committees with councillors forming the majority of the members. The aim is to place the committee in a direct relationship with a Borough Police Committee of which the police will not be members and which will form views about policing policy independent of the police.

The Home Office is resisting this idea strongly and it is apparent that the police are unhappy about creating a forum where elected representatives can make a coherent critique of policing in their area, rather than just endorsing the police's actions.[20] The GLC and many Labour boroughs have rejected consultation committees set up independently of the council (as in Lambeth) as purely cosmetic exercises, controlled by the police. The Police Bill reinforced these fears, with its implied judgement that the Commissioner would be in a better position than the local council to make arrangements for consulting the community. Even the Conservative Political Centre pamphlet on police accountability quoted earlier recognised the potentially undemocratic nature of committees with a floating membership, and recommended that there should be a statutory requirement that committees be comprised of at least 60% elected councillors.[21]

But whatever the composition of the committees, they are unlikely to achieve anything without being set in the context of democratic control of the police, and with no clear role. In Lambeth the consultative committee has hardly discussed Commander Marnoch's new policing strategies which are based on those of Sir Kenneth Newman. As *Policing London* commented, the only development coming from the community representatives on the Lambeth committee appears to have been the display of Law Centre posters in police stations.[22] The existence of this and other liaison committees may actually impede progress toward police accountability by giving a false impression of democratic control when in reality there is none.

Notes

1. Police and Criminal Evidence Bill (as amended by Standing Committee J) Clause 65 (2).
2. *Ibid* Clause 65 (6) (d).
3. *Ibid* Clause 65 (6) (b).
4. *The Government Reply to the Fourth Report from the Home Affairs Committee* Session 1981-2, HC 98-1, *Police Complaints Procedures* (HMSO Cmnd 8681 October 1982).
5. Home Affairs Committee, *Police Complaints Procedures* HC 98-1 1982 paras 57-8.
6. *Ibid* para 60.

7. Government Reply *Op cit* para 16.
8. *Ibid* Annex A para 25.
9. *Ibid* Annex A para 17.
10. Home Affairs Committee *Op cit* paras 63-4.
11. Government Reply *Op cit* Annex A para 8.
12. Home Affairs Committee *Op cit* para 16 Government Reply *Op cit* para 9. See also p 179.
13. Home Affairs Committee *Op cit* para 18, Government Reply *Op cit* para 10. See also p 179.
14. *Protecting the Police* by Kenneth Warren MP and David Tredinnick (Conservative Political Centre November 1982).
15. *Hansard* Standing Committee J 15.3.83, Col 1241, Patrick Mayhew MP.
16. *Hansard* Standing Committee J 22.3.83, Col 1419.
17. Scarman Report *Op cit* paras 5.55-5.71.
18. Police and Criminal Evidence Bill (as amended by Standing Committee J) Clause 67(1).
19. *Ibid* Clause 67(8).
20. See Newman's statement quoted at p 127-28.
21. *Op cit* p 16.
22. *Policing London* No 7, April/May 1983.

23. The Police Complaints System, the Double Jeopardy Rule and Proposals for Change

The existing system of police complaints which was explained in the previous chapter was established by the Police Act 1976. But since 1980 there has been a widespread recognition that the system is not working and a number of different proposals for change have been made.

In July 1980 the first Triennial Report of the Police Complaints Board suggested that in some cases of serious injury the investigation of the complaint was not sufficiently thorough. They proposed a separate investigatory body to deal with these complaints.[1] In response to the Board's comments and other criticisms being made, the Home Secretary set up a working party under Lord Plowden, with a large number of police and Home Office representatives. This working party rejected the Board's proposal but suggested instead that either the Chair of the Police Complaints Board or the Director of Public Prosecutions should act as Independent Assessor supervising the investigation of serious complaints.[2]

Subsequently yet another working group was set up by the Police Advisory Board at the Home Office to consider the matter, with police and local authority representatives on it. This endorsed the proposal for an Independent Assessor but could not agree on who should be appointed to the post.[3] Meanwhile the House of Commons Select Committee on Home Affairs had been hearing evidence on police complaints. The majority of the Committee reached the conclusion that an Independent Assessor should have a comprehensive regional network of complaints offices in order to make an impact. They were also attracted by the Scottish model for investigation of complaints whereby these are supervised by an independent prosecutor (in Scotland the Procurator Fiscal). At the same time a minority report of the Home Affairs Committee stated that only a wholly independent system of investigating police complaints would restore public confidence.

The Present System

The view that lack of confidence in the present complaints system is widespread was also taken by Lord Scarman. In his report on the Brixton disturbances, he said:

> "The evidence has convinced me that there is a widespread and dangerous lack of public confidence in the existing system for handling complaints against the police. By and large people do not trust the police to investigate the police".[4]

Meanwhile the numbers of complaints continue to rise. In 1982 they were up by 5% over the previous year to 17,514.[5] The criticisms made of the system are firstly that the police cannot investigate themselves properly. Secondly it is said that the Police Complaints Board are too remote, have insufficient powers and do not exercise the powers they have to question or extend police investigations or findings. Finally it has been alleged that the Director of Public Prosecutions is too cautious in recommending prosecution of police officers and does not always question or extend investigation of offences allegedly committed by police officers, where this would appear to be needed.

Perhaps the most commonly voiced criticism of the system is that investigations by police of allegations against police officers are not carried out thoroughly enough and are not pursued as they would be in relation to an offence committed by a civilian. An unpublished Home Office Research Study drew the conclusion that, "in a significant minority of cases, investigations are not as thorough as might have been expected".[6] There is considerable suspicion that implausible statements from police officers are simply accepted and that police are not cross-examined on statements, as a member of the public would be. The Research Study stated that in at least 15% of a random selection of 146 cases, more rigorous tracing of eye-witnesses and cross-examination of officers present might have produced further information leading to substantiation of the complaint. It also specifically referred to cases involving serious injury where it was equally dissatisfied by both the gathering of immediate evidence (eg, by getting a medical examination) and by the subsequent investigation.

The Police Complaints Board have the right to request "such additional information as they may reasonably require" to enable them to decide whether disciplinary charges should have been brought. They can also direct that information relevant to criminal proceedings should be sent to the Director of Public Prosecutions. This gives the Board a base which they could have used to probe into the way in which investigations are carried out. However, the Board appears to have taken virtually no initiative in this respect. It is obviously difficult for a central body of part-time untrained persons to scrutinise reports of investigations as thoroughly as is necessary. But the composition of the Board is such that its members may not be considered representative of the public as a whole.

The Director of Public Prosecutions stated in his written evidence to the Home Affairs Select Committee that he also played a role in relation to cases referred for consideration of criminal proceedings:

> "Should any apparently material evidence be lacking my officers will, of course, arrange for further enquiries to be made".[7]

He said that interviews with the suspect officers are sometimes insufficiently thorough, "and on these rare occasions, I have so informed the Deputy Chief Constable with a view to raising the standard of this aspect of the investigation". However, it appears that the DPP's ability to spot errors may also be limited. In 1982 an unnamed Nigerian man was awarded compensation by the Criminal Injuries Compensation Board in respect of an injury in Brixton in 1977 which resulted in a testicle being removed. The police gave a further substantial sum of money. It appears that the complaint alleging assault by the police had resulted in no prosecution being brought. One reason for this may have been that no attempt was apparently made to question the police involved about their testimony in the court case against the complainant or about the contents of their notebooks. This omission was not challenged by the DPP and the Board accepted both his decision to take no proceedings and the police decision to propose no disciplinary action.[8]

Another example is the failure to take any action against police involved in an incident in Leicester Square which resulted in damages of £6,000 being paid to a couple for malicious prosecution, false imprisonment and assault.[9] A television programme in June 1983 gave details of three cases where complainants whose complaints had not resulted in any action, had been awarded substantial damages (one for serious assault).[10] One case of assault, false imprisonment and malicious prosecution in 1982 resulted in £51,000 exemplary and aggravated damages being awarded against the police but no action has been taken against any of the officers.[11] Suing for damages in civil courts may therefore be a more effective remedy than the complaints system itself, even though it can take several years and result in no action against the individual police officers.[12]

A further related criticism of the police complaints procedure is that inconclusive evidence is far too readily adopted as the standard reason for not bringing proceedings. It is an intrinsic feature of any criminal system that in most cases where the accused pleads not guilty, there will be a conflict of evidence at the trial. Every day in the courts such conflicts are resolved by decisions about who is telling the truth based on other evidence and on the plausibility of the witness. However, it is said that criminal charges are not brought against police officers in situations where a civilian would have been prosecuted. In his evidence to the Home Affairs Select Committee, Peter Barns, on behalf of the Director of Public Prosecutions, stated that although complaints of assault average 2,664 a year, only about 47 are prosecuted and only 22 charges a year result in convictions. He stressed the reluctance of juries to convict police officers as a contributory reason for these figures.[13]

It is clear that the evidence required to get convictions is not forthcoming as easily as it would be in civil cases. Of course it may be that the evidence is harder to come by in these cases because of lack of co-operation by the suspect policemen who are better aware of their rights than civilian suspects. This is not to deny them the right of silence. But it is, therefore, all the more essential that all the relevant lines of enquiry are pursued and all appropriate questions are put to the suspect concerned. There are worrying indications that this is often not the case and that the DPP and the Police Complaints Board have little inclination or capacity to correct such omissions.

One result of the fact that it is the police who investigate themselves is that the investigation of a complaint and the prosecution of a case against the complainant is usually undertaken by individuals in constant daily professional contact. The standard practice is for any disciplinary hearing against the police to be postponed pending the outcome of the other proceedings. The organisation, Justice, proposed that the investigation of the complaint be carried out before the proceedings and the statements obtained in the course of it are made available to the complainant's solicitor to prevent miscarriages of justice. This recommendation was endorsed by the majority of the Home Affairs Committee but it was turned down by the government and was not in the Police Bill. Without such a provision there are obvious dangers that the complainant's guilt may be decided by a court which does not have all the evidence and that finding of guilt may then prejudice proper investigation of the complaint.[14]

Another aspect of the police investigation of complaints is the suspicion that the police may bring pressure to bear on the complainant to withdraw their complaint. Approximately 47% of all recorded complaints are withdrawn subsequently (many more unrecorded).[15] Sir Cyril Philips, in the Police Complaints Board evidence to the Home Affairs Committee, referred to fears that this is because of intimidation by the police.[16] The unpublished Home Office Research Study also reportedly stated that it was clear in one case that the police recognised that criminal charges against a complainant could be used to nullify or weaken a complaint.[17] In their Second Triennial Review 1983 the Police Complaints Board said of complaints which were withdrawn:

"We think that the proportion of cases in this category is so large that some form of scrutiny should be undertaken".[18]

A common observation about the present system of investigating police complaints is that it is not geared to satisfying the complainant. It is said that letters from the Police Complaints Board or the DPP to the complainant are uninformative and unhelpful. The complainant receives no information on the progress of the investigation or the response of the police officer(s) concerned and very little or none on the reasons for dropping the charges. The leaflet handed out for public information gives no indication of the detailed procedures or how the "independent elements" of the Police Complaints Board and the DPP can intervene. The outcome of the case is only known after very long delays; although the Police Complaints Board take an average of 34 days to complete a case, they have expressed concern that the police take an average of *190* days to deal with a complaint before it reaches the Board. This means an average of eight months after a complaint is lodged.[19]

The government have, however, rejected the recommendation of the Home Affairs Committee that the reasons for the Board's or the DPP's decision be given to the complainant,[20] and there is no proposal to speed up dealing with complaints – indeed the addition of the Independent Assessor may slow down even more the processing of serious complaints.

Double Jeopardy

What is known as the double jeopardy rule has had in the past an unexpected effect on any complaint referred to the Director of Public Prosecutions. The rule derives from S11 of the Police Act 1976 which provides that:

> "Where a member of a police force has been acquitted or convicted of a criminal offence he shall not be liable to be charged with any offence against discipline which is in substance the same as the offence of which he has been acquitted or charged".

The same Act requires the Board to have regard to any guidance given by the Secretary of State on the preferral or withdrawal of disciplinary charges. Guidance on the interpretation of S11 was formerly contained in an annex to a Home Office Circular:

> "Where an allegation against a police officer has first been the subject of criminal investigation and it has been decided after reference to the Director (or otherwise) that criminal proceedings should not be taken there should normally be no disciplinary proceedings if the evidence required to substantiate a disciplinary charge is the same as that required to substantiate the criminal charge".[21]

The result of this guidance was that 99% of cases referred to the DPP which he decided not to prosecute could not, according to the Police Complaints Board, be made the subject of disciplinary charges. This led to absurd anomalies: eg in the case of Errol Madden, a police officer who was marginally involved was disciplined; two other officers whose cases were referred to the DPP because they were more heavily involved could not be disciplined.[22]

The Home Affairs Committee recommended that this interpretation of the double jeopardy rule should stop and that only if a case was actually prosecuted in a criminal court and the officer acquitted, should they be able to claim exemption from an identical disciplinary charge on the same facts in the meantime. Errol Madden, and another complainant David Rhone, applied to the High Court for a ruling on whether the Board's interpretation of S11 was a correct one. The High Court's decision was that if the case had been referred to the DPP the Police Complaints Board could still decide to bring disciplinary proceedings against the officer concerned so long as there had been no actual criminal prosecution.[23]

The Police Bill did not include any provision dealing with the double jeopardy rule although the Home Office made available proposed revised guidelines and said the government would abide by the Madden and Rhone decision.[24] At Report Stage of the Police Bill in the House of Commons, Harriet Harman MP (previously Legal Officer of the National Council of Civil Liberties) expressed fears about whether this would be sufficient in case the judgement were overruled. She argued that police officers were better protected than members of the public because the DPP takes into account the supposed reluctance of juries to convict police officers.[25]

But even if a provision in the new Police Bill is not necessary, there may still be problems inherent in the double jeopardy rule. The new guidelines pointed out that some disciplinary charges are substantially different from their counterpart in criminal charges (eg, accepting a gratuity does not involve the mental element necessary to establish criminal corruption). On the other hand the guidelines maintained that the criminal charge of assault and the disciplinary charge of unnecessary violence are in substance the same. This would appear to give rise to some potential inconsistencies since less serious cases considered by the DPP can subsequently result in disciplinary charges, whereas the more serious cases of assault cannot. In 1982, of those complaints looked at by the Board which had also been referred to the DPP *half* alleged assault (2,796 out of 5,511 cases).[26]

The other main difference between the two types of proceeding (criminal and disciplinary) is the different chance of success on the same evidence, or at least the different assessments of the chance of success. As mentioned previously the DPP is notoriously reluctant to prosecute if there is any doubt about getting a conviction. The problem is that if he is allowed "first bite of the cherry", the Police Complaints Board attitude to bringing disciplinary charges may be governed by his decision not to prosecute, whereas if disciplinary charges had been considered at the outset a different attitude might have prevailed.

The Police Complaints Board's Annual Report for 1982 revealed that whilst 263 disciplinary actions had been taken by deputy chief constables before these complaints reached the Board, the Board recommended 46 disciplinary charges in a further 25 cases where deputy chief constables had taken no action. Of these, deputy chief constables accepted 30 recommendations, resulting in 15 officers found guilty with 4 cases outstanding.[27] These figures are roughly similar to previous years (the 46 cases were 0.25% of all complaints in 1982) and it remains to be seen whether the change in interpretation of the double jeopardy rule will result in the Board taking any more active a role.

There is a need for better protection of police officers' rights in disciplinary hearings. The Police Federation have suggested that there should be a formal hearing at which the independent investigatory body would present the case against a police officer and the officer's own representatives would present a defence. Serious disciplinary charges would be heard by a tribunal consisting of lay members as well as the Chief Officer of Police. These proposals are likely to be included in the new Police Bill.

The Independent Assessor

The system set out in the Police Bill would build on present arrangements, but minor complaints would be dealt with through conciliation, more substantial complaints would be investigated as at present, and "serious" complaints would be subject to investigation by a senior police officer from an outside force under the supervision of an Independent Assessor. However most complaints would be likely to be investigated in precisely the same way and the independent element would probably be distant and centralised and unlikely to effect any significant improvement. There would be additional practical difficulties for the Independent Assessor in directing investigations by the police and internal problems for the police in removing supervisory officers from their usual duties to deal with complaints in other force areas – a point also raised in evidence to the Home Affairs Committee by the Superintendents' Association. But worst of all, an Independent Assessor would be purely cosmetic in the absence of any substantial staff attached to the new post (see Chapter 22), a point admitted by the chair of the Police Complaints Board, Sir Cyril Phillips.[28]

An Independent Complaints System

The proposal of the National Council for Civil Liberties and the GLC is for a wholly independent body to investigate police complaints.[29] This was also supported by Lord Scarman in his Report. Objections to this proposal have centred on practical matters – resources and staffing – rather than the question of principle.

There is insufficient public information to produce reliable stimates of the costing of any new system, but some pointers are vailable. The cost to the police of the present system is estimated by he Home Officer to be about £9 million. In the Metropolitan Police District, 270 police and civilian staff are employed full-time on omplaints work, at a cost of £5.8 million. However, these figures do ot take account of the fact that much complaints work, particularly 1 the provinces, is carried out by supervisory staff in the normal ourse of duty. Given these figures, the removal of complaints work rom the aegis of the police would constitute a considerable saving on olice budgets. Apart from a tangible decrease in costs, the release of upervisory staff from complaints work would, as the uperintendents' Association pointed out to the Home Affairs Committee, increase the general standard of supervision which might a itself lead to a decrease in matters complained of by the public. However, it needs to be remembered that the police would still need o maintain adequate resources to deal with internal disciplinary natters. Thus, without a further breakdown of present costs, which nly the Home Office and the police are in a position to provide, it is npossible to estimate what resources might be available from police udgets for the new system.

There would be certain capital and running costs in establishing an ndependent system, which are likely to make it, at least initially, nore costly than the present arrangements, particularly as it is nportant to have such a system adequately financed. But, an ndependent system would also have more flexibility than the present rrangements which would be likely to make it more cost effective. 'or example, the new system, while requiring staff of a high calibre, vould not be constrained by the requirement that all complaints be nvestigated by an officer of the rank of superintendent, or above. 'he Home Office Research Study indicated that the meticulous nvestigation of complaints was in some cases carried to a wasteful nd unproductive extreme.[30] An independent investigator would be nore flexible and in a better position to be discriminatory in the use of esources to ensure that no unnecessary work was undertaken.

In the debates on the Police Bill in 1982/3 the question of costs was sed as a weapon against the introduction of an independent system. n 1976, during Parliamentary debate on the Police Act which stablished the Police Complaints Board, the cost of the Board was stimated by one Conservative MP at £2 million per annum. In fact in ne financial year 1978/79, the first year in which the Board was fully perational, the Board's costs totalled only £397,000.[31] This experience indicates that it would be irresponsible to attempt to estimate the cost of a new independent system on the basis of the information presently available. What is required is that the information available to the Home Office and the police be constituted into a proper feasibility study, and made known to the public.

It has also been suggested that only the police have the necessary expertise to investigate complaints against themselves and that, in particular, only the police have the appropriate powers and skills to deal with crime. In addition, it has been stated by some bodies that it would be unfair to subject the police to an outside investigation force, "a second police force" when the ordinary citizen can only be investigated by the police. In fact there are a number of bodies other than the police who are charged with the duty of investigating particular offences. The DHSS and the Immigration Service are obvious examples; both have had a considerable increase in their resource allocation under the present administration. The DHSS now has over 5,000 staff engaged in the investigation of fraud, and a further 250 in "specialist claims control" allocated to regional offices. Officers of the Immigration Service have the powers of a constable, to arrest and search without warrant, in relation to offences under the Immigration Act 1971.

Thus the police are not unique in respect of either their powers or their investigative capacity. Given adequate powers and resources there appears to be no reason why an independent body should not develop the expertise to mount effective investigations into complaints against the police. This point was also made by the Police Federation in their evidence to the Home Affairs Committee.

Complaints and Accountability

Police authorities have a duty, under S 50 Police Act 1964, "to keep themselves informed as to the manner in which complaints . . . are dealt with". It is true that an independent complaints system would make it less necessary for police authorities to concern themselves with individual cases alleging misbehaviour. But at the same time if police authorities were given proper powers to exercise democratic control over the police an expanded role could be given to them in overseeing and perhaps receiving complaints raising matters of policy rather than behaviour. Again this was recommended by Lord Scarman.[32] At present the formal complaints system is a means of enforcing the legal accountability of the police which bears little or no relationship to any attempted accountability on policy matters. This is particularly true in London where few people realise that the Home Secretary is the police authority. Attempts have been made by some police authorities to receive complaints directly which may or may not have been the subject of formal police complaints.[33]

Finally while it is essential that a complaints system is established which has public confidence, it will not on its own solve all the problems. Perhaps one of the biggest problems of the system at present is the inevitable confusion between rules which may be broken and rules which may not. It can be argued that since the Judges' Rules are widely broken other rules also fall into the same disrepute. The rules which may not be broken and those which may then fall to be determined by superior officers, who are sometimes primarily influenced by a desire to secure maximum numbers of convictions. As with recording of reasons, an independent complaints system will be of little use on its own in preventing institutionalised disregard for rules.

Notes

1. Police Complaints Board *Triennial Review 1980* (HMSO Cmnd 7966).
2. The Plowden Working Party Report March 1981 (Cmnd 8193).
3. Police Advisory Board Working Group, HC 98-II, 1982 p 223-230.
4. Scarman Report *Op cit* para 5-43.
5. Report of the Police Complaints Board 1982, HC 278 (HMSO April 1983).
6. *Times* 8.4.81.
7. Evidence of the Director of Public Prosecutions to the Select Committee on Home Affairs 1982.
8. *Observer* 24.1.82.
9. *Times* 10.6.83.
10. *TV Eye,* Independent Television, June 1983.
11. *Times* 24.5.82 (case of Mr and Mrs White).
12. London Borough of Camden Policy and Resources (Police) Sub-Committee Document. (PR/83/449) 31.8.83.
13. *Op cit.*
14. See p 170.
15. *Second Triennial Review of the Police Complaints Board 1983* (HMSO Cmnd 8853).
16. Oral Evidence of Sir Cyril Philips on behalf of the Police Complaints Board to the Select Committee on Home Affairs 16.12.81.
17. *Times* 8.4.81. *Op cit.*
18. *Op cit.*
19. Police Complaints Board Annual Report 1982 *Op cit.*
20. See p 170.
21. Home Office Circular 32/1980.
22. *A Fair Cop* by Patricia Hewitt (NCCL 1982) p 19-20.

23. R v Police Complaints Board *ex parte* Madden; R v Police Complaints Board *ex parte* Rhone (1983) 2 ALL ER 353.

24. *The Relationship Between Criminal and Disciplinary Proceedings. Revised Guidance to Chief Officers* Draft 1983.

25. *Hansard* 4.5.83, Col 302-3, Harriet Harman MP.

26. Report of the Police Complaints Board 1982 *Op cit.*

27. *Ibid.*

28. *TV Eye* June 1983 *Op cit.*

29. *A Fair Cop, Op cit* and GLC Police Committee Report PC 39 (5.5.82) (on which much of this chapter is based).

30. *Times* 8.4.81 *Op cit.*

31. GLC Police Committee Report PC 39 *Op cit.*

32. Scarman Report *Op cit* para 7.27.

33. eg, Merseyside Police Authority has encouraged the submission of general complaints about the police to itself direct. Home Office Circular No. 63/1977 suggested that the police authority's role was a "supervisory one" and that it would be useful for police authorities to know about the background to cases arousing local concern and about the "general pattern of complaints" in the area.

24. The Royal Commission on Criminal Procedure Report and the Concept of "Balance"

The Report of the Royal Commission on Criminal Procedure, which came out in January 1981, dealt with the extent of police powers in relation to the investigation and prosecution of offences. It did not deal with the police complaints system, police/community liaison or police accountability (other than in relation to its proposal for a public prosecutor).

The Report dealt with the framework of its terms of reference and its underlying philosophy at some length. It started from the concept of "fundamental balance" which it said had to be struck between the interests of the whole community and the rights and liberties of the individual citizens. It went on to conclude that a system of checks and balances was appropriate and that the wider police powers it often thought necessary to combat crime could be offset by safeguards built into the law. The criteria it finally adopted was that the laws governing police powers should be "fair, open and workable".

When the Report came out, it was greeted by widespread condemnation by civil liberties groups. Harriet Harman described it as a "triumph of the law and order lobby" and stated that:

> "While the new powers which the police are to receive are spelt out in uncompromising detail, the nature of any compensating obligations remains extremely vague".[1]

The Report had started from the notion that "the interests of the community in bringing offenders to justice" and "the rights and liberties of persons suspected or accused of crime" were invariably in contradiction. Having identified these as opposing forces, the

Commission went on to elaborate them in terms of utilitarian and libertarian philosophies and concluded that they were "so diametrically opposed as apparently to defy reconciliation".[2]

Critics argued that this polarisation was simplistic and incorrect. It assumed that the interests of the community were always identified with those of the police as prosecutors and that the suspect, whose rights and liberties are at stake, was always guilty. In a case where the suspect was innocent of the crime and the community consisted of persons concerned that justice is done under the law, the supposed divergence of approaches would be non-existent. Moreover since in criminal law a suspect is always to be presumed innocent until proven guilty, complete polarity of these interests can be said never to occur. It will always be an interest of the community to protect the rights and liberties of a person presumed innocent. In this context, the Commission would have more appropriately started from the basis that it was the interests of the police in proving their case and the rights and liberties of the suspect that were in perpetual potential conflict.

The Royal Commission then postulated the existence of a "fundamental balance" between two opposing points of view. They did not define balance directly but they apparently rejected the view that certain individual rights could be regarded as negotiable and that "the positions of the two main groups are capable of being reconciled by a series of compromises involving concessions by each".[3] Nevertheless subsequently they still stated themselves to be searching for the "balance" and in a concluding paragraph to the section they arrived at three standards of "fair, open and workable" to be adopted as the framework for their review of investigative arrangements. In their exposition of these three standards it was clear that the "rights and liberties of persons suspected . . ." had been reduced to the requirement that reasons be given for decisions ("openness"); that rules should apply to all persons ("fairness"); and that they should enable the police to catch criminals ("workability").[4]

The requirement that the police record their reasons ("openness") has already been discussed in Chapter 22. It was pointed out there that the requirement may be of little use to the suspect in the absence of properly defined limitations on exercise of police powers or of any means of enforcement more effective than the present police complaints system or civil actions in the courts. The requirement to record reasons might therefore be said to be a necessary component of any legislation defining (and therefore limiting) police powers but not a factor which would "balance" any failure to do so.

The Report did not specifically deal with police accountability other than in relation to prosecutions but it hinted at its importance when it said that police forces should keep records available which would "make possible general oversight of the process by the police authority by central government through its inspectorate and ultimately by Parliament".[5] The Commission's failure to deal fully with the issue of accountability may have been due to a basic misunderstanding of its importance in relation to the exercise of police power. Accountability can be said to be not just a procedural constitutional matter but the whole basis on which consent for the exercise of police power is secured. Phil Jones has written of the Royal Commission Report:

> "At fault, in part, is the concept of accountability that is utilised. Mechanisms of accountability are essentially mechanisms of delimitation. The form of accountability is important, but so too is the range of decisions regulated and this needs clear specification. For a mechanism of accountability to be effective, whatever the form of the link between supervisor and supervised, there is a need to specify the powers clearly and to specify equally clearly how they are to be regulated. The Commission does not do this, in explicitly disavowing detail in the name of principle it creates a range of possibilities. It leaves it open to police authorities how they will review the proposed records, it leaves it open to HM Inspectorate how it will report its inspections, it accordingly leaves much open to the police".[6]

The second standard needed to bring about "fundamental balance" was fairness. The Royal Commission defined it in the following way:

> "By fairness we mean that if a suspect has a right he should be made aware of it. He should be able to exercise it, if he wishes, and waive it, if he wishes. If the right is to be withheld from him he should know not only that it is being withheld but what it is. If he is being required to submit to a particular investigative procedure, he should be told under what power the requirement is made and how it can be enforced if he refuses . . . Fairness applies equally to the police officer. He should not be required to try to work within a framework of rules which are unclear, uncertain in their application and liable long after the event to subjective and arbitrary reinterpretation of their application in a particular case."[7]

"Fairness" therefore was said to be a standard which unites the interests of the police and the suspect – both need clear information as to the extent of suspects' rights and the definition of police powers. Unfortunately, however, it is open to question whether the Royal Commission Report's recommendations satisfied this standard. One of the most obvious weaknesses was in their proposal that many rights and obligations should be set out only in Codes of Practice and not in an Act of Parliament. But the Royal Commission may also have slipped into serious failures of definition. Thus for example they failed to define "reasonable suspicion" and, in relation to admissibility of evidence, the "voluntariness" rule was to be replaced by an equally vague "reliability" rule. An article in the *Criminal Law Review* pointed out that "fairness" provided no benchmark against which to measure whether there are too many or too few controls on the police, too many or too few rights for the individual.[8]

The third standard was "workability". If this was also open to interpretation, the Royal Commission may have appeared to interpret it solely from the point of view of the police catching criminals and keeping the rules. The Commission rejected the notion of the police officer as a "citizen in uniform" as being "far from reality".[9] They implied that special duties given to police officers justified special powers enabling the police to deal with "experienced and dangerous criminals" as well as to cover the circumstances of the great majority of suspects, who they admitted, were "of a very different kind".[10]

Once again accountability in its broadest sense should have been relevant since proposals for police powers cannot be "workable" if the consent of the community to them is not secured. However the Commission missed the point and concentrated purely on the mechanics of catching criminals and abiding by the rules. The suggestion created by their words, even though they were dealing with abstractions, was that police powers should be set at the highest common denominator (ie, necessary to catch the most elusive and heinous criminal) rather than at the level of the greatest support and consent from the public. Instead, it could be argued that the police would be more effective in catching criminals if they had less power and more public co-operation.

The notion of "balance" has continued to dog the discussion of the issues well after the appearance of the Royal Commission Report. Thus critics of the Police Bill claimed that it had "upset the balance" by increasing some powers and omitting some safeguards. A member of the Commission, Walter Merricks, complained that the government had "pulled apart a package we had fully stitched together".[11] Comment appeared in some of the press suggesting that the proposals in the Bill for new powers would be acceptable if only the Bill had included the Commission's proposals on tape recording of interviews in police stations and on an independent prosecutor service.

The introduction of a new Bill will be timed to coincide with the publication of government proposals on an independent prosecutor system. The content of these proposals is examined in the next chapter. However what must be questioned is whether such proposals, however beneficial, would be capable of "balancing" unacceptably wide new powers. Accountability in its widest sense must mean legal accountability as a check against abuse of police power, as well as general accountability to public opinion on policing policies and on acceptable levels of police power. The Commission, and subsequently the drafters of the Police Bill, may have taken little account of either form of accountability. As previously discussed powers were often extended by the Bill through lack of adequate definitions and through omissions of enforcement mechanisms, but there were deliberate extensions of police power. New police powers must still in the final analysis be regarded on their own merits. Thus even if the reasons judged necessary for an "intimate search" or for arrest for a trivial offence on grounds of failure to give name and address were more restricted, the acceptability of such powers *per se* to the community has still to be considered. It would be of no surprise to learn that a majority of people would reject these powers in themselves, regardless of any number of safeguards.[12]

It can therefore be argued that the notion of "balance" is a false one and impedes proper understanding of the relationship between police efficiency and police accountability to the law. A choice has to be made as to acceptable levels of police power. When that choice has been made, it will be necessary to ensure that limitations on police power are enforceable and that the individual has redress if they are breached. If this is not done unenforceable laws will fall into disrepute and the public will increasingly withdraw co-operation from the police. The "safeguards" will therefore only operate to enforce existing limitations on police powers; they will not create new ones.

General accountability of the police to the community concerns matters of policy rather than of law. It is of little protection in enforcing standards but is a means of directing police discretion. Its connection with legal accountability is explained subsequently and depends on what view is taken of the police's role in the community.

Notes

1. *New Statesman* 4.1.81.
2. Royal Commission on Criminal Procedure Report *Op cit* para 1.29.
3. *Ibid* para 1.33.
4. *Ibid* para 2.18 – 2.24.
5. *Ibid* para 2.20.
6. *Police Powers and Police Accountability: The Royal Commission on Criminal Procedure* by Phil Jones (*Politics and Power* No 4 Law, Politics and Justice, Routledge and Kegan Paul).
7. Royal Commission on Criminal Procedure Report *Op cit* para 2.19.
8. *Criminal Law Review* July 1981 p 437.
9. Royal Commission on Criminal Procedure Report *Op cit* para 2.21.
10. *Ibid.*
11. *Times* 19.11.82.
12. A poll of black people was in fact carried out by London Weekend Television's *Black on Black* programme which found that two out of three people expected relations with the police to get worse if the Police Bill became law and 70% thought more police powers would not help solve more crime (*The Times* 19.1.83).

25. Omissions – An Independent Prosecution Service, Tape Recording and Lay Visitors

In Part II of their Report published in 1981 the Royal Commission on Criminal Procedure recommended the establishment in England and Wales of a prosecution service independent of the police, organised on a local basis and responsible to local police and prosecutions authorities in each police area.[1] One of the most frequently voiced criticisms of the Police Bill was that it did not implement the proposal for a public prosecutor. The government said it accepted the principle of an independent prosecution service but had not settled how it should be organised.

The tape recording of interviews with suspects in police stations was first proposed by the Eleventh Report of the Criminal Law Revision Committee. Since then proposals for tape recording have been the subject of constant feasibility studies, experiments and consultations. The major deterrent factor has been cost. This led the Royal Commission to recommend only that a summary of each interview should be recorded. But even that proposal was not contained in the Bill nor were Lord Scarman's proposals for lay visitors in police stations.

Independent Prosecution Service

In December 1982 the Home Office issued a consultation paper on the organisation of an Independent Prosecution Service.[2] Three options were set out in the paper:

    (i) *an integrated national system* of locally based prosecutors from a single central department who would conduct cases in the magistrates' courts and the Crown Court;

   (ii) *a decentralised national system* with regionally based prosecutors as independent office holders under the Crown having a degree of autonomy and also conducting cases in the magistrates' courts and the Crown Court;

  (iii) *a local system* with a prosecutions department in each police area independent of the police, with functions similar to the above and accountable to a local supervisory body.

The paper explored these options on the basis of what it said to be "widely expressed" reservations about a local system under (iii) above as put forward by the Royal Commission. The way in which the opinions are propounded makes it clear that the Home Office probably favours a national system.

At present the vast bulk of criminal prosecutions are initiated by the police and responsibility both for policy and its implementation rests with the particular Chief Constable who heads the local force (in the case of London, the Commissioner of Police of the Metropolis). This means that the decision as to whether or not a person is to be charged with an offence is taken by a police officer – effectively often the person in charge of the investigation. The proceedings may be conducted in one or more of four ways:

    (i) The police may themselves conduct the prosecution (sometimes being a witness as well as the advocate). In practically all police forces including the Met this is the practice in summary cases and in many of the less serious indictable offences tried summarily.

   (ii) The police may employ private solicitors to act on their behalf who will instruct counsel should this be necessary. In this type of situation one firm of solicitors often becomes the regular police prosecuting agent in the particular district.

  (iii) The police authority may employ a prosecuting solicitor with a small organisation who will farm out most of the work to local solicitors whom they will instruct.

  (iv) The police or local authority may employ a prosecuting solicitor with a substantial staff who will themselves conduct all or virtually all the police prosecutions of indictable offences. This is the position in the Metropolitan Police District where Scotland Yard has its own solicitors' office.

The prosecutor has two separate roles; as independent prosecutor in the court and as policy-maker in taking the decision whether or not to prosecute. In relation to the former, prosecuting solicitors employed by the police are said to lack the complete independence which they should enjoy. This independence is based on the idea of the prosecutor as an impartial officer of the court whose duty is to be fair to both sides and arrive at the truth, not to obtain a conviction regardless of the defence case. But instead the relationship between police and prosecuting solicitor is one of solicitor and client and the solicitors consider that they are acting for and on behalf of the police. Although the solicitor may offer advice to the police they are under no obligation to accept it. The police may refuse to accept advice not to bring or continue with a prosecution. Conversely there are cases in which a solicitor would consider that a prosecution was warranted and where no proceedings are brought.

Police officers who have satisfied themselves that the suspect is guilty becomes psychologically committed to prosecution and thus to successful prosecution. In consequence, senior police officers may be inhibited from refusing to prosecute because they will not want to damage morale, whereas an independent prosecutor would not be influenced by such considerations. The English system is the only one in Europe where the interrogation of suspects, the interviewing of witnesses, the gathering and testing of scientific evidence, the selection of evidence to be laid before the court, the decision as to what charges shall be brought and the conduct of the prosecution may be entirely under the control of the police. McConville and Baldwin, comment that it is:

> "the police who assemble the evidence, control its content, select, authenticate and validate it. They interrogate the suspect on their own territory and on their own terms and their record of the encounter is virtually unchallengeable and for the most part unchallenged".[3]

The increasing shift in policing styles towards obtaining evidence via admissions and confessions, a process which could gather pace if the provisions of the Police Bill were enacted,[4] makes the overall control of the criminal prosecution process by the police even more of a threat to civil liberties. The dominance of the police in the prosecution process exposes them to temptation. They may seek or be prepared to bargain with a suspect, promising to refrain from prosecuting, or to "let them down lightly" or to "put in a good word with the magistrates", or to grant them bail (or not to oppose it).[5] The risk of abuse, however well-intentioned the motives, is manifest in such a situation.

In addition the police sometimes fail to disclose relevant information, which could have been of material assistance to the accused. This happens particularly in magistrates' court cases where the accused is not legally represented, and does not have the benefit of pre-trial proceedings or the service of witness statements upon him or her. It is not practicable for the police to be legally trained as advocates and would be undesirable in view of the existing problems of short training for proper police duties.

At present there are very considerable regional variations in prosecution policy according to the different attitudes of individual chief constables. In an attempt to enforce some standardisation the Attorney General issued guidelines on prosecution policy in February 1983. The new guidelines referred extensively to the principles operated by the Director of Public Prosecutions when he decides whether or not to prosecute a case. At present decisions on prosecution for all cases of murder, conspiracy and certain other kinds of difficult or "political" offences as well as all cases of prosecution of police officers are made by the DPP. The DPP is a political appointment by the government.

The guidelines provided that a prosecution should be brought only if "a conviction is more likely than an acquittal before an impartial jury properly directed in accordance with the law" (this is known as the 50% rule). An even higher standard is to be adopted if an acquittal would or might produce "unfortunate consequences". One example given is a trial for perjury where an acquittal might cast doubt on a previous conviction. The likely expense and length of a trial and the gravity of an offence are also to be taken into account as well as "availability, credit and credibility of witnesses and their likely impression on a jury; the admissibility of any admissions if necessary having regard to the age and intelligence of the defendant; the reliability of any identification". These kinds of considerations are legal and technical rather than matters of policy and need expert legal knowledge of previous cases for a proper assessment to be made.

Secondly, as the guidelines revealed, the prosecutor has an important policy role and the guidelines sought to pass on to the police some of the principles adopted by the DPP in this area instead of leaving it to their sole discretion. A former Attorney General, Lord Shawcross, was quoted as authority for the importance of prosecution policy:

"It has never been the rule in this country — I hope it never will be — that suspected criminal offences must automatically be the subject of prosecution. Indeed the very first Regulations under which the Director of Public Prosecutions worked provided that he should . . . prosecute 'wherever it appears that the offence or the circumstances of its commission is or are of such a character that a prosecution in respect thereof is required in the public interest'. That is still the dominant consideration''.

The guidelines then set out the factors to be taken into consideration in deciding whether or not to allow "a disposal less than a prosecution, for example a caution". These were, likely penalty (ie, how serious was the offence), staleness of the offence and the youth, old age, infirmity, mental illness or mental state of the offender. Factors such as consent and age of the offender and victim were also relevant in sexual offences. Finally the attitude of the complainant was also to be taken into account.

Setting out these considerations was obviously an attempt to bring the exercise of police discretion into line with the DPP's policies, but is unlikely to do much to stop the enormous differences in prosecution policy between different police forces.

Following the publication of these guidelines the Met Police Commissioner, Sir Kenneth Newman, issued a special order requiring a higher standard of evidence for bringing a prosecution and giving greater discretion to police officers in deciding whether or not to prosecute. Up to now the official position of the Met has been that they have automatically brought a prosecution wherever there was a *prima facie* case and this has led to concern about the rate of acquittals in court.

By contrast Devon and Cornwall police have for some time operated a policy of "cautioning" instead of prosecution for adults; in 1979 the Met cautioned only 46 people over the age of 21 years for indictable offences whereas Devon and Cornwall police cautioned 816. The Met will now use the 50% rule and the Attorney General's guidelines to caution far more people.[7] Recognition of the necessity for the exercise of discretion will however only increase the degree of unaccountable power being given to the individual police officer. Chief Inspector Brian Plaxton, the Scotland Yard officer in charge of implementing the new policy, said that, "It will require every London police officer to be something of a sociologist".[8]

It is clear that the establishment of an independent prosecutor system would be a considerable advance over what occurs at present. It is still too early to judge the effect of the new enlightened guidelines but they seem unlikely to make much difference. On principle it still seems wrong that the aims of vigorous investigation of crime and the careful and impartial prosecution process should be confused. Arguably the whole basis of an accusatorial system, such as operates in the criminal courts in this country, is the separation of investigation (by the police) and prosecution (by the state). Nevertheless the argument for an independent prosecution service becomes considerably less clear cut in relation to prosecution policy making.

Policing and prosecutions policies are inextricably linked, so that the identification of particular crime categories as priorities (eg, racial attacks, burglaries) should lead to priority in both resource allocation and consequently in prosecution decisions. There are also strong arguments for having locally variable policing and prosecutions policies, so that the different character and policing needs of different areas can be recognised.[9]

The Royal Commission recognised the difference between prosecution policy on social and policy grounds and the "legal elements of the decision to prosecute, especially the evidentiary issues". However they concluded that:

> ". . . it would not in practice always be possible to make the distinction. Discussion with our witnesses suggests that the line between law and policy is not necessarily sharply drawn (and we know of no other jurisdiction where prosecution responsibilities are divided in this way). Drawing the line at the point of charge both recognises the need for the police to continue to have discretion over the initiation of proceedings as an essential element of their law enforcement role and has the merit of being clear cut. We do not imagine it will eliminate all disputes since whenever issues are delicately balanced one must expect there to be consultation, as there is now".[10]

The Royal Commission appeared to be evading the issue somewhat, because the whole rationale of an independent prosecutor service is to separate off the prosecution process (which should be impartial) from the policing role, which is one where policy and the exercise of discretion are of paramount importance. The issue is complicated by the tendency of many of those who are in favour of police accountability to argue for a locally controlled independent prosecution system as a means of increasing accountability. The Home Office's reasons for rejecting the Royal Commission's proposals may also be connected to a government desire to strengthen the degree of *central* not local police accountability.

Meanwhile senior police officers who have been very opposed to the idea of an independent prosecution service may be coming to see the advantages of a nationally controlled system in deflecting demands for more local accountability. Dr P A Waddington stated in the Police Federation journal that:

> "The price may however be worth paying, provided that such a Prosecution Agency was not locally accountable, but directly accountable to Law Officers of the Crown, preferably the Attorney General. This connection would enhance the legal accountability of the police and provide a countervailing power to that of local politicians, because through the process of submitting cases to the prosecutor the police would be accountable to him for the quality of their evidence and thereby for the effectiveness of their policing".[11]

Dr Waddington considered that dual accountability to a local police authority and a national independent prosecutor would enable the police to bring out the adverse effects of "political meddling" by the police authority. The example he gave was that if the police authority denied the police cameras for the use of identifying suspects in public order situations then the cases the police were forced to bring would be significantly weaker:

> "This could well result in the local prosecutor refusing to proceed against suspects and his refusal could then be used as support in trying to change the Police Committee's mind. Of course the local prosecutor is not bound to support the police in this, or more direct ways, all the time, but dual accountability to the local authority and a representative of the legal system, could allow chief officers valuable *room for manoeuvre* in protecting the independence of his force".[12]

Police authorities are of course not in a position to prevent the police using cameras in public order situations or to affect operational policy in any other way (except possibly the purchase of equipment).[13] But they can try to influence the police and the police's intention would apparently be to prevent their demands gaining support by recourse to the independent government controlled public prosecutor. The supposition that this might happen is strengthened by criticisms of the way in which the DPP carries out his policy role eg, in relation to his decisions to bring "political" conspiracy charges in such cases as the "ABC" secrets trial or the Bradford 12.

There would be likely to be little means of making the nationally controlled prosecutor accountable to parliament for his policy decisions especially if it functions like the DPP's office. Thus ironically the establishment of a centrally controlled independent prosecutor service may well hamper rather than extend police accountability on matters of policy. The long-term solution to this problem might be to allocate to the prosecutor a purely legal role in terms of assessing the evidence. If in addition the police were made properly accountable to police authorities (ie, democratically controlled by elected local government bodies), democratic control could then extend to the formulation of both policing and prosecutions policies. The independent prosecutor would be restricted to deciding whether or not a case would succeed in court, while the police, under the control of the police authority, would determine in what circumstances prosecutions should be dropped, regardless of the likely outcome (the police authority would of course only be able to determine policies, not to interfere in individual prosecution decisions[14]).

Meanwhile so long as local police authorities have few real powers and in London there is no locally elected police authority, it is quite possible that the establishment of a national independent prosecutor service will be a retrograde not a progressive step in achieving accountability. That is not to say that there will not be benefits. Clearly a more professional approach to prosecution in the courts will result in more safeguards for accused persons (particularly those unrepresented). But the independent prosecutor service is unlikely to provide any real check on police power and may even aggravate the situation by (in Dr Waddington's words) "giving the police more room for manoeuvre".

The lack of any provision in the Bill either for an independent prosecutor or for tape recording of interviews in the police station was most commonly cited as evidence that the Bill had got the "balance" wrong. In the 1983 general election the SDP and Liberal Alliance manifesto included commitments to bring in both kinds of "safeguards"; an Alliance spokesperson Alan Beith MP said on a BBC 'Newsnight' television programme during the election campaign that if these measures were brought in, the Alliance would support other parts of the Bill.

Tape Recording

The results of experiments in tape recording interviews carried out in Scotland show very clearly the dangers of any great reliance on this as a "safeguard". An interim report prepared by the Scottish Home and Health Department contained findings on the tape recording of

2,149 interviews in police stations in Dundee and Falkirk since May 1980. The Report, which was made public in November 1982, found that:

"there is evidence to suggest that introduction of tape recording has led to an increase in the interviewing of suspects by the police outside the police station or in the police station but not on tape".[15]

In Falkirk the proportion of suspects who made relevant statements *before* their arrival at the police station rose from 14% to 44%. In Dundee the increase was from 34% to 43%. These findings show what the Report called an "overwhelmingly negative" reaction by the police. The police explained that they adopted the tactic of engaging in preliminary interviews outside the station to avoid the restrictions that questioning certain subjects on tape would impose.

Even more striking were the findings relating to the length of interrogations. In Dundee the average length of an interrogation before tape recording was introduced was 24 or 25 minutes. With tape recording it fell to 10 minutes. In Falkirk there was an even more dramatic reduction from 39 to only 6 minutes. One policeman quoted by the Report said:

"You are frightened to ask questions because they may become inadmissible questions and there is a record of it, whereas if the tape was not there, you really have got carte blanche. I don't say you would beat the prisoner up or throw him round the room; far from it; but you have got more leeway without the tape".[16]

Police opposition to the introduction of tape recording has, in the past, been on both an organisational and an individual basis. The Police Federation, however, has now agreed to support the Law Society's call for the tape recording of confessions and an independent prosecution system in exchange for the Society's support for a new complaints procedure and the right to legal representation for police officers facing disciplinary charges.[17] Nevertheless senior police officers' organisations have opposed tape recording and this has influenced the Home Office.

As Peter Snape MP said during debates in the House of Commons:

"The attitude of the Police Federation to this matter shows a welcome change from its previous track record, but over the years it has expressed much opposition to the introduction of what in the past it has termed 'electronic surveillance' of its activities. That opposition, rather than any technical or operational considerations, has been the main reason for the long period of Government inactivity. The intensive police lobbying over the years has persuaded successive Governments of both political hues that the proposals to introduce such tape recording would be controversial. . . . such opposition from that quarter undoubtedly persuaded the Home Office that the game was not worth pursuing. That, in principle, if not alone, has been the reason for the 11 years of inactivity so far and the further four or five years of inactivity if the Home Office gets away with the delays".[18]

The "further four or five years of inactivity" which Peter Snape mentioned may occur because of more experiments or "field trials" which have been set up by the Home Office in police stations in the Met area (in Holborn and Croydon), Merseyside (Wirral), Leicestershire (Leicester Central) and Hampshire (Winchester). The Home Office claimed that sufficient feasibility studies had not yet been conducted and also that a tape machine of the kind required was not available (ie, one with two tapes – one for use by the officer and one to be kept independently and showed to the suspect's lawyer).

The proposals of the Royal Commission on Criminal Procedure to establish tape recording in police stations were defective in that they suggested that only a summary of the interview would have to be recorded by the police officer with comments from the suspect added. The National Council for Civil Liberties called this "verballing by tape recorder" and said it would be worse than useless in preventing disputes between defendants and police as to what was said in interrogation.[19] The government seems to have accepted this point and to be proposing full recording of interviews. Nevertheless they ignored the Commission's strong representations that the time for further experiments to test feasibility was past and that taping could and should start immediately. The Commission's own research had shown that the cost of running a scheme for the whole country for the taping of full interviews (including the crucial transcription cost) would be about £6.5 million, offset by potential savings from changes in the plea rate estimated to be about £4.4 million.[20]

While tape recording of interviews is a long overdue reform, it may also be the subject of exaggeratedly high expectations. In order to be effective it will require a provision excluding other (unrecorded) evidence. But even this will not guarantee its effectiveness if inducements (allowed under the codes – see p 84) or threats can be made by police outside the recording room. Nor will a link-up between tape recording and an independent prosecutor necessarily help. The report on the Scottish experiment quoted earlier also commented on the reaction of the Procurators Fiscals, whose role as independent prosecutors has been much cited in support of a similar system here. It said that they:

> "do not feel that the introduction of tape recording has given the Scottish prosecutor a greater degree of practical control over the police than he presently enjoys. . . . most fiscals . . . considered that the methods adopted by the police when questioning supects were not the rightful concern of the fiscal".[21]

It could therefore be argued that tape recording will only really be effective if it is combined with adequate rules governing procedures during questioning, measures for their enforcement and proper police accountability. Such accountability is, as we have seen, unlikely to be improved by an independent prosecutor system, particularly a nationally controlled one.

Lay Visitors

Lord Scarman's proposal for lay visitors to police stations[22] was not included in the Bill but voluntary schemes have been set up and there is a suggestion of legislation to come.[23] The idea is for a panel of people to be given authority to visit police stations at will and speak to detainees in private. In the Brixton pilot scheme the lay visitors are ultimately vetted by the Home Secretary and report to the Police Consultative Committee. They are apparently to be allowed to sit in on interviews, and the Report to the Lambeth Police Consultative Committee on the scheme stated:

> "The possibility that a visitor present at an interview could be a compellable witness in subsequent proceedings is accepted. This is an extra benefit of the scheme, not a drawback. The visitor might appear for the prosecution or the defence but this would not diminish the value of the scheme; it would enhance it by underlining its impartial nature".[24]

The problem is that the "impartiality" of lay visitors in these circumstances will take place outside of any context of proper police accountability. Lay visitors may be used, unknown to them, to validate dubious procedures or to substantiate confessions obtained in the absence of a lawyer. As noted on p 110 the confessions in the Confait case were signed in the presence of the defendant's parents even though they were not allowed to be present at their children's interviews. The dangers of this aspect of the lay visitor scheme may well outweigh any benefits accruing from more public knowledge of the condition of police station cells, which is certainly to be welcomed.

Notes

1. Royal Commission on Criminal Procedure Report *Op cit* part II.
2. *The Organisation of an Independent Prosecution Service: A Discussion Paper* by the Working Party on Prosecution Arrangements. (Home Office 3.12.82).
3. *Courts Prosecution and conviction* by M. McConville and J. Baldwin (OUP, 1981).
4. See Chapters 11 and 12.
5. See p 85.
6. *Criteria For Prosecution* Home Office Circular No 29/1983.
7. *Observer* 31.7.83.
8. *Ibid.*
9. See also *A New Police Authority for London: A Consultation Paper on Democratic Control of the Police in London* GLC Police Committee Support Unit Discussion Paper No. 1. March 1983.
10. Royal Commission on Criminal Procedure Report *Op cit* para 2.17.
11. *The Proper Way to Police Accountability* by Dr P A Waddington (*Police* June 1983).
12. *Ibid.*
13. *A New Police Authority for London, Op cit,* para 69.
14. *Ibid* paras 237-242.
15. *Tape Recording of Police Interviews: The First 24 Months* Scottish Home and Health Department 1982.
16. *Ibid.*
17. *Guardian* 15.6.83.
18. *Hansard* 5.5.83, Col 324, Peter Snape MP.
19. *Times* 23.10.82.
20. *Police Interrogation. Tape recording* by J A Barnes and N Webster (Royal Commission on Criminal Procedure Research Study No 8).
21. *Op cit.*
22. Scarman Report *Op cit* paras 7.7-7.10.
23. *Police Review* 5.11.82.
24. Report to Community/Police Consultative Group for Lambeth *Lay Visitors to Police Stations* (1.3.83).

26. Police Accountability and the Police Bill

As has been seen, the Police Bill was primarily designed to give the police new powers they claim to need to legitimise existing practices and to carry out new policing strategies. At the same time it represented the culmination of a process whereby the constitutional identities of the police in England and Wales have been transformed. This process, which began in the 1960s, can be said to have changed notions of police power from those of quasi-judicial to executive functions. The change in ideas has been preceded by changes in practice and relationship. The rules limiting police powers have long been ineffective so that, in practice, the police have held a special position in society, even if in theory they were said to be "citizens in uniform".

Nevertheless the theory of the "citizen in uniform" has had some influence in the past. In the 1960s the English police were often compared favourably with their continental counterparts. There was no mass student confrontation with the police as in France and West Germany and the trouble between police and public during anti-Vietnam War demonstrations in 1968 was mild in comparison. A minister in the present Tory government, Norman Fowler MP, was able to write: "The British police has never been seen as the instrument of a repressive government".[1]

His book on the police argued that the trouble in the 1960s between police and public on the continent was deliberately provoked by militant students, but that provocation of this kind in Britain was unsuccessful because of the British police's extraordinary high reputation.[2] The book was written in 1979 before the riots of 1981 and was complacent about police/public relations in Britain.

His views are interesting because they provide an insight into the process of rationalisation that has accompanied changing establishment ideas of the police. Thus his chapter on "Crime and the Law" relied heavily on the police portrayal of their own role and in particular on the ideas of Sir Robert Mark. He claimed that specialist squads, such as the SPG, were "the only way open" to police to respond to the "challenge" of serious crime and in relation to obtaining convictions:

> "The case put by some policemen today is that as well as protecting the rights of the innocent, the government must also concern themselves with protecting the public. The public's rights, they argue, are not protected if the legal system makes it possible for the guilty to escape".[3]

He went on to quote extensively and uncritically from Sir Robert Mark's notorious attacks on lawyers and the Judges' Rules and ended by praising the Criminal Law Revision Committee Report of 1972, which recommended the abolition of the right of silence.[4] Most interesting of all his definition of balance in police-public relations was that where policemen, "must earn the public's respect . . . At the same time governments must keep the respect and support of the policemen upon whom they rely".[5]

In other words the police were almost equal partners with, not servants, of the people.

Although the English constitution is theoretically subject to the doctrine of the "separation of powers", the application of it has always been far from clear. Wade and Phillips state that, "In the absence of a written constitution, there is no formal separation of powers in the United Kingdom".[6]

The constitutional position of the police demonstrates that executive and judicial functions can overlap. England and Wales have never had a national police force, as on the continent. The police originally were under the control of the local JPs and developed their role as officers of the Court as well as law enforcers as the accusatorial system developed. Thus as explained previously the English and Welsh police both investigate and prosecute cases, whereas in Europe prosecution is conducted by a separate government agency. Modern critics of the English system say that the executive policing function should not be combined with the judicial prosecution role. Yet the Police Bill would have drastically extended the executive power of the police without removing the judicial function by creating an independent prosecutor.

But the police's quasi-judicial role is not just confined to prosecution nor is that even the most important part of it. Most important the purely judicial functions provided the main rationale for the constitutional independence of the police. Whereas on the continent the police are employees, in England and Wales they are holders of public office with a direct responsibility to enforce the law placed on each individual constable. As early as 1965 Geoffrey Marshall saw the dangers of the lack of any control over the police on a "judicial" not "executive" model:

> "If it is accepted that law enforcement may have aspects which place it closer to the executive than to the judicial function, it cannot in its entirety demand the isolation and immunity accorded to purely judicial decision. . . . One cannot . . . defend a rationale of police independence from control or instructions simply on the ground that in enforcing the law there is no sense in which the law imposes responsibility or corrects error. The analogy with judicial independence is defective. Although no one believes that judges exercise no discretion their whole activity – at least in principle – is rule governed . . . But in executive policy making the choice of principles may include feelings of morality and common sense and when one executive decision is substituted for another it is not normally thought as correcting it".[7]

He concluded that the status of constable implied a "rationally indefensible relationship" between the functions of police and government.

The quasi-judicial role of the police long discouraged the placing of any limitations on their powers, still theoretically conceived as those of the "citizen in uniform". Indeed it was the judiciary who made the only serious efforts in this direction in the Judges' Rules. Wade and Phillips point out that:

> "In the field of police powers, on which Parliament has never been asked to legislate in a comprehensive way, not only have the courts had to apply ancient precedents to modern conditions, but in England the judiciary has twice exercised a plainly legislative function in making the Judges' Rules, which are not rules of law in strict sense, but which give authoritative guidance to the police in questioning and taking statements from suspects. Indeed the improvised procedure by which new Judges' Rules were formulated in 1964 was open to criticism since it afforded no opportunity for democratic participation or consultation with all interested parties: but Government and Parliament have evidently not wished to challenge this unusual procedure".[8]

The dangers of the lack of any control over the police are now being reaped in full measure. Under the guise of political independence the police have become one of the most powerful political lobbies in the country. A letter to *The Times* about the Police Bill commented that:

> "For a long time there has been growing within certain echelons of the police service an attitude of elitist arrogance . . . Some police leaders appear to visualise themselves as a separate state authority imposed upon the state itself".[9]

The political power of senior police officers is matched by an occupational culture which separates the police as a body from the community. The government sees its role as "supporting" the police and appears to accede to all their demands. No control over the police (legislative, executive or judicial) is being proposed and yet dramatic new powers will be given to the police in a new Police Bill. Even more worrying, the powers are to be backed up by specific parliamentary approval for the use of force by police in situations where it would be wholly unlawful for the citizen to use force. The police therefore will be placed by this Bill almost "above" the law.

Theoretically the police are accountable to the law. However as the Greater London Council observed, in its response to the Scarman report, it is the failure of accountability to the law which has led people to place more stress on accountability through statutory mechanisms such as the police complaints system and through local police authorities. It is now widely recognised that the complaints system fails to afford the individual adequate redress, let alone deal with complaints of public concern. The provisions in the new Police Bill are likely to make things worse by removing limitations on police power and increasing emphasis on redress through internal discipline and on police discretion within the command structure.

Whereas accountability to the law and to the complaints system primarily affords protection of and redress for the individual, there should also be collective consent to methods and style of policing, and to exercise of police powers. Law enforcement policies necessarily entail selectivity, because factors such as lack of information, time or resources mean that in practice the police are unable to deal with all offences. Modern conditions have meant that the exercise of discretion in allocating priorities has become an even more important part of the police's role. The most contentious questions which have to be decided are the use of special units and technology and the policing of demonstrations and pickets.

The provisions in the Police Bill will add to the area of potential discretion by giving to officers (sometimes of a certain rank) power to make decisions such as when to set up a roadblock or what is a "serious arrestable offence". Discretion on this scale is at odds with impartially applying the law, the concept of which is the basis of the "quasi-judicial" role given to the police. Political as well as professional policing decisions are now made by the police alone. The GLC and other bodies believe the police should be brought under democratic control whereby the community, through its elected representatives, directs the process of selection through which a policy of law enforcement is constructed.[10]

In the case of local government services (eg, education, social services, housing) it is elected representatives who define the issues and formulate policy. In social services, for example, individual decisions whether or not to take a child into care are made beneath the umbrella of democratic control. Yet in the case of the policing of London it is an unelected Commissioner who prioritises the various policing functions, without being accountable to locally elected representatives. Outside London police authorities are two thirds elected but have limited powers.

Because of the localised nature of police organisation, there are recognisable and substantial differences between, for example, the policing of Greater Manchester under James Anderton and the policing of Devon and Cornwall under the ex-Chief Constable John Alderson. Even within the Metropolitan Police District there are differences between districts and even within districts, in terms of the prioritisation of the various police functions. The principle in question is the very one on which policing in Britain is supposedly based, that is: on whose behalf do the police, police. The instructions issued to the Metropolitan Police in 1829:

> "made it clear that every police officer was to regard himself as both servant and guardian of the public and to treat all citizens with civility and respect".[11]

The notion of the "citizen in uniform" may appear to be a naive historical anachronism in conditions of modern technology and advanced urban crime. But it is worth remembering that when the police forces were set up in England in the 19th century it was established as a principle not just to limit their power, but to define the whole basis of their relationship to the rest of the community. When a new Police Bill removes this concept, there will be left no model – judicial or executive – on which to base the unparalleled degree of power in the hands of undemocratic and almost autonomous institutions – the police forces of England and Wales.

The situation that will be created by the new Police Bill is an extremely dangerous one. It will legitimise the position of the police outside the community and with special powers, yet it will not even bring them under the control of central government, let alone make them locally accountable.

At a time of severe economic depression, rising unemployment and civil unrest, the agencies of the state which were once benevolent and concerned with "welfare" are increasingly adopting a "policing" role and coming under police influence and control. While crime is becoming more of a problem in depressed inner cities and the clear up rate is dropping the police are concerning themselves less with crime detection and more with social control and public order. Their new position and role mirrors the new philosophy of policing in the Police Bill. It is a philosophy of coercion and not of consent.

If the police are to become part of the community in local areas and are to win back consent from the people, it is essential that they be brought under democratic control. But is is not just committee structures that are required. So long as the police are not properly accountable to the law and do not have limitations placed on their powers they will not be accepted by the whole community. The new powers proposed by the Police Bill do not just make police accountability essential; they run contrary to it because of the special position in which the police are placed by them. Democratic control of the police can be said to involve both legal control of their powers and electoral control of their policies. The police should be made the servants of both the law and the people.

Notes

1. *After the Riots: The Police in Europe* by Norman Fowler (Davis-Poynter 1979) p 63.
2. *Ibid* p 66.
3. *Ibid* p 128.
4. *Ibid* p 133-136.
5. *Ibid* p 67.
6. *Constitutional and Administrative Law, op cit,* p 53.
7. *Police and Government* by Geoffrey Marshall (Methuen 1965) p 119.
8. Wade and Phillips *Op cit* p 52.
9. Letter from Sir Kenneth Thompson *The Times* 4.4.83.
10. *A New Police Authority for London, Op cit.*
11. *The Metropolitan Police Community Relations Branch* by Superintendent Roach (*Police Studies* Vol 1 No 3 1978).

Appendix

Summary of the Provisions of the Police and Criminal Evidence Bill (As Amended by Standing Committee J)

PART I – POWERS TO STOP AND SEARCH

Clause 1 (Power of constable to stop and search persons, vehicles, etc) would empower a constable, on reasonable suspicion, to search any person or vehicle found in a public place, for stolen or prohibited articles, and to detain a person or vehicle for the purpose of such a search. The "prohibited articles" referred to were offensive weapons or articles made or adapted for use in burglary, theft, taking a motor vehicle without authority or obtaining property by deception.

Clause 2 (Provisions relating to search under Clause 1 and other powers) provided that a constable proposing to conduct a search under Clause 1, or any other power, to detain and search, should state his/her name, the purpose of the search and, if asked, grounds for undertaking it. A constable not in uniform should also produce documentary evidence that s/he was a constable. A constable could, using reasonable force, detain a person or vehicle for such time as was reasonably required to permit a search to be carried out.*

Clause 3 (Duty to make records concerning searches) would oblige a constable who had carried out a search to make a record of it in writing on the spot or, if that is not reasonably practicable, as soon as is reasonably practicable thereafter. The record of the search was to include the name of the person searched but the constable should not detain the person to find out their name. Where the name was not known a description of the person should be given. The record should also state the object of the search and the grounds for making it. A person who had been searched, or the owner of a searched vehicle, could obtain a copy of the record within three months of the search.**

---

*A subsequent government amendment would also allow a constable to use reasonable force if necessary in carrying out a search.

**A government amendment was subsequently proposed to extend this to 12 months.

Clause 4 (Road checks) would enable a police officer of at least the rank of superintendent, and a police officer of any rank in a case of urgency, to authorise the setting up of a road check (the obstruction of a road to stop all or any selected vehicles passing along it), if they had reasonable grounds for suspecting that a person suspected of having committed a serious arrestable offence, or who was unlawfully at large, was in the area. A police officer of at least the rank of superintendent could also authorise a road check if, having regard to a pattern of crime in the area, s/he had reasonable grounds for suspecting that a serious arrestable offence was likely to be committed, within the period for which the road check was set up. Road checks were to be set up for a period not exceeding seven days initially renewed without limit.

Clause 5 (Reports of recorded searches and of road checks) provided that annual reports made by Chief Constables and the Commissioner of Police of the Metropolis should contain information about searches recorded under *clause 3* (other than information about specific searches), and about road checks set up under *clause 4* (including information about the reason for authorising, and the result of, each road check).

Clause 6 (Statutory undertakers, etc) would enable constables employed by statutory undertakers to stop, detain and search any vehicle before it left a goods area in their premises.

PART II – POWERS OF ENTRY, SEARCH AND SEIZURE
Clause 8 (Powers to enter without warrant) would make provision for a constable in certain circumstances to enter and search any premises, using such reasonable force as was necessary, for purposes of arrest or recapturing a person unlawfully at large, or of saving life and limb or preventing serious damage to property.

Clause 9 (Power to enter premises, etc to search for evidence of serious offences) would empower a Justice of the Peace, if satisfied that a serious arrestable offence had been committed, to issue a warrant authorising a constable to enter and search premises for *evidence* other than that to which clause 10 applied. The JP should be satisfied that the police could not communicate with the occupier *or* that the occupier had "unreasonably refused" entry or access to the police or that the evidence was likely to be concealed or destroyed if the police asked for entry without a warrant. **Clause 10** applied to evidence held on a confidential basis and the clause would empower a circuit judge, if satisfied that a serious arrestable offence had been committed, to issue either an order for the production to the police of the evidence, or a warrant under *clause 9* of the Bill (for subsequent government amendments see p 43-5).

Clause 11 (Entry and search after arrest) would make provision for a constable to enter and search any premises occupied or controlled by a person who had been arrested for an arrestable offence, if s/he had reasonable grounds for believing that there was evidence on or in the premises relating to that offence or to some other offence connected with that offence.

Clause 12 (Search warrants – safeguards) provided that where a constable applied for a search warrant, s/he should state the ground on which s/he was applying and so far as possible, the nature of the articles sought. At the hearing of their application, s/he should answer any questions on oath. The warrant would be to authorise an entry on one occasion only. **Clause 13** provided that entry and search under a warrant must be within 28 days of its issue and at a reasonable hour, unless it was suspected that the relevant evidence could not be found at a reasonable hour. A constable executing a warrant should identify him/herself if asked to do so and, if not in uniform, should produce documentary evidence that s/he was a constable. A search should only be to the extent required for the purpose for which the warrant was issued, and would be unlawful if it did not conform to this Part of the Bill. **Clause 14** provided that when searching premises the police could seize evidence of any offence if they believed seizure necessary to prevent concealment, loss or destruction. Communication between a legal adviser and client was exempt.

PART III – ARREST

Clause 16 provided powers of arrest without warrant for certain classes of offences. **Clause 17 (general grounds for arrest)** would enable a constable to arrest any person whom s/he had reasonable grounds to suspect of having committed or being in the course of committing any offence, if any of the general arrest conditions was satisfied. These included:

(a) that the name and address of the suspected person is

> unknown and cannot be ascertained by the constable;
>
> (b)   that the name and address supplied are not believed to be correct;
>
> (c)   that it is believed that arrest is necessary to prevent physical harm, loss of or damage to property, an affront to public decency or an obstruction to the highway;
>
> (d)   that it is believed that arrest is necessary for the protection of a child or other vulnerable person from the person arrested.

Clause 19 (Arrest without warrant for fingerprinting) provided that if a person had been convicted of a criminal offence which would be recorded in national police records and refused a request made within one month of the conviction to go to a police station for fingerprinting, a constable could arrest them without a warrant.

Clause 20 (Information to be given on arrest) provided that an arrest by a constable would not be lawful unless the person arrested was informed that they were under arrest and given the ground of their arrest, except where it would not be possible to convey that information by reason of their condition or behaviour. Under **clause 21 (Voluntary attendance at police station, etc)** where a person attended voluntarily at a police station or other place without having been arrested, they would be entitled to leave at will unless they were placed under arrest. **Clause 22 (Arrest elsewhere than at police station)** provided that where a person was arrested by a constable at a place other than a police station, they should be taken to a police station by a constable as soon as practicable but this would be delayed if the suspect's presence elsewhere was necessary to investigate an offence. Under **clause 23 (Search upon arrest for an offence)**, where a constable had arrested a person they could search them and any premises or vehicle in which the arrest takes place, using such force as was reasonably necessary.

PART IV – DETENTION

Clause 25 (Limitations on police detention) provided that a person arrested for an offence should not be kept in police detention unless one or more of certain conditions, referred to as "the detention conditions", applied to them. These included:

> (i)   that their name and address cannot be ascertained; or that

the name and address supplied are believed to be incorrect;
(ii) that there are reasonable grounds for believing:
  (a) that their detention is necessary to prevent them from causing physical harm to any person including themself or damage to property;
  (b) that they will fail to appear in court to answer bail;
  (c) that their detention is necessary to prevent them interfering with witnesses or otherwise obstructing the course of justice;
  (d) that their detention is necessary to secure or preserve evidence or to obtain such evidence by questioning them.

Clause 26 (Custody officers) would require at every police station, and at all times, the attendance of an officer known as the "custody officer", who would perform functions assigned to them by **clauses 27 to 29** of the Bill. These duties related to arrested persons, before and after being charged, including their release or continued detention **(clauses 27 and 28)**. Under **clause 29** the custody officer should ensure that all detained persons are treated in accordance with the provisions of the Bill and any code of practice issued by the Secretary of State. **Clause 30** would require reviews of the detention of persons in police detention to be carried out by the custody officer or, in the case of a person who has not been charged, by an officer of at least the rank of inspector. The first interview should be not later than six hours after detention was first authorised, the second not later than nine hours after the first and subsequent reviews should be at intervals of not more than nine hours.

Under **clause 31 (Limits on periods of detention without charge)**, subject to **clauses 32 and 33**, a person should not be kept in police detention for more than 24 hours without being charged. **Clause 32 (Authorisation of continued detention)** would empower a police officer of the rank of superintendent or above to authorise the keeping of a person in police detention for a further 12 hours, if they were satisfied that the offence for which the person was under investigation was a serious arrestable offence, that the keeping in police detention was necessary to preserve or obtain evidence, and that the investigation was being conducted diligently and expeditiously. **Clause 33 (Warrants of further detention)** would empower a magistrates' court to issue a warrant of further detention for a period not exceeding 96 hours after the suspect was detained at the police station concerned. **Clause 34** would enable a magistrates' court to extend a warrant of further detention issued under **clause 33.**

Clause 35 made provision for legal aid for detained persons in cases where an application was made to a magistrates' court for a warrant of further detention or extension of such warrant.

Clause 36 (Detention after charge) provided that persons detained after being charged should be brought before a magistrates' court as soon as practicable. **Clause 37** would amend provisions in the Magistrates' Courts Act 1980 relating to police bail. **Clause 39 (Records of detention)** would require police forces to keep written records concerning the annual number of applications for warrants of detention and the number of persons detained without charge for more than 24 hours. **Clause 40** provided that the right to apply for a writ of *habeas corpus* would be unaffected but that special powers of detention under the Immigration Act 1971 and the Prevention of Terrorism (Temporary Provisions) Act 1976 would remain.

PART V – QUESTIONING AND TREATMENT OF PERSONS BY POLICE

Clause 42 provided for the searching of detained persons. Searches were to be carried out if the custody officer considered it necessary in order that the record required could be complete. *Intimate searches* (involving physical examination of body orifices) could be carried out in suspected serious arrestable offence cases where there were reasonable grounds for believing the search would produce evidence relevant to the offence or to establish the suspect did not have on him or her any article for causing injury. Intimate searches could be carried out by a doctor or a person of the same sex as the suspect.

Under **clause 43** a person arrested and held in police custody would be entitled on request to have one friend or relative told without delay of their arrest and detention, except in certain cases. **Clause 44** provided that where a child or young person was detained after arrest, their parent or guardian should be informed of their detention as soon as was "reasonably practicable". **Clause 45 (Access to legal advice)** provided that a person arrested and held in police custody would be entitled, on request, to consult a solicitor privately as soon as practicable and in any case within 36 hours from the time when the police first detained them, except where the police believed that this would lead to interference with evidence or witnesses.

Clause 46 provided for the taking of *fingerprints*. The fingerprints of a person detained could be taken at a police station without their consent:

(a) if an officer of at least the rank of superintendent authorises them to be taken; or

(b) if they have been charged with an offence a conviction for which would be recorded in national police records; or

(c) if they have been informed that they will be reported for such an offence.

Clauses 47 and 48 allowed the taking of body samples from suspects without their consent except intimate samples. Under **clause 49** fingerprints (and copies of them) and samples taken from a person should be destroyed as soon as practicable after s/he was cleared of an offence in connection with which they were taken. A person who asked to be allowed to witness the destruction of their fingerprints or copies of them should have a right to witness it.

PART VI – CODES OF PRACTICE

Clause 51 would empower the Secretary of State to issue codes of practice in connection with the treatment, questioning, identification and detention by police forces of persons suspected of the commission of criminal offences. S/he should prepare and publish a draft of any proposed code, consider any representations made about the draft and could modify the draft accordingly. S/he should lay the draft before both Houses of Parliament and could bring the code into operation by order made by statutory instrument, which would have effect if approved by each House of Parliament. A failure by any person to observe any code of practice would render them liable to disciplinary proceedings, but not to any criminal or civil proceedings although it could be admissible in evidence in any proceedings.

PART VII – EVIDENCE IN CRIMINAL PROCEEDINGS

Clause 59 (Confessions) provided a statutory basis for the law on the admissibility of confession evidence. It required the exclusion of a confession obtained by oppression or in consequence of anything said or done that was likely to render it unreliable.

PART VIII – POLICE – GENERAL

Clause 65 (Police complaints procedure) would amend the Police Act 1976 to introduce new arrangements for handling complaints against the police. It provided for the nomination by the Secretary of State of an independent assessor to supervise the investigation of certain complaints. Regulations could be made by the Secretary of State which would, *inter alia,* prescribe descriptions of complaints that were to be referred for consideration to the independent assessor, and set out the procedure to be followed by him or her in supervising an investigation.

Clause 67 provided for arrangements to be made by the police authority in each police area for obtaining the views of local people about police matters in the area and for obtaining their co-operation with the police in preventing crime. Arrangements for the *Metropolitan Police* District would be made by the Commissioner of Police of the Metropolis, who should make separate arrangements for each London borough, after consultation with the borough council, and take account of any guidance issued by the Secretary of State. In the *City*, the arrangements would be made by the Commissioner of Police for the City of London after consultation with the Common Council.

PART IX – MISCELLANEOUS AND SUPPLEMENTARY

Clause 74 (Interpretation) defined a ''serious arrestable offence'' as one which the person contemplating the exercise of the power had reason to consider to be sufficiently serious to justify their exercising it, having regard to:

(a) the nature of the offence
(b) the scale
(c) the degree of the organisation
(d) the degree of violence used or likely to be used
(e) the gain derived or likely to be derived
(f) the harm caused or likely to be caused to persons
(g) the harm caused or likely to be caused to the security of the state, the administrations of justice or public order
(h) the prevalence of similar offences.

Index

Accountability of the police, 6, 164, 167, 171, 172, 173, 184, 185, 187, 189, 190, 191, 192, 198, 200, 203, 205-10

Adams, Len Commander, 116

Affront to public decency, 3, 63, 65, 66

Alderson, John, ex Chief Constable, 124, 138, 209

Amnesty, 138

Anderton, James, Chief Constable, 118, 209

Arrest, new powers of, 3, 13, 63-70, 75-76, 145

Association of Chief Police Officers, 8, 14, 15, 79, 133

Baldwin, J, and McConville, M., 94, 195

Barns, Peter, 178

Beith, Alan, MP, 200

Bennett Report, 137

Black people, 2, 3, 23, 36, 39, 80, 104, 115-21, 132-34

Blake, Nick, 85

Blom-Cooper, Louis and Drabble, Richard, 119, 120

Body samples, 4, 88, 92-93, 158, 165

Bonsor, Sir Nicholas, MP, 41, 42

Bradford 12, 16, 199

Brazil, Karen, 90, 113-14

British Crime Survey, 119

British Medical Association, 44, 88, 148

Brown, John, 126

Cain, Maureen, 117

Caution, 10, 17, 99, 101

Children, see Juveniles

Codes of Practice, 78, 84, 93, 94, 95, 100-04, 105, 106, 190

Community Alliance for Police Accountability, 74

Computers (police), 34, 66, 130, 137, 148, 149-52

Confait, Maxwell, 13, 50, 95, 99, 102, 103, 110-11, 203

Confessions, 10, 15, 75, 76, 82-87, 105, 112, 145, 195, 203

Confidential files, search of, 1, 15, 17, 41, 43, 44-45, 54, 128, 148

Consultative committees (liaison committees), 127, 171-73, 177, 203

Crane, Paul, 122

Criminal Law Revision Committee (seventh report 1965), 155

Criminal Law Revision Committee (eleventh report 1972), 10, 11, 12, 13, 15, 17, 73, 82, 83, 86, 206

Criminal statistics, 119-21

Critchley, T. A., 9

Curtis, Les, 4

Custody Record, 101, 103, 160, 165-66

Data protection, 147-49

Davidson, Arthur, 43

Dear, Deputy Assistant Commissioner, 47

Deaths in police custody, 72, 73, 101, 155

Demonstrators/trade unionists, 3, 33, 66

Demuth, Clare, 23, 163

Detention without charge, 3, 5, 13, 15, 72-80, 82, 164

Devlin, Lord, 10

Director of Public Prosecutions, 167, 170, 175, 176, 177, 179, 180, 181, 196, 197, 199

District Support Units, see Instant Response Units

Doctors, 1, 88, 89, 92, 101

Double Jeopardy, 171, 180-82

Drabble, Richard, see Blom-Cooper, Louis

Driscoll, Jim, 106

Drugs, 20, 22, 26, 35, 39, 72, 89, 90, 91, 116, 162

Exclusion of Evidence, 6, 10, 45, 54, 105-07, 164, 166

Fairbairn, Commander Brian, 21, 116

Fingerprinting, 4, 13, 15, 67, 88, 92, 131, 137, 158

Firearms (police), 155, 156-59

"Firebrigade" policing, 65, 124, 141, 151

Fisher, Sir Henry, 13, 95, 99, 100, 102, 103
Football supporters, 37-38
Force (use of by police), 4, 21-22, 43, 93, 96, 154-59, 208
Fowler, Norman, MP, 205
Franey, Ros, 131

Gay people, 3, 65, 90, 117
Going equipped for stealing, 19, 22, 23, 24, 29
Gordon, Paul, 132, 134
Grave offences, 6, 15, 32, 46, 77, 90, 95
Greater London Council, 3, 19, 106, 121, 124, 182, 208, 209
Greenwood, Chief Superintendent, 156, 157
Griffiths, Basil, Inspector, 122
Griffiths, Eldon, MP, 33, 90, 171

Haldane Society, 22
Harman, Harriet, MP, 181, 187
Hattersley, Roy, MP, 27
Hilliard, Paddy, 85
Hoare, Chief Superintendent, 158
Home Affairs Select Committee of the House of Commons, 168-70, 175, 176, 177, 178, 179, 180, 183, 184
Homeless people, 3, 65, 72, 130-32, 133
Home Office Advisory Committee on Drug Dependence, 115, 161, 163
Home Office Consultative Memorandum on Royal Commission on Criminal Procedure Report, 14-15, 64
Home Office Research Study on Stop and Search (*The Use, Effectiveness and Impact of Police Stop and Search Powers* by Carole F. Willis) 28, 36-38, 119, 161
Horsfall, James, 154
Human Rights, European Convention on, 74, 85, 88
Humphry, Derek, 115

Identification parades, 99, 100, 104

Imbert, Peter, Chief Constable, 14, 54, 131
Immigration 80, 126, 132-34, 148, 150, 184
Independent Assessor, 6, 167-71, 175, 180, 182
Independent prosecutor, 6, 14, 16, 191, 193-200, 202, 206
Instant Response Units, (District Support Units), 24, 65, 124, 139, 143
Institute of Race Relations, 119
Intimate samples, 92, 93
Intimate searches, 3, 4, 88, 89-92, 93, 158, 165

Jellicoe, Lord, 5, 78, 79
Jones, Phil, 189
Journalists, 1, 44
Judges' Rules, 10, 12, 13, 93, 99-100, 105, 106, 185, 207
Juries, 5, 8, 9, 11, 16, 17, 73, 107, 178
"Justice", 178
Juveniles/children, 63, 92, 93, 99, 100, 104

Kavanagh, P. B., Deputy Commissioner, 47
Kettle, Martin, 11, 13, 14, 16
Kitson, General, 136

Lambeth Council Working Party Report, 119
Lane, Lord Chief Justice, 121
Laugharne, A., Deputy Commissioner, 118
Law Society, 6, 93, 95
Lawyer, right of access to, 6, 88, 93-96, 100, 104, 165
Lay visitors, 193, 203-04
Legal Aid, 77, 163
Leigh, David, 8, 14
Leigh, L. H., 27
Lindop Committee Report on Data Protection, 149
Lyell, Nicholas, MP, 51
Lyon, Alex, MP, 75

Madden, Errol, 111, 180
Mark Sir Robert, 9, 10, 11, 12, 15, 16, 95, 118, 120, 206
Marnoch, Commander Alex, 153, 173
Marshall, Geoffrey, 207
Mayhew, Patrick, MP, 22, 42, 46, 64, 65, 66, 73, 89, 90, 157, 171
McCluskey, Lord, 5
McConville, M., *see* Baldwin and McConville
McNee, Sir David, 3, 6, 12, 13, 14, 65
Mentally handicapped persons, 101, 103, 104, 112, 113
Merricks, Walter, 191
Mikardo, Ian, MP, 24
Morris, Pauline, 73

Names and addresses, power to take, 15, 29, 63, 64, 65, 66,72
National Council for Civil Liberties, 79, 86, 106, 110, 111, 182, 202
Neighbourhood watch schemes, 128, 129-30, 141, 152
Newman, Sir Kenneth, Commissioner, 2, 3, 15, 28, 33, 124, 126, 127, 128, 130, 136-45, 147, 197

Northern Ireland, 5, 8, 15, 34, 78-80, 85, 136-38, 140, 155

Obstructing the highway, 63, 64, 66, 77
Offensive weapons, 19, 20, 22, 23, 29, 39, 116
Operation Major, 130-32

Peden, W., Chief Inspector, 128
Philips, Sir Cyril, 179, 182
Phillips, Melanie, 36
Plowden, Lord, 175
Police Complaints Board, 6, 47, 48, 52, 89, 113, 167, 168, 170, 175-84
Police complaints system, 6, 14, 164, 175-85, 187, 188, 208
Police Federation, 6, 8, 16, 33, 182, 184, 201
Pounder, C. N. M., 151
Powis, Deputy Assistant Commissioner David, 38, 46, 90, 117, 118

Plaxton, Chief Inspector Brian, 197
Pratt, Dr Michael, 119
Price, Chief Constable Barry, 156
Price, Christopher, MP, 32, 46, 65, 111
Proctor, Harvey, MP, 121
Prostitutes, 3, 90, 91

Railton Road raids, 47-48, 52-53
Road blocks, 3, 13, 15, 31-34, 139, 142, 143, 145, 152, 164, 209
Robertson, Geoffrey, 164
Royal Commission on Criminal Procedure, 3, 5, 6, 12, 13, 14, 15, 16, 19, 21, 22, 27, 28, 29, 32, 35, 42, 45, 46, 52, 53, 54, 63, 64, 73,74, 75, 76, 77, 83, 85, 89, 90, 92, 94, 95, 100, 101, 104, 105, 106, 107, 115, 143, 145, 152, 160, 163, 164, 187-92, 194, 198, 202
Royal Commission on the Police 1929, 154
Runnymede Trust, 23

Scarman, Lord, 21, 35, 38, 116, 119, 121, 124, 127, 171, 176, 182, 184
Schools, 127, 128
Search of confidential files (*see* Confidential files)
Search of homes, 3, 4, 13, 21, 39, 41-62, 142, 143, 145, 152
Serious arrestable offences, 6, 15, 31, 32, 41, 42, 43, 44, 45, 46, 55, 73, 77-78, 79, 89, 94, 96, 209
Shawcross, Lord, 196
Sim, J., 79
Simmonds, Mr , 38
Snape, Peter, MP, 201
Special Branch, 132, 148, 149
Special Patrol Group, 35, 124, 139
Speed, Chief Superintendent Tony, 141
Steer, David, 143, 145
Stop and search, 3, 19-40, 116, 139, 141, 142, 143, 144, 157, 160, 162, 164, 165
Strip searches, 88, 89-90, 91, 92, 113-14, 158, 165
"Sus" law, 20, 23, 24, 28, 163
Swamp '81, 21, 35, 38, 39, 120

Symbolic areas ("high crime areas"), 33, 39, 138-39, 142-43, 152

Tape recording in police stations, 6, 11, 14, 16, 191, 193, 200-03
Targeting and surveillance, 20, 137, 139, 140-45, 151
Telephone taps, 147, 152
Thomas, P, 79

Van Bueren, Geraldine, 74, 88
Video equipment (police), 147, 152

Waddington, Dr P. A., 199, 200

Wade and Phillips, 206, 207
Waldorf, Stephen, 158
Walker, Deputy Assistant Commissioner, 38
Warrant of further detention, 5, 52, 76-77, 164, 165
Warren, Kenneth, MP, 170, 171
Whitelaw, William, 2
Williams, Professor Glanville, 29, 115, 161
Women, 3, 23, 88, 96, 117

Zander, Michael, 94, 105

Table of Cases

R v Allen (1977) CLR 163, 105

Chic Fashions (West Wales) Limited v
Jones (1968) 2 QB 299, 50

R v Dayle (1973) ALL ER 1151, 22

Ghani v Jones (1969) 3 ALL ER 1700,
50-52

R v Haughton (1978) Cr App R 197,
105

Hussein v Khan (1970) AC 942-4, 76

Jeffrey v Black 3 WLR, 895, 105

R v Lemtasef (1977) 2 ALL ER 835,
105

McBean v Parker *Times Law Report*
4.1.83, 162

Mohammed – Holgate v Duke *Times
Law Report* 16.7.83, 76

R v Nycander *Times Law Report*
9.12.82, 74

R v Police Complaints Board ex Parte
Madden; R v Police Complaints
Board ex Parte Rhone (1983)
2 ALL ER 353, 180-81

R v Prager (1972) 1 WLR 260, 105

R v Reid (1982) Crim LR 514, 73

R v Rennie (1982) 1 WLR 64, 82

R v Sang (1979) 3 WLR 236, 107

Re Sherman v Apps (1981) 2 ALL ER
612, 74

Reed v Wastie (1972) *The Times*
10.2.72, 155

Table of Statutes

Bail Act 1976 Schedule 1, 71

Criminal Attempts Act 1981, 121

Criminal Damage Act 1971, 47, 48

Criminal Justice Act 1982, 5, 8, 11

Criminal Justice (Scotland) Act 1982,
5, 76

Criminal Law Act 1967 s3, 21, 155

Criminal Law Act 1977, 27
s62, 96, 98

Firearms Act 1968 s47, 30

Freshwater Fisheries Act 1972 s11, 30

Highways Act 1980 s137, 66

Licensing Act 1964, 47, 48, 52

Liverpool Corporation Act 1821
s507(1), 30

Metropolitan Police Act 1839 s66, 21,
26, 31

Metropolitan Police Courts Act 1839
s24, 24, 27

Misuse of Drugs Act 1971, 50, 52, 163
s23, 30

Northern Ireland (Emergency
Provisions) Act 1973, 8, 85, 155

Official Secrets Act 1911, 42

Police Act 1964 s12, 164
s50, 184

Police Act 1976, 167, 175
s11, 180

Prevention of Crimes Act 1953
s1, 24

Prevention of Terrorism (Temporary
Provisions) Act 1976, 78-80

Road Traffic Act 1972 s159, 31, 32

Salmon and Freshwater Fisheries Act
1923 s54(3), 30

Theft Act 1968 s25, 25

Vagrancy Act 1824 s4, 20, 23, 24,
27, 28, 163